The Fifth French Republic

European History in Perspective
General Editor: Jeremy Black

European History in Perspective
Series Standing Order
ISBN 0–333–65056–5 hardcover
ISBN 0–333–65057–3 paperback
(*outside North America only*)

You can receive future titles in this series as they are published by placing a standing order. Please contact your bookseller or, in the case of difficulty, write to us at the address below with your name and address, the title of the series and the ISBN quoted above.

Customer Services Department, Palgrave Ltd
Houndmills, Basingstoke, Hampshire RG21 6XS, England

The Fifth French Republic

NICHOLAS ATKIN

First published 2005 by
PALGRAVE MACMILLAN
Houndmills, Basingstoke, Hampshire RG21 6XS and
175 Fifth Avenue, New York, N. Y. 10010
Companies and representatives throughout the world

PALGRAVE MACMILLAN is the global academic imprint of the Palgrave Macmillan division of St. Martin's Press, LLC and of Palgrave Macmillan Ltd. Macmillan® is a registered trademark in the United States, United Kingdom and other countries. Palgrave is a registered trademark in the European Union and other countries.

ISBN 0–333–65056–5 hardback
ISBN 0–333–65057–3 paperback

This book is printed on paper suitable for recycling and made from fully managed and sustained forest sources.

A catalogue record for this book is available from the British Library.

A catalog record for this book is available from the Library of Congress.

10   9   8   7   6   5   4   3   2   1
14   13   12   11   10   09   08   07   06   05

Printed in China

To Claire

Contents

Acknowledgements

My thanks go first to Jeremy Black who invited me to contribute to this series. The initial idea was to write on the later years of the Third Republic, and I am grateful to Pamela Pilbeam who suggested that there was a greater need for a study on the Fifth Republic. As in the past, her advice and backing have been greatly welcomed. At Palgrave Macmillan, Terka Acton and Sonya Barker have been both supportive and patient. Patience was also displayed by Andy Knapp who read through an early manuscript which still makes me blush with embarrassment. He corrected several silly mistakes, made many suggestions for further reading and forced me to reconsider a number of my arguments. I am also indebted to all those who have written on the Fifth Republic. To have acknowledged their full contribution would have turned the text into a briar of footnotes. Thanks also go to my students on whom I have tried out several of my ideas. I have particularly benefited from the suggestions of Richard Carswell who regularly sent me reviews of books which otherwise would have passed me by. Any mistakes, shortcomings and peculiarities of judgement are my own contribution. As always, the greatest debt is to my wife, Claire, and children, Charlotte and Benjamin.

Nicholas Atkin
Windsor

Abbreviations

ACR	Association pour la Cinquième République
ADMP	Association pour Défendre la Mémoire du Maréchal Pétain
ALN	Armée de Libération Nationale
AML	Amis du Manifeste et de la Liberté
CACR	Comité d'Action pour la Cinquième République
CALs	Comités d'Action Lycéens
CAP	Common Agricultural Policy
CDP	Centre Démocratie et Progrès
CDS	Centre des Démocrates Sociaux
CERES	Centre d'Etudes de Recherche et d'Education Socialiste
CFDT	Confédération Française Démocratique du Travail
CFLN	Comité Français de la Libération Nationale
CFSP	Common Foreign and Security Policy
CFTC	Confédération Française des Travailleurs Chrétiens
CGP	Commissariat Général du Plan
CGPG	Commissariat Général aux Prisonniers de Guerre
CGT	Confédération Générale du Travail
CHDGM	Comité d'Histoire de la Deuxième Guerre Mondiale
CLEF	Comité de Liaison des Etudiants Révolutionnaires
CIR	Convention des Institutions Républicaines
CNIP	Conseil National des Indépendents et Paysans
CNJA	Cercle National des Jeunes Agriculteurs
CNPF	Conseil National du Patronat Français
CPNT	Chasse, Pêche, Nature Tradition
CRS	Compagnies Républicaines de Sécurité

CRUA	Comité Révolutionnaire d'Unité et d'Action
CSDN	Conseil Supérieur de la Défense Nationale
DOM-TOMs	Départements d'Outre-Mer, Territoires d'Outre Mer
ECSC	European Coal and Steel Community
EDC	European Defence Community
EEC	European Economic Community
EMF	European Monetary Fund
EMS	European Monetary System
EMU	European Monetary Union
ENA	Ecole Nationale d'Administration
ENA	Etoile-Nord Africaine
ENS	Ecole Normale Supérieure
ERM	Exchange Rate Mechanism
Euratom	European Atomic Energy Community
FANCA	Fédération Nationale des Anciens Combattants d'Algérie
FFI	Forces Françaises de l'Intérieur
FGDS	Fédération de la Gauche Démocratique et Socialiste
FIS	Front Islamique du Salut
FLN	Front de Libération Nationale
FN	Front National
FNF	Front National Français
FNSEA	Fédération Nationale des Syndicats d'Exploitants Agricoles
FSUD	Fédération des Syndicats Unitaires et Démocratiques
GATT	General Agreement on Trade and Tariffs
GDP	Gross Domestic Product
GIS	Group Islamique Armée
GM	Gardes Mobiles
GMs	Gentils Membres
GOs	Gentils Organisateurs
GPRA	Gouvernement Provisoire de la République Algérienne
HLMs	Habitations à Loyer Modéré
IHTP	Institut d'Histoire du Temps Présent
INSEE	Institut National de la Statistique et des Etudes Economiques
IRBMs	Intermediate Range Ballistic Missiles
JAC	Jeunesse Agricole Chrétienne
JHA	Justice and Home Affairs
MdC	Mouvement des Citoyens
MDEF	Mouvement de Défense des Exploitants Familiaux
MDF	Mouvement Démocratique Féminin

MFPL	Mouvement Français pour le Planning Familial
MLF	Multilateral Nuclear Force
MLF	Mouvement de Libération des Femmes
MNPDG	Mouvement National des Prisonniers et Déportés de Guerre
MNR	Mouvement National Républicain
MPF	Mouvement pour la France
MRG	Mouvement des Radicaux de Gauche
MRP	Mouvement Républicain Populaire
MTLD	Mouvement pour le Triomphe des Libertés Démocrates
NATO	North Atlantic Treaty Organisation
OAS	Organisation de l'Armée Secrète
ONI	Office National d'Immigration
OPEC	Organisation of Petroleum Exporting Countries
ORTF	Office de la Radiodiffusion-Télévision Française
OS	Organisation Spéciale
PCF	Parti Communiste Français
PLO	Palestinian Liberation Organisation
PPA	Parti Populaire Algérien
PPF	Parti Populaire Français
PR	Parti Républicain
PS	Parti Socialiste
PSA	Parti Socialiste Autonome
PSD	Parti Social Démocrate
PSU	Parti Socialiste Unifié
QMV	Qualified Majority Voting
RAF	Rassemblement pour l'Algérie Française
RER	Réseau Express Régional
RPF	Rassemblement du Peuple Français
RPF	Rassemblement pour la France
RPF	Rwanda Popular Front
RPFIE	Rassemblement pour la France et l'Indépendance de l'Europe
RPR	Rassemblement pour la République
RI	Républicains-Indépendants
SAFER	Sociétés d'Aménagement Foncier et d'Etablissement Rural
SALT	Strategic Arms Limitation Talks
SEA	Single European Act
SEM	Single European Market

SFIO	Section Française de l'Internationale Ouvrière
SLII	Service des Liasions Interministerielles pour l'Information
SMIC	Salaire Minimum Interprofessionnel de Croissance
SMIG	Salaire Minimum Interprofessionelle Garanti
SNESup	Syndicat National de l'Enseignement Supérieur
SPD	Social Democratic Party
STO	Service du Travail Obligatoire
TEU	Treaty on European Union
TGV	Train de Grande Vitesse
UDCA	Union de Défense des Commerçants et Artisans
UDMA	Union Démocratique pour le Manifeste Algérien
UDF	Union pour la Démocratie Française
UDR	Union pour la Défense de la République
UDR	Union des Démocrates pour la République
UDSR	Union Démocratique et Socialiste de la Résistance
UDVe	Union des Démocrates pour la Cinquième République
UFF	Union de Fraternité Française
UFNA	Union des Français Nord-Africains
UGAC	Union des Groupes Anarchistes Communistes
UJCML	Union des Jeunes Communistes Marxistes-Leninistes
UMP	Union pour la Majorité Présidentielle
UN	United Nations
UNEF	Union Nationale des Etudiants de France
UNR	Union de la Nouvelle République
VAT	Value Added Tax
WEU	West European Union
ZUPs	Zones d'Urbaniser à Priorité

Introduction

When I first envisaged writing a study of the Fifth Republic, it was very much with student need in mind. While there were plenty of texts available in French, there were few written in English.[1] Always excepting Robert Gildea's brilliant synoptic study *France since 1945*,[2] most anglophone approaches treated the regime as part of a wider history of France in the twentieth century and stopped at some convenient point in the Republic's lifespan – for instance 1969, the resignation of de Gaulle, or 1995, the end of the Mitterrand presidency.[3] As befitted the importance which the Republic attached to its constitution, at least in its early years, there were ample accounts of political life, written by political scientists, but these were naturally aimed at fellow students of political science.[4] Almost invariably, the history of the Fifth Republic would be subsumed into discussions of the constitution, the presidency, the role of the prime minister, the powers of the state, party structures, local government, the relationship between France and Europe, and so on. Additionally there were numerous excellent analyses of cultural life, designed both for the general reader and students of the French language, but these too attached less importance to historical context.[5]

The object of the present study is to fill a gap in the existing anglophone literature by providing a brisk political narrative of the Fifth Republic. In the midst of the many thematic treatments available, it is often difficult to get a sense of the way in which the regime has evolved. All too often the history of the Fifth, especially in recent years, can appear to be a merry-go round of ministerial reshuffles, ironic given that de Gaulle wanted to end the cabinet instability that had supposedly blighted France before 1958. Some overview of the Fifth Republic is even more essential given that it is fast approaching its fiftieth anniversary, and is thus in danger of outliving the most venerable of post-1789 French regimes, the Third Republic, which survived for some seventy years (1870–1940). Yet in privileging the political history of the Fifth, this study has not neglected social, economic, cultural and international developments. It has much to say about the evolving nature and practice of presidential power; the tentative steps towards decolonisation and the 'resolution' of the Algerian problem; the unprecedented prosperity of the so-called *trente glorieuses* ('thirty glorious years'), which were followed in the 1970s by a period of economic retrenchment; the gradual disappearance of the peasantry, so long a bedrock of French society; the explosion of 1968; the revival of socialism under Mitterrand; the experience of the left in power; the influx of immigrants; the rise of the extremist Front National; the painful legacy of the Vichy years; the broader relationship between France and the wider world; and the recent presidencies of Jacques Chirac.

The survival and maturation of the Fifth Republic inevitably raises questions about periodisation. Those familiar with the history of the Third Republic (1870–1940) will be aware that, in the pre-1914 era, its history is commonly broken into three phases: the Republic of the Notables (1871–79) when the nation was dominated by the aristocracy; the Opportunist Republic (1879–1899), when political life revolved around respectable *bourgeois* politicians; and the Radical Republic (1899–1914) when the Radical party rallied to defend France from perceived threats, both at home and abroad. For sake of clarity, the structure of the present study has focused on particular staging posts in the evolution of the Fifth: the background of the Fourth Republic when politics effectively 'coagulated'; the 'crisis' years of the Fifth's founding, 1958–62; the 'consolidation' achieved by de Gaulle, 1962–67; the 'contestation' or questioning of 1968; the 'confidence' restored by Pompidou and Giscard, 1969–81; the 'chameleon-style' presidencies of François Mitterrand, 1981–1995; and the 'chagrin' or disappointments of the Chirac years since 1995. The advantage of adopting such discrete episodes is that it is possible to pick up on those longer term trends mentioned earlier, for example, presidential power, decolonisation, economic developments, intellectual life, and so on.

Nonetheless, may some broader periodisation be hazarded? The obvious answer, as Olivier Duhamel notes, would be to think of the Fifth Republic in terms of its presidents.[6] Such is the approach recently adopted by British writer Philip Thody.[7] This though would be to downplay continuities between *septennats* – the name given to the president's seven-year term of office, which since 2002 has become a *quinquennat*, a five-year term. Continuities were especially evident within the social and economic domains. It was fortunate for de Gaulle that his presidency (1958–69) coincided with the *trente glorieuses* which had begun shortly after the Second World War and which endured until the early 1970s. As to foreign policy, it might even be claimed that, in its essentials, this has changed little since de Gaulle. Successive presidents have upheld the principle of *grandeur*, asserting the French presence on the international stage, notably in Europe or Africa, so as to retain an independence of the USA, even though that independence has been more illusory than real.

A more compelling perspective would be to delineate overarching political trends. It could be argued that the period 1958–74 was that of the Gaullist state, the *Etat–UNR*, in which government had no hesitation in telling its citizens what was good for them. There followed, under Giscard (1974–1981), an 'interregnum', when liberalism prevailed and the powers of the state were rolled back. Under Mitterrand, it is often said that Fifth went through a period of *cohabitation*, a time when France was governed by the president of one party and the prime minister of another (1986–88 and 1994–95). Nonetheless, the period from 1981 to the present could also be seen as one of 'normalisation' in which both a Socialist and neo-Gaullist have consolidated the 'Republic of the centre'.

Yet another approach has been counselled by Georgette Elgey and Jean-Marie Colombani who argue that we should think of the Fifth largely in terms of those social and economic trends that have dominated each decade. For them, the 1960s were a period of 'civil war' in which various groups, notably the army in Algeria, sought control of the state; 1968 ushered in a *décennie* (decade) in which the conservative elites endured an uncomfortable relationship with a prosperous society ever ready to question accepted norms; the 1980s saw the state embrace the economics of the market place giving rise to an unbridled individualism; and the 1990s have witnessed a reassertion of a moral order, a dubious claim given the exposure of widescale corruption among politicians of all parties.[8]

One final periodisation should be noted here, that recently suggested by the British historian Richard Vinen. The Fourth Republic, he writes, was the 'age of the *notable*' when the traditional elites in society still made decisions; the hegemony enjoyed by de Gaulle in the 1960s coincided with the 'era of state power'; this 'statism' faded in the period after 1968 when 'globalisation' took root, a moment when French culture and economic autonomy was dominated by multinational companies, often Anglo-Saxon in background, which were unanswerable to national governments.[9] It is these corporations which now make the decisions which would once have been the province of local *notables*, prefects, deputies or the president.[10] Viewed from this perspective, it is claimed, the Fifth is no more: it is an anachronism, a mere shell, as France moves towards a Sixth Republic.

The possibility of a Sixth Republic is a constant theme in the political analysis of contemporary France and there even exists today a pressure group, the Convention for a Sixth Republic, which urges the adoption of a very different parliamentary system.[11] The fact remains, however, that the Fifth Republic is still in existence. There have been several prophets of doom but, at each crisis, the regime has picked itself up and dusted itself down. As two distinguished American historians observed, when the Fifth was a mere 20 years of age, 'At birth in 1958', it was 'a sickly creature ... unlikely to survive either a settlement of the Algerian conflict or the retirement of its founder.'[12] In the event, the regime overcame both of those difficulties, and more. In 1968, onlookers were astonished how the powers of the state suddenly evaporated, only to resurface again within a month. After the presidency of Pompidou, it was doubted whether the Fifth could cope with a non-Gaullist president in the shape of Giscard. In 1981, it was questioned whether it could endure with a Socialist at its helm. The year 1986 ushered in the first experience of *cohabitation*. This would have spelled disaster under de Gaulle. Under Mitterrand and Chirac it became an accepted way of life, popular among the electorate. Just when it seemed the Fifth had established its legitimacy, the remarkable showing of the extreme right-wing leader Jean-Marie Le Pen in the 2002 presidential elections startled political commentators who once again began talking in pessimistic terms about the life expectancy of the Fifth.[13]

At the time of writing, it cannot be argued that liberal democracy in France is in an especially healthy condition. In 1995, the distinguished historian of the Fifth Republic Arnaud Teyssier spoke of the 'pessimism' which pervaded political life,[14] a despondency recently reinforced by the remarkable showing of Le Pen in 2002. The roots of this disaffection are not difficult to discern. Since the 1980s there has been a steady drip of revelations about government corruption which, on occasion, have threatened to turn into a flood, submerging government. If he had not won in 2002, Chirac would almost certainly have been brought to trial. The state still controls too much power, and it is questioned whether government institutions have kept pace with underlying social and economic trends. Minorities, especially immigrants, await true integration. France still has to find a world role with which it feels comfortable. Today the talk among the political classes is that 'France est malade'.

As in other western liberal democracies, many of which have undergone similar experiences, these problems have produced a deep-seated disenchantment with politicians, exemplified by extensive voter abstentions in recent elections. Yet while these difficulties should not be underestimated, and must be urgently addressed, talk of crisis can be unhelpful. As the American historian of France, Stephen Kaplan has remarked, such talk is very much a French phenomenon, which should not obscure an underlying stability.[15]

The present study illustrates that rarely has the Fifth's future been genuinely in doubt, at least after 1962. Gaullists would argue that the key to the Republic's longevity lies in the constitution which gave the French people a system of government worthy of their genius, saving them from the natural Gallic trait of constant argument. This is an exaggeration. The political structures established in the period 1958–62 were undoubtedly important but most historians agree that, over the years, the constitution has become less crucial. This is partly due to the phenomenon of globalisation, mentioned earlier, but more critically to the general evolution of political life. As the Fifth has matured, all sides have accepted its legitimacy, notably the left which had a traditional mistrust of strong presidential powers. Even the extremist Front National (FN) seems content to work within the system, although who knows what it would do if it ever achieved any meaningful power on the national stage. Unlike the Fourth Republic, which struggled against the sniping of the Communists and Gaullists, the Fifth has thus been fortunate in that no major political party has seriously agitated for regime change. Political life has subsequently developed a momentum of its own and, at difficult moments, parties have made an effort to ensure the smooth functioning of the system, witness the repeated experiences of *cohabitation*. This process has been further aided by a dimming of ideological differences, a process facilitated by the marginalisation of the extremes, most notably the Communists who today appear caught in an irreversible decline.

Politicians have also adapted, with varying degrees of success, to an economy in mutation, something neither the Third or Fourth Republics managed to achieve. As John Horne has recently written, 'Only with the advent of the Fifth Republic ... did the political system begin to catch up with the transformation of French society,'[16] although this was to be a drawn out process. This profound social change also produced unparalleled levels of prosperity which have buttressed overall stability. As Vinen remarks, to this day France continues to be regarded as an economic success story, even though the impressive growth of the *trente glorieuses* ended in the mid-1970s and even though its benefits were unevenly divided, producing moments of profound social unrest.[17] Whereas the so-called *classes moyennes* have flourished, the peasantry and small business groups have been squeezed, although they have not entirely disappeared as was once predicted, partially because successive governments have cushioned their livelihoods. As we shall see, the worst hit have been immigrants, and the working classes whose numbers have fallen, along with their standards of living, and whose influence, through trade unions, has steadily declined. Economic uncertainty, especially the fear of unemployment, continues to haunt political debate. Yet, looking at the wider picture, it is difficult to avoid the conclusion that post-1945 French society has produced more winners than it has losers.

Foreign policy has also contributed to stability at home. We shall see how the politics of *grandeur* often degenerated into tawdry threats and empty gestures, which alienated international goodwill, yet it has often given the impression to the public that French power still matters. Decolonisation has not been an easy process, but getting out of Algeria was a terrific boon, as de Gaulle understood only too well. Greater involvement with Europe has also brought benefits, facilitating the ending of a near-century of Franco-German rivalry, which had produced three wars and two regime changes in Paris. France has subsequently adopted a highly ambivalent attitude towards European integration, and the results have often been uncomfortable. As Alistair Cole observes, France today is less distinct, less insular, less French, than it was in 1958. To walk down a French high street is to encounter many of the same shops, with the same shop fronts, selling the same goods, that can be found anywhere in northern Europe. Yet at the cost of losing something of its national identity, France has come to approximate more and more with its European neighbours, Britain and Germany, 'with their stable political systems and their regular alternations in power'[18], attributes not to be sniffed at.

The Fifth Republic has achieved a stability few would have predicted in either 1958 or 1969. Institutional flexibility, a desire on the part of a majority of the political players to make the system work, the fading of ideological extremes, an underlying economic prosperity, withdrawal from Algeria, closer involvement in European integration – these factors have all contributed to the durability of the regime. In the process, France may well have discovered the answer to the quest for political legitimacy that has bedevilled the nation ever since the people of Paris stormed the Bastille on 14 July 1789.

Chapter 1: La Coagulation: *The Fourth Republic, 1944–1958*

The Fifth Republic came to life in May–June 1958 thanks to an extraordinary fusion of a colonial crisis and a domestic impasse. Overseas, in the sweltering heat of North Africa, European settlers in the French colony of Algeria had, for the past four years, been resisting calls on the part of Arab nationalists for the creation of an independent state. As fighting intensified, settlers took to the streets organising a series of demonstrations demanding the colony remain French. None of these marches had, in the past, provoked serious riot or rebellion. 13 May 1958, it is agreed, was different. Terrified that, in Paris, the new government of Pierre Pflimlin was going to do a deal with the rebels, granting Algeria its autonomy, senior army officers and right-wing politicians seized power in Algiers. Their demand was for a government of public safety under the stewardship of General de Gaulle, the leader of wartime resistance to Nazism, and a man who had disassociated himself from the Fourth Republic thanks to its supposed inability to place the interests of France before those of political parties. In Paris, the government seemed transfixed by events – unable to react, sapped of energy, and all too impotent in the face of impending disaster. Whereas earlier in its life, it might have mustered the energy to confront the protestors, the Republic's successive failure to provide strong leadership meant that few politicians, even within the cabinet itself, had any faith in the regime's capacity to resolve the Algerian conundrum. In this situation, there appeared to be little option other than to summon de Gaulle; and, momentarily, the crisis was contained. As Jean-Marie Donegani and Marc Sadoun relate, the violence raging within Algeria did not immediately infect the mainland; the rule of law prevailed; and the main political players in both Paris and Algiers rallied behind the general who set about establishing the constitution of the Fifth Republic.[1]

It need not have been like this. In the aftermath of the Liberation (1944–46), there was hope that the resurgence of liberal democracy in the shape of a Fourth Republic would bring with it a new social and economic order redressing the inequalities of the past. Few could have predicted that within 12 years France would once again have to undergo the agonising process of overhauling its political structures. What had gone wrong? As we shall see, there is no shortage of explanations, many of which believe that regime was flawed from the outset. This was not necessarily so. When the Fourth uncovered a sense of purpose, it functioned reasonably well, for instance throughout the period 1947–51 when it rallied to fend off the Communist and Gaullist menaces, and during the Mendès-France experiment of 1954 when it set about concerted reform. For the most part, however, political life was allowed to drift, degenerating into petty squalling which resulted in an extraordinary inability to get things done. Liberal democracy subsisted as the regime still represented key interest groups within society: *notables*, peasants, small-holders and artisans. Whether in the long term, the Republic could have survived, without major change to its political structures, remains a moot point. This was a period of rapid, albeit uneven, economic change, the beginnings of the *trente glorieuses*, a period marked by a rise in consumerism, demographic growth, urbanisation, economic innovation, state planning and closer ties with Europe. Inevitably these changes began to recast society, boosting new social groups (most obviously professionals and white-collar workers), radically reshaping others (for instance, the working classes) and marginalising the formerly important (both the peasantry and *notables*). As David Hanley writes, 'All these processes of modernisation impacted sharply on France from the late 1940s onwards, meaning that by the end of the Fourth Republic economic and social structures were beginning to look much more like they do today, than they had done in 1939.'[2]

Given the ingrown inertia of the Fourth Republic, it is difficult to believe that the main political parties would have readily responded to the needs of this society in mutation, and that crisis loomed at some point in the future.[3] In the event, it was the very seriousness of the Algerian dilemma that laid bare the Republic's shortcomings, most obviously its lethargy, and brought about regime change. Even so, there was no reason why politicians should have turned to de Gaulle. Having entered the political wilderness in 1946, angered that the mainstream parties were not prepared to implement his ideas on a new constitution, he dreamed that he would be called upon to rescue his country, just as he had done in June 1940. Yet there was never any guarantee that the *appel* would sound or that it would have the backing of the key political players.

The Workings of the Fourth Republic

The reasons why drama in Algiers brought about a regime change are located in the failings of the Fourth Republic. One of the least-loved regimes in modern French history, 'la mal-aimée' as Joseph Barsalou described it, the Fourth began life in propitious circumstances, especially when compared to earlier experiments in the republican government. The First Republic (1792–1804) was very much a political expedient born out the chaos of the 1789 Revolution. Bereft of popular support, lacking stable constitutional structures and confronted with seemingly intractable problems bequeathed by earlier revolutionary regimes, it was easy prey to the vaulting personal ambition of Napoleon Bonaparte who, tiring of his role as First Consul (1799–1804), established the First Empire in 1804 (1804–1814). The Second Republic (1848–1852) was, as Alfred Cobban suggested, largely 'accidental', introduced to fill the political vacuum left by the sudden disappearance of the Constitutional Monarchy. Once again, a republic lacked popular support and secure political structures. Once again, it fell victim to a Bonaparte, this time to Louis Napoleon who, in 1852, abused his position as president of the Second Republic to emulate the *coup* of Brumaire. The Second Empire (1852–1870) that ensued had its share of problems, but would not have collapsed when it did had it not been for military defeat at the hands of the Prussians. For once, Bonapartism gave way to republicanism, but the Third Republic, officially founded in 1875, was largely thought of as another temporary arrangement; few predicted its survival. Remarkably it overcame a series of crises, each episode injecting much-needed confidence into its mental make-up. In the process, the Third established republicanism as *the* mainstream political force. Although by the 1930s the regime was clearly struggling, especially in its attempts to introduce progressive economic and social reform, it is widely agreed that the collapse of 1940, like that of the Second Empire in 1870, was the result of failings on the battlefield.[4]

Historically, then, a republic had begun life as a *deus ex machina*, brought down to provide temporary scenery while the principal actors attempted to build a more permanent political backdrop. At the Liberation of 1944, when France shook off the yoke of the Nazi presence and with it the wartime government of Marshal Pétain which had sidled up to the occupier, things were very different. Nearly everyone – the main political players, the behind-the-scenes stage hands and, most importantly, the audience of public opinion – was committed to a Fourth Republic. Among the people, there was no wish to go back to the lethargic ways of the Third, a regime wholly damned by the magnitude of the defeat in 1940. In a referendum of October 1945, the electorate (comprising women for the very first time) overwhelmingly rejected a return to the 1875 settlement, and gave the green light for the drawing up of a fresh constitution. It was a task the main political parties – the Parti Communiste Français (PCF), the Socialist Section Française de l'Internationale Ouvrière (SFIO), and the Christian Democrat Mouvement Républicain Populaire (MRP) – quickly warmed to. Their leaders, predominantly Resistance heroes (Thorez, president of the PCF, spent the war in Moscow) had long been discussing plans for renewal and looked expectantly to a political framework which would enable them to build afresh. Those on the left were especially enthused by the 'Social and Economic Programme of the Resistance' which envisaged wide-scale nationalisations and a massive redistribution of wealth. For his part de Gaulle, as head of the Provisional Government which oversaw national affairs in the period 1944–46, had little interest in social reform, but was likewise committed to a new constitution – one which would place power in the hands of the executive as opposed to parliament.

The prospects for liberal democracy were even stronger given the weakness of its enemies. The extreme right was tarnished by its association with Vichy, and was decimated by the post-Liberation purges (see below). For the time being, extreme rightists could hide behind the cloak of the MRP, known as the 'Machine à Ramasser les Pétainistes' and even less charitably as 'Mensonge, Réaction, Perfidie'. On the left, there were fears that the Communist Party would exploit its considerable influence within the Resistance to launch a revolution, yet these anxieties were misplaced, something even de Gaulle appreciated. While it suited his purposes to speak publicly of a 'red menace', privately he referred to Communists as 'reeds painted to look like irons'. As he was well aware, because of healthy PCF representation in the Provisional

Government, it was in the interests of both the party and Moscow to work within the confines of liberal democracy. For Stalin, the French Communist party, so slavish in its obedience to Moscow, could be relied upon to perform its appointed task of irritating the western democracies when the occasion called. In any case, he understood that the American presence in France would forestall any attempted revolution. As to the PCF, it was indeed content with the power it already wielded. Although its claim to have lost 75,000 members in the fight against the Nazi occupier was an exaggeration, the party's resistance credentials played well with voters who returned 160 Communist deputies in the June 1946 elections. The PCF would do even better in the November 1946 elections, winning 28.8 per cent of the vote and a record number 165 representatives.

The restrained, albeit deeply cynical, behaviour of the Communists was important in enabling France to escape the indignity of civil war in 1944. Such a struggle would undoubtedly have cast a pall over the Fourth Republic but, with hindsight, it may be seen that the nation was not truly at war with itself. As Rod Kedward has shown, by 1944 public support for Vichy, if not for Pétain who was still mistakenly credited for defending his country's interests, had all but evaporated, and it was only a minority of die-hard collaborators, congregated notably in the paramilitary Milice, who dared take on the Resistance.[5] Credit for the avoidance of civil war must also be given to resisters themselves who did not overstay their welcome. The majority of partisan fighters, assembled in the Forces Françaises de l'Intérieur (FFI), local *milices patriotiques* and *maquis*, melted back into civilian life or discovered a new career in the regular army. Likewise, those on the *Comités de Libération*, established to oversee the running of government at both a communal and departmental level during the Liberation, recognised when their work was done, and in April–May 1945 relinquished authority to newly elected municipalities.[6] So too did the Gaullist super-prefects, the *Commissaires de la République* – 'my' *commissaires*, as de Gaulle later made a point of stressing – whose role had been to stymie US plans to set up a military administration in France.[7] The French were thus able to govern themselves, which proved critical in restraining the excesses of postwar justice. As head of government, de Gaulle made plain that he had no wish for the French to be re-fighting recent quarrels, and expressed a desire for the wartime trials to be expedited as quickly as possible.

For some historians the temperate nature of the so-called *épuration* (the name given to the Liberation purges) was the key reason why in

1944–45 France did not slip into an unsightly internecine struggle. While certain key Vichyites, including Laval and Petain, were put on trial in front of a High Court of Justice and sentenced to death, the marshal escaping execution on the grounds of his old age, most received modest, even token sentences. Overall, the lower *cours de justice* established by the Provisional Government sentenced 2,853 to the firing squad, but judges soon lost a taste for this extreme sanction. In the event, only 1,502 executions took place while a further 3,910 death sentences were pronounced on persons *in absentia*. Additionally 38,266 individuals received jail terms, 46,145 suffered the penalty of 'national degradation', losing property and civil rights, and approximately 22,000 civil servants were relieved of their functions. Thanks to amnesty laws of 1947, 1951, and 1953 a majority of these punishments were commuted. It was the anomalies of postwar justice that were most unsettling. Punishments were severest in those areas where resistance had been fiercest, and it was poorer members of society, who could not pay for proper legal representation, that had most to fear. Historians also point to the harsh treatment meted out to those who had given symbolic support to the New Order, notably literary figures such as the novelist Robert Brasillach who faced the firing squad. This contrasted markedly with the token penalties imposed on industrialists, who had lent far more practical help to the Germans, although admittedly the Renault car works were nationalised in part as a punishment for economic collaboration. And, there remained the phenomenon of summary justice. Some 10,000 were shot by the Resistance, fewer than in Holland and Belgium, but troubling enough. Worst treated were those women suspected of *collaboration horizontale*, some 40,000 in number, who were tarred and feathered, and occasionally paraded naked down the streets with swastikas daubed on their breasts.[8]

The moderate nature of the purges, the reluctance and inability of political extremes to rock the boat, the discrediting of the Third Republic, the avoidance of civil war, the enthusiasms for creating something afresh – these were all encouraging omens. Yet, as politicians attempted to thrash out a new constitution, problems soon arose dashing this initial optimism for the future. A first draft pushed through by the Communists and Socialists, favouring a unicameral parliament, was overwhelmingly rejected in a referendum of 5 May 1946 lest the Chamber became the plaything of an over-mighty party. Consensus among the constitution-makers seemed a long way off and was only achieved by the adoption, that autumn, of a document eerily akin to that of the Third Republic. There were differences, but they could be easily missed. Although the president was more than a ceremonial figure, much depended on what he made of his office. Vincent Auriol (1946–53), proved himself as a power-broker. His successor, René Coty (1953–58), lived for compromise choice (he was elected by a congress of the National Assembly and Senate on the twenty-third ballot!) and was as bland as his suits. Greater authority rested with the prime minister whose role was considerably augmented. As Maurice Larkin recalls, no longer could governments be toppled at the impulse of parliament: it needed the premier to turn a parliamentary vote into one of no confidence, otherwise it required the passing of a censure motion, both procedures requiring an absolute majority.[9] As will be seen, this proved no safeguard against the ministerial instability which had been a fundamental part of life under the Third Republic. Although votes of no confidence were rare, and although there were never any motions of censure, when in rough waters prime ministers tended to resign before they were pushed, an acknowledgement of the overwhelming influence still wielded by the lower house, known as the National Assembly from 1946. To be fair, there was an upper house, named the Council of the Republic rather than the Senate, which was stripped of many of its former powers in the hope that it would not block legislation as in the past. Within two years, it reverted to its former name and, while less obstructive than before, remained a stronghold of business and agrarian interests.

The public was not fooled. In the referendum of 13 October 1946, the new constitution was approved by nine million votes, yet there were some 7.8 million abstentions and a similar number of 'no' votes. It was not an encouraging start. 'So many years lost', bemoaned François Mauriac in *Le Figaro*, 'simply to arrive at this patching together, this reupholstering.'[10] It was a view shared by de Gaulle who had repeatedly spoken out in favour of a strong executive which would rule over a weakened chamber and weakened parties. Earlier in January 1946, tired of the factionalism of political life, he had resigned from office, perhaps hoping that his absence would bring the politicians to sense.[11] If this was his intention, and many historians doubt it, the ploy failed and he was forced into a political wilderness which endured 12 long years. Residing at his country retreat at Colombey where he composed his war memoirs, he visited Paris each Wednesday to catch up on all the latest political gossip, but he deliberately kept a distance from the 'regime or parties'. This unwillingness to support the Republic at the outset, and to engineer reform from within, has also been seen as extremely damaging to the Fourth, yet it is difficult to see how de Gaulle could have ever worked within its structures.[12] As he himself remarked to the Chamber, 'There are two conceptions. They are not reconcilable. Do people want a government that governs, or do they want an Assembly that is all powerful.'[13]

Thereafter de Gaulle never lost an opportunity to denounce the factionalism of the Fourth Republic mocking the political parties for 'boiling up their little soup, over their little fire, in their little corner'.[14] For many, this sectarianism damned the regime. That ministerial instability was rife cannot be disputed. During the period 1946–58, there were no fewer than 25 ministries and 18 prime ministers. One cabinet managed to last an afternoon. The most successful survived for little more than a year – there were but two of these, those of Henri Queuille and Guy Mollet. As we have noted, prime ministers were inclined to resign rather than suffer the stigma of losing a vote of confidence. Nor did it help matters that they lacked the right to control the timetable of parliamentary business, that prerogative belonging to party chiefs. It was a brave premier who, in consultation with his cabinet, invoked articles 51 and 52 in order to exercise his full powers, for instance the right to disband parliament and announce fresh elections. It is frequently pointed out the one man do so, Edgar Faure, never occupied the premiership again. Accordingly, the parties in the Chamber seemed all powerful, ready to bring governments down at a moment's provocation. Larkin recalls the joke, popular in the Third Republic, that American tourists, newly arrived to Europe, travelled first to London to watch the changing of the guard at Buckingham Palace and then to Paris to watch the changing of the government. A cruder joke doing the rounds in the 1950s was that you always knew when a new cabinet had been formed as that was the day they changed the lavatory paper in the Archives Nationales.

Ministerial instability does not in itself, however, constitute a satisfactory explanation for the failings of the Republic. Many historians point out that postwar Italy has suffered far greater cabinet instability, yet the system there has continued to function. Historians also stress the underlying consistencies behind these cabinet turnovers: the collapse of government did not mean a fresh general election (the example of Faure was the exception that proved the rule), together with the remarkable continuity of personnel. As Auriol remarked to the US vice-president Alben Barkley, the regime was like a carriage pulled by horses. When the

horses grew tired, new ones were found; when new ones were not available, the original ones were used again.[15] As Peter Morris used to joke,
when Harold Wilson remarked that a week was a long time in politics he
clearly did not have France in mind.

Far more serious to the good health of the Republic than the coming
and going of ministers was the way in which the constitution was used by
the political parties. Thanks to the spirit of cooperation fostered by the
Resistance and a shared desire to promulgate progressive reform, the
new structures functioned reasonably well. In 1946–47, the three principal parties, the Socialists, Communists and MRP, worked within a
coalition known as *tripartisme*. In 1947, however, the Cold War started in
earnest. As David Bell observes, the Socialists now felt they had no other
option but to align with the MRP and other centrist parties, thus exclud-
ing the PCF from ministerial office.[16] This gave comfort to Washington
which was placing enormous pressure on the French government for the
removal of Communist ministers. Yet it should also be added that the
PCF position in government was virtually untenable following the 1947
Renault strikes which were supported by Communist ministers who
voted against the Ramadier government. They could hardly complain
about their subsequent expulsion from cabinet.

The Communists had expected their exclusion to be short-lived; it
proved permanent, till 1981. This meant that one of the most powerful
political forces was now arraigned against the system. Nonetheless, anti-
communism, sustained by the fears of the Cold War, lent the Republic a
fresh sense of purpose. Instead of *tripartisme*, the regime moved to
another coalition, known as the 'Third Force', comprising Radicals,
Socialists, and Christian Democrats, whose *raison d'être* was to resist the
far left. The Third Force soon had another enemy. On 14 April 1947,
Gaullists organised themselves into a 'movement' (in truth, a party) the
Rassemblement du Peuple Français (RPF), committed to the reform of
French institutions, a new constitution and the recovery of national
grandeur. The workings of this party will be discussed in more detail
later. What must be noted here is that the party failed to build on its
initial electoral successes and predicated its triumph on the eventual collapse of the system. When meltdown did not happen, when the RPF
started to behave in an indisciplined manner, de Gaulle disbanded the
movement.

Paradoxically, then, when confronted with danger, the 'regime of
parties' was capable of mustering a sense of purpose. It was in the period
1952–58, when these threats diminished and the Cold War became a

permanent part of the scenery, that political life degenerated into ill-discipline. In the words of David Hanley, 'Party logic was working much as it had been in 1939; short-lived coalitions, often giving way to broadly similar combinations of men, all based on compromise with mainstream regime parties, were the accepted norm.'[17] Even within the parties them-selves factionalism was rife, something skilfully summarised by Richard Vinen.[18] Although the right managed to set aside its differences to form the Conseil National des Indépendants et Paysans (CNIP), which did well in the elections of 1951, this was nothing more than a temporary settling of differences. Factions, continues Vinen, gathered around per-sonalities, notably Antoine Pinay and Joseh Laniel; disagreements raged over how best to protect business and agricultural interests; the ghost of Vichy still had to be exorcised; and opinion was divided on how to react to de Gaulle. In the centre, the MRP struggled to reconcile its commit-ment to progressive social reform with its conservative electoral base; its ties with the Church were another distraction, committing the party to a policy of proselytisation among the working class, a forlorn and expen-sive task; and the obsession with European integration meant that the party often sought ministerial office even if this meant aligning itself with unpopular governments. The other centre party, the Radicals, was more concerned with self-preservation, recognising that its traditional supporters in the shape of the peasantry and small shop-keepers were no longer as numerous as in the past.[19]

In this regard, the Radicals were assisted by the electoral system adopted in 1946 which dispensed with the single-member constituencies of the Third Republic in favour of multi-member ones through the so-called *scrutin de liste*. This encouraged yet further horse-trading at both a local and national level, something at which the Radicals were undisputed masters. They thus clung to power political office even though their vote was in free-fall. And, on the left, the Socialists, remained divided as to overall strategy: ought they work alongside the 'bourgeois parties' so as to protect social reform, even though this incurred the wrath of the Communists and disenchanted core voters? In the event, it proved difficult to influence national debate. With the Communist menace ever present, and in an attempt to create some party discipline, the mainstream parties revived old and sterile argu-ments: the quarrel between clericals and anticlericals, especially over the privileges of Catholic schools, and the dispute between resisters and former Vichyites, rehabilitated by amnesty laws. A new issue was that of the European Defence Community (EDC), which looked towards some form of common European defence policy independent of the USA. This raised the bogey of German rearmament which worried politicians of all hues.

The one concerted attempt to break this *immobilisme* came during the premiership of Pierre Mendès-France (June 1954–February 1955). Although Mendès-France is occasionally ridiculed for his Saturday evening radio homilies to the nation and fruitless attempts to get the French to drink milk instead of wine in order to curb alcoholism and absenteeism at work, he was a youthful and energetic premier, who wisely kept a distance from his supporters in the Radical party. Given a huge vote of endorsement by deputies at the start of his time in office, 419 votes to 47, he was determined to end the coalition of parties that were acting against the nation's interests. 'To govern is to choose' was one of his favourite sayings. With a degree in economics, he was also unusually knowledgeable about the condition of French industry and was committed to an economy that successfully harmonised state and private initiatives. He further recognised the need for France to pull out of its disastrous war in Indo-China and, in July 1954, signed the Geneva agreements enabling France to withdraw from Vietnam. Historians have since questioned whether Mendès-France was as far-sighted as is some-times argued, suggesting that his premiership was more a triumph of style over substance, the creation of the highly influential political weekly *L'Express*. What is not in doubt is that the 'New Deal' Mendès-France promise ultimately proved too radical, both for the right who sneered at his Jewishness and for his own party bosses who worked to undermine his position, leading to his resignation in 1955. The Fourth Republic was always more at ease with Henri Queuille, premier no fewer than four occasions in the period 1948–54. A provincial doctor from the Corrèze, one of the sleepiest rural departments, a veteran Radical politi-cian and member of numerous pre-1940 cabinets, his public demeanour and bedside manner reassured his colleagues that France was not in need of major surgery. His comment that, 'It is not a question of resolv-ing problems but of silencing those who raised them', more or less summed up his political philosophy.[20]

The premiership of Mendès-France is at least a reminder that the record of the Republic is not altogether a negative one. Born amid the euphoria of the Liberation of 1944, the Republic had promised a new dawn. In the words of the economic planner and advocate of European integration Jean Monnet, 'France had in fact become a new country, full of fresh energies'.[21] Many of these were epitomised in the 'Social and

Economic Programme of the Resistance'. Promising the 'creation of a true economic and social democracy, entailing the eviction of the great economic and financial feudalities', this resulted in the nationalisation of the coalfields, the state take-over of gas and electricity companies, the public ownership of the principal banks, an extension of the social security system and limited worker participation in the running of factories. For some resisters, the failure to implement this wide-ranging project of renewal in its entirety seriously weakened the Fourth. This might be so, but it cannot be disputed that the state – through subsidies, regulation, protectionism and national ownership – interfered in the running of the economy on an unprecedented scale, and on a level which would be deemed unacceptable today, even by socialists. Crucially, these polices contributed to the so-called *trente glorieuses*, a sustained period of impressive economic growth, a time when France appeared to break free from the sleepy rural world so evocatively portrayed in Marcel Pagnol's novel, *Jean de Florette*, Gabriel Chevallier's *Clochemerle* and André Chanson's *Les Hommes de la route* to enter a new age of modernisation. Economic planning, consumerism, demographic boom, urbanisation, a communications revolution, the proliferation of technocrats often trained in the Ecole Nationale d'Administration (ENA) – these were the features of a new France. Founded by an ordinance of 9 October 1945, the object of the highly elitist ENA was to form the bureaucrats of the future who would oversee the smooth running of French interests at both home and abroad.[22]

The inequalities and societal changes produced by the *trente glorieuses* will be discussed in chapter three, yet some mention should be made here of Pierre Poujade, a hitherto unknown stationer from Saint Céré in the Lot, who had flirted with various right-wing groups before abandoning Doriot and Pétain for de Gaulle and service in the RAF.[23] In 1953, angered that shopkeepers like himself had to collect Value Added Tax (VAT) and account for themselves to visiting tax inspectors, he formed the Union de Défense des Commerçants et Artisans (UDCA), an alliance of farmworkers, artisans, small wine merchants and shopkeepers. With some 200,000 members, in 1955 this was transformed into a political party, the Union de Fraternité Française (UFF), which aimed to be more than an anti-fiscal movement; instead it stood for a defence of the small man against the capacious designs of the state, the preservation of an old world dominated by small businesses and the maintenance of the empire which had covered France with glory. Although it unexpectedly won 53 seats in the 1956 elections, success proved fleeting. The historian

Annie Collovald has shown how in the Chamber, Poujadist deputies, among them artisans and peasants, were easily outfoxed by their more sophisticated counterparts; Poujade himself could not exert a discipline over his supporters who were divided over Suez, Algeria and de Gaulle; Poujade himself lost his seat in 1957; and there remained a limited constituency to whom the movement could appeal.[24] Although de Gaulle famously quipped that 'in my day, grocers voted for solicitors; now solicitors vote for grocers',[25] Poujade largely recruited among the lower middle class, discontented leftists and Algerian settlers. Others were put off by the movement's tub-thumping rhetoric, its resort to violence in breaking up rival political meetings, its underlying racism and the vagueness of its programme which all too often recited grievances without providing answers other than the summoning of an estates-general. Poujade had become a figure of fun, 'Poujadolf', and retreated from the limelight.

With hindsight, it may be argued that the Republic had less to fear from Poujade than from the frustrated ambitions of other social groups whose lives had been transformed by underlying economic change, notably white-collar workers, professionals and a reconstituted working class. For all Poujade's talk that the Republic was out of touch with everyday realities, politicians of the main parties still retained links with traditional social groups such as the *notables*, peasants and artisans. In this sense it was uncannily like the Third Republic which had also established 'transmission belts' between itself and these communities. As suggested earlier, it must be seriously questioned whether the political structures of the Fourth could have survived unchanged, given that these social groups were no longer all dominant. Had it not been Algeria, it is tempting to believe that some other matter would have provoked crisis bringing about regime change. It is even possible that the regime would have faced national unrest akin to that of May 1968 which, as we shall see, was in one sense a reaction against a 'blocked society'.

The Republic Overseas

The balance sheet of the Fourth Republic overseas is a mixed one: within the new international order, shaped by the Cold War, France had little choice but to accept its role as a second-rate power, although it never entirely complied with the wishes of the USA; within Europe, France achieved some measure of prestige and influence, taking the initiative in moves towards integration; and within its empire, it woefully mismanaged the processes of decolonisation, reluctant to abandon its colonies even though this created intolerable pressures at home and dented the nation's international standing.

Image was everything to the regime. At its birth in 1946, the Fourth was eager to put France's recent ignominious past behind it. In 1940 the country had undergone the most calamitous defeat in its history, one which had shocked world opinion and destroyed France's international status. During the four long years of enemy occupation, the collaborationist government of Pétain had failed to achieve any meaningful concessions from the Nazis and had merely succeeded in turning France into the milch cow of Hitler's Germany. When liberation was achieved, principally through the efforts of Allied troops, the outlook appeared bleak, France a mere bystander as the Anglo-Saxons and Soviets got on with the serious business of creating a new world order. It was a terrible, terrible snub when in, February 1945, the 'big three' (Britain, the USA and USSR) assembled at Yalta to decide on the post-war settlement for Europe without extending any invitation to France.

It was thanks to de Gaulle that France, in 1944–46, retained some measure of independence from the USA. We have already noted how, through the *commissaires de la République*, the general thwarted plans for an American-led administration at the Liberation. As Robert Gildea notes, he also insisted that French troops played a part 'in the final defeat of Germany' and secured a permanent seat for France on the Security Council of the newly-formed United Nations (UN).[26] Yet, as de Gaulle himself would discover on becoming president in 1958, there was only so far his country could travel in defying the realities of the new bi-polar world dominated by the two superpowers of the USA and USSR. In 1947, the nation had little choice but to enter the US-sponsored North Atlantic Treaty Organisation (NATO), acknowledging that the Soviets were henceforward the real enemy. While Marshall Aid was gratefully received, the influx of other American economic interests in the shape of Camel cigarettes, Wrigley's chewing-gum, Hollywood films, Disney cartoons and Coca-Cola, gave rise to fears among intellectuals and politicians that France, once the fountainhead of western civilisation, was in danger of becoming a US colony.

If in the international arena, France no longer wielded the power it once had, at least within Western Europe there was a possibility of re-establishing its influence. Excepting de Gaulle, who possessed his own 'idea of Europe', that is a Europe of nation states, in 1945 all politicians agreed on the desirability of closer European integration, a process in which France would take the lead. As has been suggested, this was driven by two considerations. On one level, it was hoped that European relations would be freed of the intense nationalism of the past which had resulted in periodic bloodshed, notably the three wars which France had fought with Germany in 1870–71, 1914–18 and 1939–45. 'Peaceful, tolerant cooperation for the benefit of all' was the desired ideal. On another plane, European integration might enable France to 'catch up, and if possible ... overtake, more industrialised neighbours,'[27] once again Germany constituting the prime rival. Beyond these general goals, however, politicians were in disagreement over how cooperation could be best accomplished. Integrationists, centred around Monnet and the MRP 'observes Guyomarch,' favoured a coming together of nations to produce a single economy, a single currency, a single defence policy – in essence a United States of Europe. Federalists, to be found among the Radicals and centre right, favoured some less rigid construct which would bolster indigenous economies and harmonise standards of living. Confederalists, largely located in the RPF, advocated looser ties, investing European institutions with little more than advisory functions, so as to preserve the autonomy of nation states.

The intensity of these debates surfaced in 1949 when Washington, anxious to cut its military commitment to Europe, pressed for West Germany's entry into NATO. The Pleven government in Paris preferred the creation of the EDC, which would oversee the creation of a European army in which Germans would serve under a centralised command. It was an ingenious proposal, but one that bitterly divided both country and parliament. The Gaullists and Communists are usually credited with the ditching of the plan by the National Assembly in August 1954. Yet critically many Socialists and some Radicals, together with a handful of MRP deputies, were likewise opposed, and the support of Mendès-France was never wholehearted. Ultimately, the debates over EDC were fruitless as, in 1955, it was decided to include West Germany into NATO. At least, progress was made in achieving closer economic ties by which the economic recovery of West Germany could be contained and re-distributed so as to benefit its European partners. On 9 May 1950, the Christian Democrat foreign minister Robert Schuman took France into the European Coal and Steel Community (ECSC) which pooled natural key resources; this paved the way for the Rome Treaties of March 1957, establishing the European Atomic Energy Community (Euratom) and the European Economic Community (EEC). As one of the six original signatories of Rome (along with West Germany, Italy, Luxembourg, Belgium and Holland) France was thus in pole position to mould any further integration.

The other means by which France could reassert its international standing was through empire. This had long been a source of national pride. Historians frequently remind us that it was second largest after Britain's, comprising lands in South-East Asia (Laos, Cambodia and Vietnam), North Africa (Algeria, Morocco, Tunisia), so-called 'Afrique Noire' (Senegal, Sudan, Guinea, Ivory Coast, Gabon, Congo), the Levant (Syria and the Lebanon), the Atlantic (St-Pierre, Miquelon), the Indian Ocean (Madagascar) and the Pacific (for instance, New Caledonia).[28] Empire had also come to the assistance of the 'mother' country on more than one occasion. After the *débâcle* of 1870 and subsequent diplomatic isolation at the hands of Bismarck, France looked to its overseas possessions to recover a sense of national pride. In 1914–18, some 172,000 Algerians fought in the French army, together with nearly 300,000 troops drawn from other African colonies. In 1940, the colonies were vital bargaining counters in Vichy's fruitless quest for collaboration. To Pétain's chagrin, much of the empire subsequently slipped into the hands of the Free French to form a valuable platform in the eventual liberation of metropolitan territory.

Uncomfortably for the French, the liberation of the metropolis gave rise to expectations among colonial peoples for their own liberation. This was never going to be straightforward. Apart from the national prestige conferred by empire, France had long seen itself as imbued with certain universal truths and understanding. In the words of de Gaulle himself, 'The magistrature of France is moral. In Africa, in Asia, in South America, our country is the symbol of equality among races, of the rights of man and of the dignity of nations.'[29] As Anthony Clayton writes, it was thus France's 'mission to pass on these truths and wisdom to others, even if necessary by force.' Thanks to this conception, 'France and French possessions must form an indivisible whole ... Secession to the French mind was not an emancipation, it was a heresy.'[30] This attitude perhaps explains why, in January 1944, French colonial administrators (significantly no African representatives were given a real voice), gathered together at Brazzaville in the Congo, refused to think in terms of granting independence. Instead they contemplated various administrative reforms and looked ahead to renaming the empire the 'French Union', something confirmed by the constitution of the Fourth Republic. As Gildea observes, in defiance of that constitution, which promised that France would never use force to suppress the liberty of any people, French troops were quickly, and brutally, re-imposing control in Algeria, Madagascar, Syria and the Lebanon, a campaign that was approved by de Gaulle himself.[31]

Real difficulties began in Vietnam where, in March 1945, Vichy control passed to the Japanese, then to the Communist and nationalist forces of the Vietminh, led by Ho Chi Minh who, in September that year, announced the creation of an independent Vietnamese Republic. Historians have since acknowledged that the requirements of the insurrectionists were restrained, especially as the rebels envisaged the new Vietnam would remain within the French Empire, albeit with its own government, parliament and budgetary powers. With hindsight, Paris should have jumped at this compromise and, in March 1946, it appeared that such a settlement had been conceded. Yet both central government and local administrative and military chiefs agreed on the need to rebuild French authority in the area. To this end, in June 1946 the new Commissioner for the area, Thierry d'Argenlieu, announced the creation of a republic of Cochin-China, to be governed from Saigon (for which, read Paris), a move which effectively divided Vietnam into two, confounding the hopes of the nationalists. Unperturbed that this initiative flouted international law, in another cack-handed attempt to display French resolve, in November that year Thierry d'Argenlieu bombed the northern port of Haiphong, leaving up to 6,000 dead. The conflict that ensued proved unwinnable. Struggling to cope with the Maoist guerrilla campaign of General Vo Nguyen Giap, by 1950 French forces had relinquished sizeable chunks of the countryside to the Vietminh. As historians point out, that same year matters were compounded by the fact that a localised colonial struggle became part of the emerging Cold War when Communist China and the USSR recognised the Democratic Republic of Vietnam. This prompted significant US aid to France, and inevitable PCF criticism of the war effort at home. Catastrophe came in May 1954 when large numbers of French paratroopers were encircled and defeated at Dien Bien Phu. At the subsequent peace conference of July 1954, some honour was rescued when Mendès-France secured a largely favourable settlement for France: Vietnam was split into two, the north being occupied by the Vietminh and the south placed under US protection.

While the politicians could draw some comfort from the withdrawal, the generals were enraged. Having suffered catastrophe in 1940, the army had not had a chance properly to reconstitute itself. All too soon it had suffered a fresh humiliation, beaten this time not by the might of Guderian's Panzers but by an inferior enemy, a rag-tail army of 'little yellow men'. Just as in 1940, there was a search for scapegoats, especially among the political body. As General Boyer de Latour, Commissaire de la République for North and South Vietman grumbled, 'The loss of Indo-China was due to the incoherence of our politics under the Fourth Republic, to military errors resulting in part from the regime.'[32]

The omens were not good for what was to unfurl in North Africa, especially when the composition of the *Armée d'Afrique* is taken into account. This had long enjoyed a distinctive identity, assimilating elements of Arab culture without losing a sense of racial superiority. It had felt betrayed by the politicians in 1940 and was loyal to Vichy until the Allied landings in November 1942 left it with no choice other than to go over to de Gaulle. Traditionalist in its opinions, contemptuous of politicians and hostile to outside interference, such attitudes had been hardened by new recruits in the post-1945 period. Analysis has shown that these were often men who were alienated by the consumer mentality sweeping across France – men who were searching for 'a purity in the bled', men who wanted to enjoy some good old-fashioned soldiering, men who were contemptuous of Algerian nationalism, believing it nothing more than a front for Soviet Communism.[33] After Indo-China, they had also begun to learn the secrets of guerrilla warfare which meant they became even more attached to the land, its people and traditions, as they waited to fight the enemy within. These, then, were not soldiers who would leave Algeria voluntarily. As General Lorillot, the French Commander in Algeria, remarked, 'They (ie the politicians) made fools of us in Indo-China ... They will never screw us in Algeria. I swear to you.'[34]

At least in Tunisia and Morocco, the French managed to withdraw from their protectorates without any serious difficulties, as they were from their Sub-Saharan possessions. Algeria, it is commonly said, was different. Here, on 1 November 1954, Algerian nationalists belonging to the newly-formed Front de Libération Nationale (FLN) began an uprising, the ultimate objective of which was nothing less than an independent state. Thanks to the unwillingness of the French state to grant Muslims equal rights, so that they became 'citizens' rather than 'subjects', there had been nationalist movements aplenty, but none on the scale of the FLN. As Martin Evans reminds us, the very first had been the left-orientated Etoile Nord-Africaine (ENA), founded in 1926 by Hadj Abel Kader, and later fronted by Messali Hadj, the son of a cobbler from

Tlemecen.[35] Recruiting among immigrant workers in Paris, continues Evans, the ENA called for the liberation of Morocco, Tunisia and Algeria, and initially enjoyed close relations with the PCF; these relations turned sour in 1936 when, in a crackdown on extra-parliamentary bodies, the ENA was outlawed by the Popular Front. Not to be thwarted, it re-emerged as a political party, the Parti Populaire Algérien (PPA), renaming itself in 1945, after another crackdown, as the Mouvement pour le Triomphe des Libertés Démocrates (MTLD). Alongside this left-wing brand of nationalism was an Islamic strain, known as the Ulama movement, initiated in 1931 by Sheik Abdulhamid Ben Baddis, which believed Algeria could only be cleansed of colonial rule by the assertion of the strict ideals of the Koran. As Evans concludes, a more 'reformist' wing congregated around Ferhat Abbas, a pharmacist from Constantine, and a onetime admirer of French civilisation. Disappointed by the limited reforms of the Popular Front, he abandoned gradualism and came to advocate full-blown independence, a view hardened by the Second World War which revealed the vulnerability of the French empire. In 1943 he authored the 'Manifesto of the Algerian People' advocating the direct representation of the Arab population and the inspiration behind the Amis du Manifeste et de la Liberté (AML), founded a year later, which brought together the many elements of Algerian nationalism.

This unity was short-lived. When in May 1945 the Allied victory in Europe inspired a nationalist uprising in Sétif, resulting in the deaths of 21 settlers, French retribution was severe. Some 40,000 Algerians lost their lives in the ensuing barbarity. This legimated violence and gave rise to a generation of die-hard militants who had little time for either the MTLD or the Union Démocratique pour le Manifeste Algérien (UDMA), a new political party created by Ferhat Abbas. There thus emerged the Organisation Spéciale (OS) of Ahmed Ben Bella, a guerilla-style organisation. After this too was overcome by the French, militants founded the Comité Révolutionnaire d'Unité et d'Action (CRUA) which mobilised the many strands of Algerian nationalism into the FLN. While unity remained fragile, the FLN oversaw a resistance army, the Armée de Libération Nationale (ALN), which prepared for an armed insurrection in Algeria on 1 November 1954, the Feast of All Saints, when the largely Catholic colonist community would be caught unaware.

Apart from the new-found zest of the Arab nationalists, there were other reasons why this protest was so serious. First, unlike much of the remainder of the Empire, Algeria was more or less regarded as a fully-

relinquish their gun-boat diplomacy. Even such international condemnation did not prevent the French airforce from bombing the Tunisian village of Sakhiet, on a busy market day, in February 1958. Supposedly an FLN base, 69 civilians lost their lives.

After 1956, 'like a British prime minister at Suez', a snipe at Anthony Eden, became a popular phrase in this country to mean someone in a fluster. In France, the sobriquet 'national molletism' became popular to denote government ineptitude. Cabinets appeared to favour an ostrich approach to North Africa, burying their heads in the sands of national politics, ignoring what was happening in the *bled*. After Sakhiet, confusion reigned supreme. Prime minister Gaillard resigned over the issue, and it was 38 days before the next ministry was formed, the most protracted spell the Fourth Republic ever went without a government. In this situation, the military in Algeria became more and more powerful. As Douglas Porch has remarked, generally speaking the French army stays out of national politics so long as governments remain strong and do not intervene in military affairs.[42] In 1958, government was weak, and the army was determined to make a stand. It will be recalled that the moment came on 13 May when Pflimlin, an MRP deputy and a liberal on Algeria, became the new prime minister. Frightened that a deal with the FLN was on the cards, that very same day *pieds noirs* demonstrators stormed government buildings in Algiers, shortly to be joined by Massu and his paratroopers. Initially, the demonstrators were not especially keen on de Gaulle. As noted, several *pieds noirs* were Giraudist or Pétainist, while the army itself doubted the general's commitment to Algeria. It was largely thanks to the manoeuvrings of influential Gaullists, such as Jacques Soustelle, Jacques Chaban-Delmas and Delbecque, that on 15 May the cry from Algeria was for de Gaulle.

Similarly, on metropolitan soil, several key politicians, including Mendès-France, had come to accept that the general was the only man capable of resolving the crisis; the public likewise. In a *sondage* of January 1958, 13 per cent of those interviewed hoped for his return; no other politician did as well. In March, *Le Monde* printed an article simply called 'When?', the question being at what point, not if, de Gaulle would return. Such editorials were highly reminiscent of the late 1930s when leading politicians and newspapers had seen Pétain as the answer to the sense of crisis overwhelming France. Then, as in 1958, confidence lay with a man who had deliberately stood outside of a discredited political system, and whose patriotism seemed beyond reproach. Interestingly, both men had also refused to put themselves forward. Instead, they had

to be called upon at a moment of crisis. For de Gaulle, May 1958 was the
defining hour as June 1940 was for Pétain. The difference between the
two was that the marshal was a supremely ordinary individual, overly
confident in his own abilities and woefully prepared to lead his country.
De Gaulle was anything but.

De Gaulle

Who was the man that the politicians, public and *pieds noirs* were clam-
ouring for? Born in Lille on 22 November 1890, he came from a minor
northern, aristocratic family which, not surprisingly, was monarchist and
deeply Catholic in sympathy, ill-at-ease with the anticlerical Third
Republic which had been in power for some 20 years. His father, the
descendant of a long line of writers, taught at a Jesuit college, which
Charles himself attended for a short while. 'Give the Jesuits a child at the
age of seven and they will show you the man', so the saying goes. It would
be in the best traditions of clerico-military conspiracy theory to suggest
that one of France's most celebrated sons was part of a Jesuit plot to
infiltrate the army, and ultimately the Elysée, yet by the time he entered
the prestigious military college of Saint-Cyr in 1909 it is already possible
to see something of the adult de Gaulle. A tall, albeit slightly awkward
figure, with the angled nose that would later be a target for caricaturists,
he possessed unlimited self-confidence, and was certain that one day he
would serve his country. A deep-rooted patriotism was always part of his
make-up, and helps explain his choice of career in the army and faith in
French *grandeur* and the nation state. Although a sense of pragmatism led
him to accept the European Economic Community (EEC), as historians
stress he had no liking for supra-national bodies such as the EDC or
NATO – 'supranationality is absurd', he later quipped – and he remained
suspicious of the influence of the USA.[43] Nor did he have much truck for
ideologies such as communism which transcended national boundaries.
'Ideologies pass and people remain', he once stated.[44]

Remarkably, given his upbringing, he did have time for republicanism, yet he was no admirer of the Third Republic. As a man of the north,
albeit one who spent much of his early life in Paris, it is said that he
inherited a regional reserve, and was contemptuous of the garrulous
republican deputies, many of whom sprang from the socially affable
south. As Serge Berstein has shown, this distaste was evident as early as
1913.[45] As a patriot, he had little patience with political parties, whose

alleged pursuit of selfish sectarian goals diluted national interest. His preference was for a republic guided by a strong leader who would be assisted by a weakened legislature, and who would have occasional recourse to plebiscites. As several commentators have pointed out, notably Arnaud Teyssier, his vision was not that dissimilar from the authoritarian republic favoured by such right-wing writers as Maurice Barrès and Paul Déroulède, and it is not difficult to see why he would later be accused of dictatorial tendencies.[46] To Alain Peyrefitte, his minister of information in the 1960s, he made a habit of quoting Péguy, the Catholic nationalist poet popular before 1914, 'Order, and order alone, guarantee freedom. Disorder creates servitude.'[47]

Because of his ambition, patriotism and desire for adventure, the First World War should have been a liberating experience for de Gaulle, yet it proved frustrating. Captured at Verdun in 1916, he spent the remainder of the conflict in a prisoner-of-war camp where he bided his time perfecting his German, making frequent escape bids, all unsuccessful, and writing. On return from captivity, he enjoyed a varied, but largely unspectacular military career, serving on Pétain's staff (1925–27) and sitting on the secretariat of the Conseil Supérieur de la Défense Nationale (CSDN) (1932–73). At the outset of war in 1939 he was a colonel and tank commander in the Fifth Army. Meanwhile, he pursued a literary career, publishing *The Edge of the Sword* (1932), a compendium of his Saint-Cyr lectures, *Towards an Army of the Future* (1934), a critique of French strategic thinking, and *France and her Army* (1938), originally a piece a staff work written for his one-time mentor Pétain, which appeared in de Gaulle's name causing a bitter quarrel between the two men. Indeed, this foray into publishing signalled de Gaulle's increasing preparedness to question the wisdom of his betters, a trait unwelcome in military circles. His superiors especially resented the theme of *Towards an Army of the Future*, which rejected the defensive tactics favoured by France's military gurus and advocated the creation of an elite professional force which would deploy tanks in an offensive capacity. Historians have shown that such unorthodoxy was not as original as is sometimes believed. What perhaps was of greater significance was de Gaulle's willingness to seek a wider audience for his views among politicians. In the event, many deputies were frightened off, fearing that a professional army might be used for political purposes. At least he found a champion in the maverick politician Paul Reynaud who, as prime minister in June 1940, appointed the newly-promoted brigadier-general de Gaulle to the post of Under-Secretary of State for National Defence.

Disturbed by the desperate nature of the military situation, despondent at the defeatism he discovered inside the cabinet, and despairing at Reynaud's resignation in favour of Pétain, on 17 June de Gaulle flew to England and, on 18 June, broadcast an appeal to France inviting his countrymen to join him in continuing the struggle.

Although few people heard this message, there was no disguising the remarkable position that he had adopted. An unknown in England, he had cast himself into the role as his country's saviour, regarding himself as the embodiment of the 'true France'. It was a brazen move, and one which initially paid few dividends. While Churchill acknowledged de Gaulle as leader of the Free French, he did not bestow upon him the title of head of a government-in-exile; the Foreign Office was mistrustful of this little-known figure; and there remained the hope that a more prestigious, and less arrogant, politician would somehow make the difficult journey from France to London. Nor, to begin with, did de Gaulle have much success in recruiting to the Free French. In this situation, lacking military clout, de Gaulle conducted what has often been called 'a diplomatic war', one that can be broken down into two stages.

In the first period, June 1940–November 1942, he was concerned with strengthening his position, especially in the empire, resisting British attempts to 'colonise' his movement. Relations with Churchill reached a low point in 1941 as disagreements broke out over the future of Syria, which de Gaulle feared would become a British colony, a fear that resurfaced when British troops invaded Madagascar the following year.

In the second phase, November 1942–August 1944, de Gaulle had to fend off several threats, the most serious being that posed by the Americans. Roosevelt, highly suspicious of de Gaulle's commitment to liberal democracy and bewildered by the arrogance of a man who compared himself to Joan of Arc, was determined to outwit the general and discover a more compliant French leader. The moment came in November 1942 when American forces invaded North Africa. Anxious to exclude de Gaulle, the USA attempted to govern the area first with the help of ex-Vichyite Admiral Darlan and then with the cooperation of General Giraud, a general of undoubted patriotism and astonishing political naivete. It was not long before de Gaulle supplanted Giraud to take charge of the recently-formed Comité Français de Libération Nationale (CFLN), a body on which both men were supposed to share equal power. As a government-in-waiting started to take shape under de Gaulle's aegis in Algeria, the general took care of other dangers to his authority, in particular by extending his control over the rapidly developing resistance in metropolitan France. When the Liberation drew closer, the general's concerns mushroomed. As his biographer Andrew Shennan recalls, these were to ensure the smooth transfer of authority between himself and Vichy; to restrict Anglo-Saxon meddling in French affairs; to guarantee his own place as France's next political leader; and to make certain that France played a part in the final defeat of Germany. As noted, not all of these objectives were met, thus forcing his resignation in January 1946. While the war years might have transformed de Gaulle into a national leader and 'given him a unique symbolic identity', as Shennan observes, they had also left him an 'inexperienced politician without an organised and cohesive following'.[48]

De Gaulle subsequently entered a 12-year political wilderness, yet was far from inactive. It was his expectation that a global crisis would usher him back to power, most probably international tension over nuclear weapons, not such an unlikely prospect given the freezing over of the Cold War. Meantime, ever the opportunist, he was not averse to exploiting lesser crises to engineer his return. Following the rejection of the first draft of Fourth Republic's constitution in the referendum of April 1946, on 16 June that year de Gaulle travelled to Bayeux, the town where he had landed at the Liberation. Here he delivered a speech clearly intended to influence the decision-making process. With his mind cast on the inadequacies of the Third Republic, the message championed a presidential regime in which the head of state would stand above both parties and parliament, and would be selected by an electoral college. To avoid chronic ministerial instability, parliamentary authority would be reduced, the right to appoint the prime minister and his cabinet colleagues belonging to the president. Yet lacking any organised support in the Provisional Government or the countryside, his words fell on deaf ears and, as noted, in October the new constitution of the Fourth was approved, albeit by a narrow margin.

Bowing to the inevitable, in 1947 the general established a political movement, the RPF. To avoid accusations of factionalism, his new 'party' was called a 'Rassemblement', a rally. In this way, de Gaulle viewed his creation as a continuation of the Free French, both movements committed to the restoration of French *grandeur*. Yet, unlike the Free French, the RPF immediately won over many recruits, doing handsomely in the municipal elections of 1947, becoming the largest parliamentary force in the 1951 elections with 119 seats. Its moment, however, had passed. Much of its early support – the product of a 'red scare', economic uncertainty and de Gaulle's tireless campaigning – had tailed off.

International relations had eased; American economic aid had kicked in; and, as we have seen, the Fourth Republic proved capable of defending itself through the Third Force which engineered subtle changes to the electoral laws to minimise Gaullist success in 1951. The Fourth Republic had not imploded as de Gaulle had intended. As a result, 'the party that was not a party', as it has been aptly called, became increasingly ill-disciplined, 27 of its deputies breaking ranks in 1952 to support the conservative prime minister Pinay, behaviour all too reminiscent of other political groups in the Chamber. The following year, de Gaulle disbanded his movement, clearly a difficult decision.

Retreating to Colombey-les-deux-Eglises, he spent the next four years writing his war memoirs, seemingly an old man with little ambition, yet keeping in touch with events in Paris through his *petite bande* – Olivier Guichard, Jacques Foccart, Pierre Lefranc, and Georges Pompidou. Indeed, de Gaulle 'the politician' had matured during his time in exile. In the course of the Second World War, he had learned much about diplomacy, but little about politics, and in the early days of the Fourth Republic he was repeatedly outclassed by the 'pint-sized' politicians he despised. He was not about to let this happen again.

The Investiture

Older and wiser, in 1958 de Gaulle was immediately aware of the need to allay the fears of the main political players. He thus presented himself to the *pieds noirs* and Algerian military as of the same mould, a formidable army figure who would keep the colony French and who would silence the chattering politicians in Paris. When it came to the politicians, he sought to avoid charges that he was a Boulanger or Bonaparte by presenting himself as a champion of liberal democracy, a man who would save France from the danger of a *coup d'état*.

It was always going to be a difficult task to keep so many people happy, yet de Gaulle played a skilful hand, allowing events to unfurl in such a way as to accentuate the sense of crisis, thus hardening the belief that he was the only person capable of solving the problem. When, on 15 May, the *coup* leaders came out in his favour, he quickly issued a *communiqué* denouncing 'the degradation of the state' and making clear his readiness 'to assume the powers of the Republic'. On 19 May, he held his first press conference since June 1955, in which he told reporters that he was happy to be 'useful again to France'. To reassure the politicians, he joked that at the age of 67 he had no idea of beginning 'a career as a dictator' and insisted that if he resumed power it would be through legal processes, that is through a delegation of exceptional powers by parliament. Significantly, however, he avoided an outright condemnation of the *putschists*, a ploy to keep the military happy and to keep alive the threat of a military takeover. Such fears were heightened when, on 24 May, paratroopers from Algeria landed in Corsica. Meanwhile, in Algeria General Massu threatened to repeat the operation, codenamed 'Ressurection', dropping paratroopers into the streets of Paris to occupy key government buildings.

Whether de Gaulle would ever have given the green light to 'Ressurection' has remained a question of endless fascination, one of those counter-factual situations in which historians delight.That he knew about the plot is not in doubt. It is also clear that he was prepared to use it as a stick with which to beat the republican politicians. It also seems likely that his contempt for the Fourth Republic and his determination to avoid the mistakes of 1946 were such that he would have been prepared to have come to power on the back of such an invasion. In the event, he avoided a *coup*, thanks largely to his own brinkmanship and the action of those politicians he so despised. As John Keiger and Martin Alexander remark, his coming to power was 'less the outcome of plots, more a case of being the only credible political force at that moment rushing into the vacuum left by the foundering of the Fourth Republic in April–May that year.'[49] On 26 May, after a fruitless interview with Pflimlin, he announced that he had begun the regular process of forming a government and appealed for order in Algeria. The prime minister refused to budge, buoyed by a parliamentary majority and Socialist backing in the Chamber, yet many senior politicians on all sides were reaching the conclusion that the general was the only person of resolving the crisis. This belief was hardened on 28 May when some 200,000 protestors took to the streets of Paris in a Communist-organised demonstration denouncing de Gaulle as 'a putschist'. Now that France faced the spectre of a communist insurrection as well as a military one, politicians agreed that the time had come to act. On 29 May President Coty – thoroughly disillusioned with the regime over which he presided – showed some independence of spirit and requested de Gaulle to assemble a new government, a move reminiscent of Albert Lebrun, the Third Republic's final president, who had summoned Pétain on 16 June 1940.[50]

On 1 June 1958, the general presented himself to the Assembly where he was invested with full powers for a period of six months, a time in which he promised to restore order and draft a new constitution to be approved via a plebiscite. Bewildered, frightened and out-manoeuvred, the deputies agreed his requests by 329 votes to 224. In this way, de Gaulle became the last prime minister of the Fourth Republic, and effectively the executor, of the Fourth Republic, tidying up the regime's affairs as it was laid to rest.

Conclusion: La Mal-Aimée

Had Napoleon III not been defeated at Sedan in 1870 there is every likelihood that the Second Empire would have stumbled on for several more years. Had not Guderian's Panzers crushed Allied troops so convincingly in June 1940 it is almost certain that the Third Republic would have celebrated further birthdays. Had not Algeria erupted into crisis in 1958 it is also possible that the Fourth Republic would have lived to see another day. Yet this does not hide the fact that there was something fundamentally wrong internally with all three regimes. While the fear of both Communism and Gaullism had given the Fourth a sense of purpose, after 1951 politics had become characterised by their *immobilisme* and inability to promote radical change. Confronted with the conundrum that was Algeria, admittedly a problem frightening in its complexity, it had no answer but to fall on its sword and hand power to de Gaulle who had long predicted that the Fourth would end in tears. As Philip Williams suggests, perhaps no regime could have overcome the Algerian headache.[51] Yet to attribute the fall of the Republic entirely to the failings of the political system is misleading. As noted, it overcame the challenges of Communism, Gaullism and Poujadism. It was unfortunate that this success perpetuated 'traditional republican behaviour (in the sense of deference to the chamber and a general mistrust of firm government)' and did not persuade those in power to adapt their party structures to reflect new social realities.[52] Economic change, urbanisation, consumerism, a growth in communications – all of these things were beginning to alter the landscape in such a way that tension would almost certainly have erupted between an inert political system and an energetic society. Algeria notwithstanding, a crisis was thus looming in the future. It has been one of the achievements of the Fifth Republic that it has achieved political elasticity, enabling it more or less to keep pace with underlying economic developments, something de Gaulle could not truly have envisaged when he drew up a new constitution in 1958.

Chapter 2: La Crise: *The Founding of the Fifth, 1958–62*

On drafting his recollections of the Fifth Republic, de Gaulle's intention, as in his earlier *Mémoires de guerre*, was to present himself as a man of vision, a man of destiny, who had single-handedly salvaged his country on two occasions – the first was in June 1940 when he had defied the authority of the Pétain regime to restore the honour of France; the second was his accession to power in May 1958 when he rescued his country from crisis over Algeria.[1] As the historian Andrew Shennan observes, this historical parallel might not necessarily have been accurate, but it soon became part of the Gaullist mythology.[2] In the eyes of his supporters, the general had twice delivered the French from their inability to devise a political system worthy of their intelligence and genius: from the bickering of the Third Republic which had led to military collapse and the unacceptable solution of Vichy, and from the political instability of the Fourth Republic.[3] The Fifth Republic was, then, the true beginning of modern France, the point at which the country relinquished being an unruly, churlish and feckless adolescent to enter into adulthood, assuming responsibility, discipline and pride. To borrow de Gaulle's own words, it was the time when France 'married its century'.

This is how an old man at Colombey-les-Deux-Eglises might have wished to present matters, and it may have been how his acolytes chose to interpret things, yet in 1958 there was no certainty that the Fifth Republic would endure, at least in its Gaullian vision. As René Rémond observes, the historical parallel with 1958 was less 1940 than that of 1870. Then, too, a new republic seemed to be the most opportune solution to crisis; then, too, the French had turned to a charismatic old man, on that occasion Adolphe Thiers, a stalwart of the July monarchy (1830–48), who became the new regime's first president.[4] As in 1870, a period of stability would ensue allowing the elites to mull over the future, the end of their deliberations being the moment when the general would step down. De Gaulle had no intention of emulating Thiers, who had lasted as president little over two years, but much would depend on how the new political structures functioned, together with his success in handling both Algeria and his opponents.

Constitution-Making

During exile, de Gaulle had enjoyed plenty of time to think about the new political structures he wished for France but, as Rob Turner asserts, his ideas had changed little since he delivered his famous speech on 16 June 1946, the so-called Bayeux Constitution.[5] In this, he had fore-warned of the dangers within the Fourth Republic's institutional frame-work and, in his mind, it was these failings that had exacerbated the crisis of 1958, affronting his very conception of the state. Although no disciple of Charles Maurras, the right-wing ideologue who had been so widely read during the general's youth, de Gaulle agreed with the Action Française leader in seeing the state as a living organism, similar to the family, school or workplace, a natural product of the human con-dition, with all its faults and weaknesses. The problem for the French had been that successive regimes, notably the Third and Fourth Republics, had 'exacerbated the natural Gallic temperament which is so prone to divisions and quarrels.'[6] Unlike Maurras, de Gaulle did not wish to split France from its past by renouncing the principles of the 1789 Revolution through a restoration of a monarchy; he sought instead to unite his country by a strong presidential regime which would not be held hostage by sectarian parties which were characteristic of the national habit of 'questioning everything and thus all too often over-shadowing the major interests of the country.'[7] Only such a system, he maintained, would permit his people to rediscover their genius. In this sense, de Gaulle never aspired to be a dictator as elements of the left fre-quently charged. During the 1960s, he recalled with bitterness how, during his wartime residence in London, fellow exiles such as Raymond Aron had charged him with wanting to be a Bonaparte.[8] To Peyrefitte, he said that it would, in any case, be impossible in a modern-day demo-cracy to repeat the *coup* of Napoleon III of December 1851, not that he wanted to.[9] He accepted that the democratic form of government, underpinned by universal suffrage, was the only true basis of political power.[10] It is also telling that de Gaulle, intensely involved in the new institution-making despite the pressing problems of Algeria, still allowed a wide range of jurists and ministers a say in the drafting of the constitution. This perhaps accounts for its complexity, and also for its ambiguity; in the longer term, historians suggest, this ambivalence has proved no disadvantage.

Presented to the people on 4 September 1958 – significantly, the same day on which the Third Republic had been proclaimed in 1870, and, symbolically, unveiled in the Place de la République, Paris, the site of the huge bronze monument to the theme of a Republic – the new constitution expressed its commitment to the *Declaration of the Rights and Man of the Citizen*, the key charter of 1789.[11] As Peter Morris reminds us, article 2 reasserted the new regime's commitment to republican symbols: the flag of the tricolour; the national anthem of the *Marseillaise*; the values of liberty, fraternity and equality; and the separation of church and state. For good measure, article 89 declared that the republican form of government remained immutable, all constitutional amendments being the prerogative of parliament to which the government was responsible (article 20).[12]

In this way, de Gaulle set out to deflect left-wing taunts that he was a Bonaparte. Yet, naturally, he had no wish to adopt a document which mimicked those of 1946 or 1875 as this was to invite the same kind of instability which, in his opinion, had afflicted the nation for too long. To avoid this, the presidency, increasingly an honorary office since the 1880s, was invested with considerable authority. The president had the right to call referenda, dissolve parliament (albeit only once in a 12-month period), assume emergency powers, appoint the prime minister and, in consultation with the premier, nominate other ministers who did not necessarily have to be plucked from the ranks of deputies and senators. Those deputies who did become ministers were obliged to hand over their seats to an alternate thus emphasising, as Larkin states, the separation between 'legislative and executive function',[13] although this distinction never truly worked in practice. And in another attempt to protect the nation from the sectarian whims of parliament, the president was to be elected by an electoral college of 80,000 *notables*, responsible representatives of the people supposedly free of party political ties. To elect the supreme office-holder by universal suffrage, went the Gaullist line, was again to play into the hands of parties as he would then be nothing more than an incarnation of the 'political majority of the day'.[14] Instead, the president would serve as an independent 'arbiter', standing above petty disputes and acting in the interests of the whole nation. To reflect this notion, it is said that de Gaulle would have opted for the title 'chef de l'état' had not this conjured up unfortunate memories of Pétain who had also termed himself thus. Pétain had, of course, exploited his position to promote political change while his country was under enemy occupation; to safeguard against this, article 5 stated that the president was 'the guarantor of national independence'.

Ever since 1958, the extent of presidential power has been a lively subject of debate among political scientists.[15] There is no doubt de Gaulle intended to invest himself with considerable authority, so that he could determine both the composition of his government and the nature of policy. Yet, even at the very start, there were limits to what the president could do.[16] It should not be forgotten that the constitution provided for a dual (bicephalous) executive in which the president ruled alongside a prime minister. Although the latter was intended as the junior partner, those framing the constitution ensured that the pre-miership had greater authority than de Gaulle originally intended. As David Howarth and Georgios Varouxakis remind us, through articles 37 and 38 the premier was invested with considerable authority with the right to sign a majority of decrees and ordinances. It is the premier who coordinates government's business and it is he or she who presides over most government meetings.[17] De Gaulle was fortunate in that the prime ministers he chose were so-called 'unconditionalists', not prepared to use their office to mount a serious challenge to the president. This though did not mean they were mere satraps, as de Gaulle himself was acutely aware. They had minds of their own and, as we shall see in chapter three, they enjoyed a high measure of independence especially when it came to day-to-day business. So, too, did the president's minis-ters. It was an unfortunate secretary of state who found that an aspect of his particular portfolio was also an interest of de Gaulle's. More often than not, however, the general was preoccupied with the so-called *domaine réservé*: foreign, colonial and defence policy. It was here that he used his presidential authority to the maximum.

The other break on presidential power was, of course, the National Assembly. Inevitably, given de Gaulle's concerns, the 1958 constitution considerably reduced the authority of parliament. While the Chamber of Deputies, the lower house, still had the right to initiate legislation, details were left in the hands of civil servants and, if feeling secure, a government could proscribe unwelcome bills and even legislate by ordinance, albeit for a limited period. The president could also assume emergency powers, although this has happened only once, at the time of the general's *putsch* in Algiers in 1961. Hitherto, as Larkin recalls, it had been the budget that had consumed so much parliamentary time; now debate on this matter was curtailed to 40 days. Should deputies wish to bring down a government, he continues, they could still turn a bill into a vote of no confidence, yet this had to be followed up by a censure motion within the next 24 hours. This, in turn, needed to secure an overall majority. Cleverly, it was decided that abstentions – a favourite procedure under the Fourth Republic whereby timorous deputies hid their true colours – were 'yes' votes for the cabinet. On the single occasion during de Gaulle's presidency when there was a successful censure motion, that of October 1962, the president merely reselected his prime minister. Small wonder that, in the 1960s, cabinets could expect to last some three years as opposed to the average six-month life expectancy of the Fourth Republic. Pompidou survived as prime minister for six years, a republican record, although he did oversee a series of major cabinet reshuffles. As we shall see in chapter three, this stability was not all that it seemed, yet it was undoubtedly augmented by a new electoral law favouring single-member constituencies which eliminated some of the horse-trading endemic in the former system of proportional representation. As to senators, they were elected for a period of nine years by means of departmental colleges, a third of their number coming up for reelection every three years. Once at the Palais de Luxembourg, they discovered their powers to amend bills, approved by the lower house, severely restricted, though to be fair this had also been the case under the Fourth Republic. What was new in 1958 was the Consitutional Council, a nine-member body, appointed by the president, Chamber and Senate, whose job was to approve the legality of all legislation. Often likened to the Supreme Court in the USA, its role under de Gaulle was strictly circumscribed, but it would grow steadily in influence after 1969, pronouncing on a whole range of issues from government economic policy to European matters, and in 2001 stepping in to save Chirac from prosecution.

Although the 1958 constitution seemingly did much to clip the wings of parliament, there was no escaping the fact that both the president and his prime minister were ultimately responsible to the National Assembly which had the final say in approving legislation. To ensure the smooth running of government, it was thus vital that the president choose a prime minister who was acceptable to the majority of deputies, and that the president himself could count on majority support within the Assembly. De Gaulle was fortunate that, during his term of office, he and his prime ministers could depend on the newly formed Gaullist party, the Union de la Nouvelle République (UNR) which, in alliance with other right-wing parties, dominated parliament throughout the 1960s. Yet, given that the lower house was to be elected every five years, and the president every seven, there was always the possibility that the president would be forced to govern with opposition parties which, in turn, selected the prime minister. This eventuality, the so-called phenomenon of *cohabitation*, would first arise in 1986 and, as we shall see, proved far less destructive than many had predicted.

Whether in 1958 de Gaulle contemplated the prospect of *cohabitation* is a moot point. We know from Peyrefitte's memoirs that the possibility crossed his mind, but in 1958 he could draw reassurance from the fact that he enjoyed widespread popular approval, a further factor that would prove critical in defining the nature and scope of presidential power. It was largely thanks to his prestige, coupled with a desire to break from the unstable politics of the past, that the electorate, voting on 28 September 1958, approved the new constitution by an overwhelming 80 per cent. This document also drew the approval of the mainstream political players. Because it was so open-ended and untried, it was possible to read into it whatever one wanted. Whereas de Gaulle's first prime minister Michel Debré argued that it had laid the foundations for a British parliamentary system, Mollet and other Socialists tried to convince themselves that government was still beholden to parliament.[18] In the event, the constitution has proved extremely malleable, both in the hands of de Gaulle and his successors, and herein lies one of the underlying factors behind the durability of the Fifth. Commentators agree that the constitution remains central, but stress that it is less axiomatic than before, and it has benefited from a willingness on the part of the key political parties to make it work, a rare occurrence under the Fourth.

Algeria

With constitution-making more or less resolved, de Gaulle could get on with the pressing business of Algeria. Once again, he must have been struck by historical parallels, especially the similarities between 1944 and 1958. On both occasions, his overwhelming task was to restore order, paradoxically by taking action 'against the very forces which had helped him to power: in 1944 the Resistance, in 1958 the Algerian rebels.'[19] The task was to preoccupy him for the next four years and, as Michel Winock reminds us, 'the stakes could not have been higher.'[20] If de Gaulle failed, it would not just be the fate of Algeria and the Fifth Republic which were in jeopardy. The state itself would be at the mercy of those who – in a manner uncomfortably reminiscent of those Spanish nationalists two decades earlier – had strayed from the path of legitimacy: recalcitrant army officers and extra-legal bodies, such as the local committees of public safety, which had been formed in Algiers. Might such examples be imitated in mainland France, and how would the left react, especially the Communists? De Gaulle liked to boast that, in 1944, he had already blocked one Communist revolution; he did not want to create the conditions in which a real uprising might take place.

Even if he could keep the state together, albeit by brutal means, would he be able to sustain the internal cohesion of the nation? While one of the adolescent characters in Louis Malle's semibiographical film *Le Souffle au Coeur*, set in the mid-1950s, could sneer 'Colonies they're so passé', this was not a widely-shared view. An opinion poll revealed in 1958 that 52 per cent favoured retaining Algeria, while 41 per cent supported independence. At long last people were sitting up and taking notice of what was happening. While the start of the war had aroused little interest, the 'mad, nihilist destruction' being perpetrated by all sides, the use of torture, the calling up of reservists, the disloyal behaviour of the army and the spiralling sense of crisis meant that from 1955 onwards Algeria was frequently in the news.[21] As Alistair Horne relates, François Mauriac repeatedly denounced the army's behaviour in the pages of *L'Express*,[22] accusations echoed by the liberal Christian Democrat journal *Témoignage Chrétien* which also took issue with members of the Catholic hierarchy for not criticising human rights abuses, just as they had failed to condemn Vichy's dismal treatment of the Jews.[23] Then, in 1957, came the publication of Servan-Schreiber's *Lientenant en Algérie*, closely followed the next year by Henri Alleg's *La Question*. A Jew, a communist and a journalist, three things hardly likely to endear him to the army, Alleg recounted his own torture at the hands of Massu's paratroopers when he had electrodes placed on his ear and fingers and then in his mouth, before being submerged for long periods in a water trough. Yet whether everyone fully took on board the horrors being played out across the Mediterranean remains doubtful. In Simone de Beauvoir's 1962 novel, *Les Belles Images*, a brilliant portrayal of young Parisian *bourgeois* life, the principal character Laurence absent-mindedly reads an article on torture in Algeria before taking a keener interest in adverts for shampoo.[24]

While the political elites were focused on what was happening, they were also deeply divided, their positions cutting across traditional party boundaries. Many on the left, such as Mollet and Mitterrand, were initially in favour of Algeria staying French, as were those Socialists committed to the vision of *la France civiliatrice*, most famously the Popular Front veteran Paul Rivet. Only as the affair dragged on, and as more revelations of French brutality appeared in the press, did the left more generally come to endorse independence. It was on the right that Algeria prompted most soul-searching. Whereas elements in the MRP, together with some Gaullists, favoured independence, a majority of conservative opinion wished to keep hold of the colony. This sentiment often led former right-wing resisters to align with former Pétainist adversaries. For instance, the Christian Democrat Georges Bidault, who had recently quarrelled with the MRP, joined with the Pétainist Tixier-Vignancour to create the Rassemblement pour l'Algérie Française (RAF) which campaigned tirelessly for the retention of the colony. Even de Gaulle's cabinet was split. While Pierre Guillaumat, Bernard Cornut-Gentile and Jacques Soustelle rallied to the integrationist path, others headed by the prime minister Michel Debré were wary of making any irreversible position.

Commentators have been divided over whether de Gaulle had any pre-brewed medicine for the Algerian headache. His detractors, notably Soustelle, one of those resisters who aligned with former Vichyites, argue that his former idol reneged on the promises he initially made to the Algerian settlers, notably the sentiment contained in his speech of 4 June 1958 when he proclaimed to a crowd of *pieds noirs* in Algiers, 'Je vous ai compris.'[25] Ultimately, it is alleged, de Gaulle betrayed the whole of the French empire, facilitating far speedier and far more extensive decolonisation than was necessary at the time. His supporters counter by portraying a Bismarckian figure, with a series of fixed notions in his head, determined to see these through at whatever cost, a veritable statesman who recognised that the age of decolonisation had arrived, just as the German chancellor had understood, in the 1860s, that the age of nationalism had surfaced. Such was the image of himself that Bismarck created in his memoirs. In his *Memoirs d'Espoir*, de Gaulle is more cryptic, allowing the best possible gloss to be made of his diplomacy, although he is also at pains not to overdramatise the affair. As

Winock and Shennan observe, this was not one of the finer moments in
French history. On the one hand, de Gaulle writes that he came to the
question 'with no strictly pre-determined plan'; on the other, he adds
that, 'no other policy but one which aims at replacing domination by
association in French North Africa' was 'either viable or worthy of
France.'[26]

Historians have since scrutinised de Gaulle's every move over the
1958–62 period, poring over his speeches, 'great gusts of words' as de
Beauvoir sneered,[27] in the hunt for clues as to whether his policy
remained basically the same, the procedures merely changing, or
whether it underwent a veritable sea-change. This is no easy conundrum
to resolve. The situation was so delicate that de Gaulle was obliged to
play a subtle hand. While he was often profoundly depressed by events
in Algeria, he kept himself regularly informed of what was going on – he
made five visits to North Africa in 1958 alone – and excelled in adopting
a flexible strategy, delighting in the fact that commentators frequently
misread his intentions. De Gaulle was Molière's Don Juan, wrote one,
promising 'marriage to five or six women' and avoiding being 'pinned
down by any of them.'[28] As the general himself quipped to Louis
Terrenoire, 'If I have a plan, I won't tell anyone about it.'[29]

Although the evidence remains contradictory, a series of factors can
be identified in de Gaulle's thinking. First, he appears to have rejected,
from the outset, the remedy favoured by the *pieds noirs* and Algerian
army officers, that of full-blown assimilation. Conscious that the Algerian
and French populations did not mix easily, he was further aware that
Algeria's population was rising at a rapid rate and might be in danger of
swamping metropolitan France. To Peyrefitte, he remarked that the
Arab peoples were 'unassimilable'.[30] (This of course is the argument
now used by Le Pen who in 1958 had stood for a French Algeria).
Second, de Gaulle was enough of a nationalist himself to appreciate the
nationalism of other peoples, and realised that the age of colonialism
was dying. This did not make him a supporter of left-wing plans for
decolonisation; his preference was for Algeria to take its place in a
revamped French Union, a construct which would resemble the British
Commonwealth. This way former imperial possessions would maintain
links with Paris, thus retaining France's influence in far-flung parts of
the globe. Third, de Gaulle had no intention of allowing Algeria to
undermine the Republic he had created. No supporter of outright independence, he reluctantly accepted that this would have to be conceded if France's internal political settlement was imperilled by the

behaviour of the *colons*. This was always a much bigger consideration than the fate of the *pieds noirs*, not all of whom could claim French ancestry, and the sensibilities of the *Armée d'Afrique*, whose views did not necessarily reflect those of the military more generally, notably the airforce. Fourth, at no point was he going to allow historical sentiment – the fact that the colonies had come round to the support of the Free French in the Second World War – cloud his judgement. In this respect he may have recalled that Algeria had been stubbornly Pétainist and Giraudist. This ability to rise above emotional attachments, although not always out of a slough of despair induced by the barbarity of events in Algeria, was much in evidence throughout the crisis, and was notably absent among those keen to keep Algeria French. Several historians cite the following anecdote. When he was informed the *pieds noirs* were suffering, he abruptly replied, 'well you will suffer then.' On another occasion, he dismissed the settlers as 'babblers'.

On close inspection, and indeed on careful listening to the inflections of his voice, such thinking, most particularly his preference for Algeria to become part of a French Union, may be discerned in de Gaulle's famous television speech of 16 September 1959. Here, he announced that Algeria's future lay in 'self-determination' to be realised by one of three solutions – these would be put to the people in a referendum four years hence when tempers had cooled and peace established. The alternatives were 'secession', by which it was understood 'independence'; 'Francisation', the option favoured by the *pieds noirs*; and, finally, 'the government of Algerians by Algerians, supported by French aid and in close union with France.'[31] To ensure that everyone saw the advantages of this last possibility, the army was urged to build on earlier initiatives, notably the five-year investment plan for Algeria, authored at Constantine on 3 October 1958. In future, it was declared, the army should treat the indigenous population with respect, something which French officials had repeatedly failed to do. (Indeed, the French were paying the penalty for having earlier dismantled an Arab aristocracy and an Arab professional elite, thus handing the initiative to the extremists.)

It must remain questionable whether, in 1958–60, de Gaulle really believed in diplomacy as the best *means* of attaining his preferred solution of an Algeria in association with France. He wanted to negotiate from a position of strength and that meant humbling the FLN through force; hence the appointment of General Maurice Challe as Commander-in-Chief in Algeria, significantly an airman free of the prejudices of the colonial forces, although that did not ultimately stop his joining the army rebels in the generals' *putsch* of 1961. Instructed by Debré to produce significant military victories before Spring 1959, Challe's plan involved the deplacement of Arabs to concentration camps, all too similar to those used in the Boer War, the institution of free-fire zones and the systematic rooting out of FLN fighters in the *bled*. So it was that negotiations over Algeria's future were played out against a background noise of continuing violence.

By 1961 the FLN might have been militarily broken but was stronger politically than ever before. Now calling itself the Gouvernement Provisoire de la République Algérienne (GPRA), and demanding nothing less than complete autonomy, it interpreted any hand-over of arms as surrender and urged Muslims to boycott elections. As many Arabs knew to their cost, the FLN/GPRA was not to be meddled with. Punishment beatings and summary executions were dished out to so-called collaborators who worked with the French, either in Algeria or mainland France, where nearly 4,000 Arabs had been murdered by 1962. Meanwhile, the *pieds noirs* and their army supporters were as defiant as ever. When in January 1960, General Massu was withdrawn to Paris, following his criticisms of Algerian self-determination, their response was the so-called 'week of the barricades' in which the settlers occupied key government buildings and undertook a general strike, actions in which the elements of the army happily colluded.

De Gaulle's response was to don his military uniform, and undertake another trip to Algeria in March 1960, the so-called 'tour de messes', in which he reassured the army that there would be no Dien Bien Phu in Algeria. This has been seen by some as return to an uncompromising policy of keeping Algeria French. Other historians have suggested that it was at this point that he understood there was little alternative but to grant Algeria full independence. In late 1960 he confided to Peyrefitte, 'French Algeria, that is not the solution, that is the problem.'[32]

His thinking was conditioned by a series of other developments. Further afield, Madagascar and the sub-Saharan states of the French empire were in the process of obtaining autonomy without the difficulties experienced in North Africa. The UN was also putting pressure on France, the sympathies of several member states, notably former colonies, naturally being with independence. Within France itself, intellectual critics of French brutalities were becoming ever more vocal, taking up the case, in 1960, of Djamilia Boupacha, a young Algerian girl, whose punishment for throwing a bomb into a restaurant was to be starved, used as a human ashtray and repeatedly raped with a bottle, a mutilation that outraged Simone de Beauvoir.[33] Later that year, de Beauvoir, Jean-Paul Sartre and Laurent Schwartz, among others, published the *Manifeste des 121* which supported the secondary-school teacher Francis Jeanson, who had been put on trial for raising FLN monies in France. De Gaulle had little respect for these protests, but it must have irked him that several resisters, among them Paul Teitgen, Claude Bourget and Philippe Viannay had likened French treatment of the Arabs to the behaviour of the Gestapo in occupied France.[34]

Worryingly the outrage in North Africa seemed to be infecting metropolitan soil. On 17 October 1961, a mass demonstration by Algerians in Paris, was severely dealt with by the police chief Maurice Papon, who would later be indicted for 'crimes against humanity' for his role in the deportation of Jews as Vichy's police chief at Bordeaux. The protest resulted in 11,538 arrests, 69 wounded and at least 40 dead. This latter figure might even be higher, as over the next few weeks the Seine relinquished its grisly catch of 60 protestors killed while in police custody and simply dumped in the river.[35] Some estimates place the death toll at over 400.

Meanwhile, in Algeria, the army and *pieds noirs* gave further proof of their unreasonableness. In April 1961, elements of the military (Challe, Jouhaud, Salan and Zeller, a 'tetrad of superannuated generals' in de Gaulle's own words) launched a *putsch* in Algiers. After this was crushed, the campaign to keep Algeria French went underground, resulting in the formation of the Organisation de l'Armée Secrète (OAS), headed by Salan, who claimed to be following in the footsteps of the great colonial administrator Marshal Lyautey. Through his approval of a sustained campaign of violence – the organisation of bank-raids to raise money, attacks on prominent intellectuals such as de Beauvoir who had dared challenge the cause of French Algeria and numerous assassination attempts on de Gaulle – Salan seemed to owe more to Al Capone.[36] A protest against the OAS on 8 February 1962, organised by the left, and much better known than the one of 17 October the previous year, led to a further eight dead, nearly all communist militants, and countless others nursing cracked heads, broken ribs and the after-effects of tear-gas.

If at some point in 1960 de Gaulle came round to the conclusion that Algeria had to be given its independence, he still had to work at a solution, outside of a military one, and was fortunate that additional factors came into play which made a settlement achievable. The first, and perhaps most notable of these, was the referendum of January 1961, promised in 1959 and hurriedly brought forward, in which 75.26 per cent of voters on mainland France approved self-determination; most others abstained. Within Algeria itself, 72 per cent favoured the colony remaining a part of France, yet it was understood that these were nearly all *pieds noirs*. Tired of the quarrels over empire, the public was also beginning to appreciate the costs of keeping Algeria French, both in terms of high taxes and the conscription of young men. As already noted, to many parents the assembling of the cream of French youth at railway stations, destined for foreign parts, conjured up unfortunate images of the forced deportations under German rule. These conscripts, some 400,000 of whom travelled to Algeria, further strengthened de Gaulle's strategy. Unhappy to be in Algeria in the first place, the more politically aware feared that they might become part of a new fascist army which would march on the mainland in the manner of Franco.[37] Others were contemptuous of their professional colleagues who were preoccupied with their financial security and who were not prepared to trust a conscript army with any real fighting. As Vinen astutely points out, there was an irony in that de Gaulle, the one-time champion of the professional army in the 1930s, could now appeal 'over the heads' of the officer elites to a 'nation-in-arms'.[38] Nor was the navy or the airforce especially enamoured of the army's antics in Algeria, despite the fact that Challe himself was an airman. The French airforce, which had successfully reconstructed itself after the disaster of 1940, was the most technically advanced of all three forces, and was especially irritated by the regressive thinking displayed within the colonial army. Such sentiments undoubtedly protected the Fifth Republic from a military takeover, for instance during the crisis of April 1961, although admittedly the containment of this particular *putsch* required another dramatic intervention from de Gaulle himself, a speech which went down well among the conscripts listening to their radios in Algerian barracks. Indeed, the failed *coup*, together with 'the week of the barricades', had demonstrated the limits of extremism. The renegade army leaders in Algeria could not topple democracy in France; the *pieds noirs* could not carry public opinion; and, within France, political parties, always excepting maverick right-wingers, drew reassurance from the president's handling of the crisis. Even the Communists were mollified, fearing that Salan, not de Gaulle, was the new Boulanger.

So it was in 1960–61 that a solution was tantalisingly close: sections of the FLN, headed by the dissident rebel Si Salah, indicated their readiness to talk to Paris, and Paris itself overcame its moral scruples about talking to 'terrorists'. Realistically, there was little else it could do, although discussions conducted at Melun between 20 and 29 June 1960 resulted in naught. Negotiations, held up because of the failed *putsch*, resumed at Evian in May the next year, and endured for ten, cheerless months in which yet more died. This delay was partly due to petty disagreements, but more critically to de Gaulle's reluctance to concede the points demanded by the FLN – its sole right to negotiate on behalf of the Arabs and its refusal to grant a ceasefire before negotiations could truly get under way. He could never truly stomach the pretensions of the GPRA. Only too aware that de Gaulle now wanted out of Algeria as fast as possible, the FLN held unswervingly to its position, intensifying its terror campaign both in Algeria and mainland France in an attempt to put yet further pressure on Paris. As Martin Alexander and John Keiger have observed, for both sides the conflict was always 'a mental, nervous and psychological war of attrition', and it was the French whose resolve ultimately cracked.[39]

On 18 March 1962, the Evian agreements were unveiled to an expectant nation. Algeria was to be granted full independence; European settlers were given three years in which to settle upon French or Algerian nationality (dual citizenship was not an option); the Constantine Plan was still to be implemented; French technical and bureaucratic help would be available if required; Algeria would remain part of the *franc* zone; and the newly-independent nation would protect the property of the Europeans, plus reimburse them for any losses. Although, on 26 March, the OAS attempted to thwart the agreements by goading the police to launch further violence against Algerian protestors marching in Paris, the Evian Accords were accepted by 90 per cent of French voters in a referendum of 8 April, and by 99 per cent of Algerians on 1 July.

There were several winners and losers in this 'savage war of peace'.[40] It is believed that 17,456 French soldiers were killed; astonishingly, almost a third of this number died as a result of what the American military euphemistically calls 'blue on blue' or 'friendly fire'. In Algeria, this meant jittery conscripts, unused to guerilla war, blowing themselves up or unwittingly shooting their fellow soldiers. A further 64,985 troops were wounded and 1,000 listed as 'missing in action'. Civilian casualties, caused by acts of terrorism, amounted to over 10,000 dead; another 500 'disappeared'. Among Arab casualties, 141,000 were killed in action; the figure was so high partly because the FLN did not have the facilities, helicopters and armoured cars, to sweep its wounded off the battlefield.

It is further calculated that the FLN was responsible for the deaths of nearly 66,000 Muslims, including 12,000 of its own supporters suspected of treason. A further 30,000 *harkis*, those Arabs who had soldiered along-side the French, were also summarily murdered, the remainder were ghettoised in shanty towns in Algeria where their bitterness is still evident today.

Sadly violence and acrimony were to remain features of the newly lib-erated state of the Democratic and Popular Algerian Republic. Initially governed by the FLN leader Ben Bella, who attempted unsuccessful modernisation policies and a wholly pointless war against Morocco, in 1965 he was replaced by General Boumedienne. His ability to strike fear among Arab nationalists won him friends in Paris, and he himself valued good relations with France. Yet economic mismanagement, falling gas prices and government corruption ensured that, in the late 1980s, Algeria was again at war with itself. In this situation, the FLN was unable to prevent Algerian nationalism becoming infected by Islamic funda-mentalism. This unholy mixture led to the setting up of the FIS (Front Islamique du Salut, and known less reverentially Fatima, Interdit de Sortir), whose early electoral successes ensured its speedy dissolution, only for it to reemerge as the terrorist Groupement Islamique Armée (GIS). It soon conducted a campaign against both the Algerian govern-ment and French nationals found on Arab soil. Eventually, it waged war on France itself, organising a bombing campaign in Paris during 1994–1995. As we shall see, in the 1990s the activities of such terrorists contributed to a growing racism in French society.

If Algerians were not welcome in France in the 1990s nor, in the 1960s, had there been any joyful homecoming for the one million *pieds noirs*.[41] As Vinen observes, the antics of the OAS ensured that they were linked with violence, political extremism and villainy. Their strange accents and poverty also marked them out. It was not what they were used to. Originally descendants of immigrants, they had forged a com-fortable way of living in North Africa benefiting from cheap housing, servants aplenty, and closely-knit communities. The Mediterranean sun of the southern French departments, where a majority congregated, was no compensation. (Some 30,000 settled in the Spanish resort town of Alicante, as it was said to resemble Oran.) Having arrived, often with little more than a suitcase – it was said the alternative, if they were to stay in Algeria, was a coffin – they discovered that their lack of professional qualifications, no bar to work in North Africa, forced them to accept menial and semi-skilled occupations. Even the well qualified had to

carve out a different living. Horne cites the example of one ophthal-
mologist in Alicante who ended up running a night club. Nor did the
Algerian government keep its promise of financial compensation. Small
wonder they became an embittered community, whose politics gravitated to the far right although, as Vinen says, few understood that they
were on the extremes. It was the *pieds noirs* who, in the presidential
elections of 1965, voted for the Pétainist Tixier-Vignancour, (a man
renowned during the Occupation for his outspoken antisemitism), and
who, in the early 1970s, were the initial disciples of Le Pen.[42]

Their contribution was not, however, entirely negative. Reminiscent of
those Ugandan Asians expelled by the cannibalistic dictator Idi Amin,
and resettled in Britain during the early 1970s, these reluctant *émigrés*
often settled in unpopular and cheap regions, for instance the Vaucluse
where their natural drive and ambition, especially for their children,
revitalised local economies, although their presence often caused resentment on the part of the indigenous population. *Pieds noirs*, who had of
course wanted to remain 'French', were especially disliked in Corsica,
where there was a long-standing separatist movement.

For France itself, the exit from Algeria was undoubtedly a boon for
the economy more generally. Thereafter there was no expensive army of
occupation to support; the influx of *pieds noirs* and Algerians eased the
lack of domestic manpower; and industries began to shift their attention to European, as opposed to imperial, trading partners. In other
ways, too, the Evian Accords were a release for France. On the whole,
historians agree that Algeria never truly became another Vietnam.
There were several reasons for this which revolved around context,
timing and depiction. As Gildea has pointed out, the context of Algeria
was that of a civil war: 'The Algerians against whom war was waged were
regarded as Frenchmen, even if they were bad ones.'[43] As to timing, it
has been pointed out that the final defeat in Vietnam (1975) happened
when the USA, in the aftermath of the Watergate Scandal and the oil
crisis of the early 1970s, was undergoing a crisis of self-confidence.
France in 1958 might have appeared chaotic, wracked by self-doubt, yet
shortly afterwards de Gaulle was able to put the Fifth Republic on a sure
footing. While at home the economy boomed, abroad France embarked on an ambitious foreign policy, hopelessly unrealistic in some
respects, yet successful in placing the country at the heart of European
and global affairs. Depiction was important, in that the horrors of Indo-
China were regularly played in front of American television screens
every evening, the so-called 'first living room war', whereas in the 1950s

and early 60s it was left to French intellectuals to overcome government censorship to recount the horrors of Algeria, not through the televisual media, but through petitions, articles and books.[44] There was thus little film representation of the Algerian war at the time of the fighting itself. As Philip Dine reminds us, the first films to portray the conflict, Gillo Ponteorvo's 1965 *La Bataille d'Alger* and Mark Robson's 1966 *Lost Command*, were both made by foreign producers.[45] While the films of Jean-Luc Godard and Louis Malle might have made subliminal references to the Algerian war, it was not until *Mon Cher Frangin* in 1989, continues Dine, that the conflict was depicted in mainstream, popular cinema, and there remain few films that compare with the American depiction of Vietnam: *The Deer Hunter, Full Metal Jacket, Apocalypse Now* and *Born on the Fourth of July*. Thankfully, there has been no real attempt to emulate the *Rambo* trilogy.

While Algeria might not have become another Vietnam, the memory of the war was an intensely distressing one.[46] It is precisely because the memory has been so painful that it has been suppressed. Throughout the 1960s and 70s, the conflict was alluded to not as a 'war', but as 'the troubles', an echo of Britain's ongoing difficulties in Northern Ireland. Veterans, both among the regular army and the *pieds noirs*, found it hard to gain official acknowledgement of their role. The Fédération Nationale des Anciens Combattants d'Algérie (FACA), which dared question aspects of the Algerian war, was often targeted by right-wing activists. For their part, politicians generally avoided bringing Algeria into the limelight, fearing that it might inflame passions between those who saw the war as an attempt to promote France's civilising purpose and those who understood that this mission had depended upon the methods of the Gestapo. Some measure of objectivity was achieved in the 1980s, prompted by the findings of the highly prestigious research body, the Institut d'Histoire du Temps Présent (IHTP), which looked into the impact of the war on French society.[47] As Martin Evans writes, the findings of historians gave rise to media interest and, in the 1990s, a series of documentaries appeared, among them Benjamin Stora's *Les Années Algériennes*, commemorating the thirtieth anniversary of the war, Bertrand Tavernier's *La Guerre sans nom*, exploring the lives of conscripts from Grenoble, and Richard Copan's *Les Frères des Frères*, which investigated the Jeanson network.[48] Nonetheless, Algeria still has the power to shock and bitterly divide French opinion – witness the recent debates in *Le Monde* between the veteran generals Massu and Bigeard over the deployment of torture.[49] It has been human rights abuses that have most shocked public opinion. A real furore followed the publication of General Paul Aussaresses' memoirs in 2001, which freely admitted to the use of torture on FLN suspects.[50]

While there are signs that Algeria is moving to the forefront of the nation's collective memory, it is striking that France has not chosen to recollect the war in the same way as it has lingered over Vichy. This, too, was a taboo subject but, as we shall see in chapter 6, since the 1980s the Occupation has become a matter of fascination. As Sudhir Hazaressingh speculates, there are several reasons why the French public chooses to remember Vichy over Algeria.[51] Vichy is now defunct, discredited, a part of 'history', he writes, whereas Algeria is still 'living', a fundamental aspect of the extant Fifth Republic. Vichy was part of a wider war, which engulfed the whole of Europe, while Algeria was a French phenomenon. Under the Occupation, misdeeds were perpetrated by fascists; in Algeria, torture was carried out by the French army, although it might be objected that members of the police and other security agencies often colluded with the Nazis in the round-up of Jews and resisters. It could also be added that the Resistance saw its cause as a war of liberation, inspired by the principles of 1789, whereas the FLN struggle was one against these very same values. Hazaressingh is surely right, however, to stress the fact that, at Vichy, violence was directed at Europeans; in Algeria, it was against Arabs. Given that France has a large Muslim population, the nation has no urge to go raking through its past highlighting past injustices against Islam.

De Gaulle was another who had no desire for his compatriots to be pawing over the past, as this would call into question his own leadership. He was well aware that the Evian Accords were not what he had sought at the outset. His initial hope had been for Algeria to remain part of France in some form of association, only for the colony to be granted full independence. Many unnecessary deaths had occurred as he groped for a solution; he himself had initially intensified the military campaign; and it was his later prevarication that cost yet further lives. Nonetheless, the result achieved at Evian further strengthened the political settlement of 1958. Algeria was thus both a defeat and a victory for de Gaulle, although at the time he was too skilled a propagandist to permit this interpretation. It was not a humiliation for France, as the general said it was not. By his deft manipulation of the media and his shrewd use of language, he presented an unavoidable political outcome as a political triumph. It was a technique that he would perfect over the coming years.

The Après-Guerre: De Gaulle on the Attack

Algeria 'absorbs and paralyses us'.[52] So noted de Gaulle to himself. In truth, an enormous amount of governing was done in the period 1958–62. This was partially because of the president's undoubted energy, which was especially evident in the domain of foreign policy where he pursued his so-called politics of *grandeur*, withdrawing the French Mediterranean fleet from the NATO command structure, cementing good relations with West Germany (see chapter three) and acquiring independent nuclear weapons, the *force de frappe*. Government was also busy in the domestic arena thanks to the premiership of Michel Debré who used the distraction of Algeria to enable the Republic to break with the political issues which had immobilised the Fourth Republic. One such was the clerical-anticlerical debate, especially the privileges granted to Catholic schools. By no means a fervent Catholic, in 1959 Debré exploited the goodwill felt towards the government over Algeria, to secure a law by which private schools could secure government subventions for teachers' salaries and maintenance costs by signing contracts with the state. In so doing, he drew the poison from a largely hackneyed debate which would not resurface until the 1980s.

Proud of his achievements in what has been termed the *après-guerre* of 1958–62, de Gaulle was not going to make the same mistakes as he had done during the Liberation period, when he had been outsmarted by political parties.[53] As Shennan emphasises, two factors concentrated the general's mind on the fragility of his achievement. The first was the OAS terrorist campaign which threatened the general's own life, a threat far more serious than the isolated shots fired during his triumphal march down the Champs Elysée in 1944. On 8 September 1961 at Pont-sur-Seine, and on 22 August 1962 at Petit-Clamart, he was subject to assassination attempts, the second of which saw a bullet miss his head by a whisker. While such a campaign might have given rise to a brilliant piece of thriller writing in Frederick Forsyth's *Day of the Jackal*, which was made into an equally brilliant film despite the fact that the ending was never in any doubt, the question arose as to whether the Fifth Republic could survive the death of its originator so soon after its founding. To Peyrefitte he mused on what would happen 'si l'OAS me zigouille'.[54] Second, adds Shennan, the easing of the Algerian question reignited parliamentary opposition, thus raising the prospect of a return to the fractious politics of the Fourth and Third Republics. Despite the strength of the UNR and despite Debré's skilful handling of the

Assembly, as Serge Berstein relates de Gaulle was confronted with enemies everywhere: the Communists who saw the Republic as a form of absolutism and a front for big business; the newly-created Parti Socialiste Unifié (PSU), a group of left-wing dissidents which held themselves together through their opposition to de Gaulle and the SFIO; the mainstream Socialist Party which took issue with most of the government's domestic initiatives; the rump of the Radical Party, now only 39 deputies strong, which was outraged by the Debré schools law; the MRP, sympathetic to de Gaulle on Algeria, but protective of parliamentary privileges and hostile to the general's vision of Europe; and the Conseil National des Indépendants et Paysans (CNIP), in truth more a loose assemblage of right-wing personalities than a party, but the one group least happy about the Algerian solution. As Berstein argues, it was obvious that 'a trial of strength' between the president and parliament was now 'inevitable'.[55]

De Gaulle's answer was an offensive strategy. The first indication of this came in the aftermath of the April 1962 referendum on Algeria. The general's response was to dismiss the faithful Debré, lest he used the 'yes' vote to further his particular vision of the 1958 constitution, which privileged the role of government over that of the president. The replacement was the little known Georges Pompidou, an influential financier but a man with no experience of parliament. While highly intelligent and well equipped to turn de Gaulle's grandiose projects into legislative reality, the impression lingered that Pompidou was no more than a satrap; he was frequently portrayed in political cartoons as a valet with a feather duster in his hand. Parliament was outraged that such an outsider should have been called to office, especially as Debré had not lost a parliamentary majority. When Pompidou appeared in the Chamber, the deputy Jean Legendre asked, during a debate on Europe, 'Monsieur, le président, we do not know your ideas.'[56]

Further outrage was inevitable when, on 22 September 1962, de Gaulle announced that a referendum would be conducted the following month over whether the president should be elected by universal suffrage rather than by the electoral college specified in 1958. The general had almost certainly toyed with this idea in 1958 but had rejected the vehicle of universal suffrage believing the presidency would merely be the embodiment of the political majority of the time, and thus vulnerable to party manipulation. Buoyed by the popularity he enjoyed over Algeria, he now saw how an overwhelming vote in his favour would be additional protection against parties. He also appreciated that, should

he die, future presidents would benefit from this type of public endorsement which he, as the embodiment of France and its 'saviour' in 1940
and 1958, more or less took for granted. In this way, he recognised how
public opinion would be a critical factor in delineating the powers of the
president, and so it has proved.

De Gaulle's arrogance in 1962 ensured a stormy reception. All the
major parties, with the exception of the UNR, came together in a
defence of the 'principles of republicanism', the spokesperson of this
campaign being none other than de Gaulle's former mentor, the centre-
right deputy Paul Reynaud. Opposition focused not so much on the
issue of how to elect the president, but the manner in which de Gaulle
had put forward his proposal. De Gaulle argued that article 11, permitting the president to initiate referenda, allowed him to instigate the
change, whereas his opponents claimed that, through article 89, only
parliament was authorised to amend the constitution. By invoking
article 11, and through his by-passing parliament to speak directly to the
people, de Gaulle appeared to be rejecting the very bases of liberal
democracy in favour of an elected dictatorship. So it was that, on
5 October 1962, the parties passed a censure motion, bringing down the
Pompidou cabinet. De Gaulle's response was to retain his prime minister, dissolve parliament, and announce elections after the referendum
on presidential voting.

Historians agree that while, in his invocation of article 11, de Gaulle
had behaved unconstitutionally, such legal arguments were hardly the
stuff to capture the electorate's imagination. This, too, was an electorate
which, in the aftermath of the Fourth Republic, was still suspicious of
parliament, and shared the general's view that France required a firm
steer, something which the president had provided through his handling of the Algerian war. Even though this crisis was now receding, the
need for direction remained; and it was understood that, if the general
subsequently lost the vote, this would bring about a return to political
uncertainties. While left-wing and centrist politicians still feared strong
leaders, worried lest they used abused their authority in the manner of
Louis Napoleon, many voters did not share the same anxieties.

It was, then, a relief to de Gaulle when he won the October referendum: 62 per cent of voters approved the change, some 46 per cent of
the total electorate. It was not the landslide he might have wished for:
there were many abstentions and the 'no' camp was fuelled by those
who had opposed him over Algeria. But it was still a majority and
encouraged him to take an active role in the parliamentary campaign of

November 1962 which the Gaullists won handsomely. Rewarded with a
233 seats, only nine short of an absolute majority, the UNR could
depend on the support of the Independents to dominate parliament.
There is irony, however, in that the 1965 presidential election, fought on
the principle of universal suffrage, saw de Gaulle forced into a run-off
with Mitterrand. This was something the general had always wanted to
avoid, knowing that this process would undermine some of the mystique
that had hitherto cloaked his leadership, turning him into little more
than another politician.

Conclusion: The Gaullian Achievement

Historians agree that the referendum of 1962 was a crucial turning point
in the history of the Fifth Republic. It has even been called its 'second
foundation' whereby the presidential interpretation of the constitution
triumphed over 'the old institutional model of parliamentary republicanism'.[57] Indeed, the creation of a directly-elected president marked
the passing of a political culture dominated by parliament and the
arrival of a system whereby a popularly elected president could claim a
legitimacy superior to that of the National Assembly. Even so, France was
not quite the presidential dictatorship that was alleged. Ultimately, government was responsible to parliament, and could only truly function
with a parliamentary majority. There also remained the possibility of
cohabitation, not such an unlikely possibility given that the president was
elected for seven years and the deputies for five. As we have seen, de
Gaulle almost certainly fretted over this possibility. In 1962, however, he
had reasons to feel confident. With his presidential power guaranteed,
with the parliamentary opposition outwitted, with Algeria more or less
behind him, with a compliant prime minister at the helm, with a UNR-
dominated Chamber, the way seemed open for the general to realise his
wider ambitions for France. It would not prove an easy ride.

Chapter 3: La Consolidation: *De Gaulle's Republic, 1963–1967*

In 1965, the writer Georges Perec published his novel, *Things. Story of the Sixties* which recounted the experiences of an upwardly mobile young Parisian couple Jérôme and Sylvie, both in their early twenties, who were unable to resist the lure of advertisements, buying every new product that came on the market.[1] Contemporaries interpreted the lives of these so-called 'hommes nouveaux' as a critique of the consumerism sweeping across France, while historians have come to view the book as a valuable social commentary, reflecting the changes which were overcoming France during the 1960s.[2] This was a time when the country appeared ready to slough off a sleepy past to embrace a brave new world dominated by a fashion-conscious and hedonistic young, interested in gadgets and eager to climb the social ladder.[3] In the words of the influential sociologist Henri Mendras, in the mid-part of this decade France embarked on a 'second revolution' which was, in its own ways, just as 'profound' as that of 1789.[4] Economically, the country was enjoying an unprecedented period of economic growth; in its foreign policy, there was a confidence and a swagger; at home, de Gaulle's highly personalised style of leadership played well with the people; and, in politics, governmental instability appeared a thing of yesteryear as parties learned the arts of self-discipline. The 1960s were, then, an eventful period where, in many respects, France caught up and overtook developments in the twentieth century. Yet the extent of change was not everywhere the same and, inevitably, there were winners and losers. Among the latter we might even include de Gaulle.

The Politics of Gaullism: A Republican Monarchy?

Any study of the presidential politics that dominated France in the mid-1960s must begin with an analysis of de Gaulle himself. Although his position looked unassailable in 1962, he remained conscious of his growing age and was fearful of his compatriots. The general thus wished to establish his own vision of France before it was too late. As his biographer Andrew Shennan writes, above all this meant articulating a sense of purpose.[5] This could only be achieved by keeping himself fully abreast of what was happening both in France and the world, reading both the foreign and French press, listening to the radio, viewing the television news and digesting reports in a manner that would have left that other great bureaucrat Napoleon Bonaparte exhausted. It is said that de Gaulle even died while watching television, although he was not always engrossed by the news. Peyrefitte recalls that he watched films, sports, football and boxing, complained that the Opéra and Comédie Française were not televised, and was dreadfully excited at the prospect of colour pictures.[6]

Once he had assimilated such information, he frequently retired for long weekends at Colombey where observers were struck by his silence, meditation and aversion to the telephone – in Andrew Knapp's words 'that greatest intruder on solitary thought'. Fortunately for de Gaulle, he lived in a world where instant reactions to domestic or world events were less expected, thus permitting him the time to ponder over possibilities. Interestingly, de Gaulle's mentor Pétain had also been noted for his 'silences'; it was one of the characteristics that had given rise to a mystique of the marshal. In a similar manner, respect for de Gaulle emanated from this outward impression of calm. The difference was that, when silent, Pétain's mind was often in a day-dream or simply mulling over his contempt for his interlocutor; de Gaulle was genuinely thinking matters over, arriving at a decision that could hardly be labelled opportunistic.

Having reached that decision, it would be communicated to the relevant ministers and civil servants, and eventually presented to the Council of Ministers where alternative viewpoints were not welcomed. Debate was more forthcoming in the Cabinet Council, largely abandoned after 1961 as it did not include the president himself, and in the improvised Interministerial Councils where the general met his prime minister, together with selected ministers and bureaucrats, to discuss a particular issue. As Shennan says in this way, de Gaulle was able to keep himself informed of policy initiatives, especially in those domains, such as economics and finance, where he had no true expertise. It was also a means of alerting himself to impending problems, allowing time for the president to distance himself from government failure. It further helped that he was no micro-manager. The actual implementation of policy was always left to others.

In this personalised system of government, the prime minister was intended as the junior partner, reflecting de Gaulle's concept of the chain of command. As a mere minister, Peyrefitte was told that he was situated between 'the tree' (the president) and 'the bark' (the prime minister).[7] Such a concept also circumvented the problem inherent in the constitution that the prime minister might become a rival base of authority, deriving his authority from the elected deputies, as had been the case under the Third and Fourth Republics; and it was partially because of this fear that, in 1962, de Gaulle dismissed the independent-minded Debré. In this regard, it is perhaps no surprise that Debré's successors, Pompidou (1962–1968) and Couve de Murville (1969), stemmed from outside the party cadres although, to be fair, Debré had kept his distance from the UNR. It would though be wrong to think of Pompidou and Couve as satraps, taking a back seat in policy formulation. As already mentioned in chapter two, the 1958 constitution had provided for a dual executive, and government operated as such. While in the so-called *domaine réservé* (foreign policy, defence issues and colonial matters), de Gaulle's prime ministers were little more than *exécutants* of the president's will, in other areas Pompidou and Couve exerted considerable influence in the crystallisation and delivery of policy. Pompidou, who actually understood business having worked for Rothschild's, played a critical role in economic and industrial strategy, facilitating mergers and blocking reforms which would have provided some limited workers' participation in the workplace. Ministers likewise enjoyed quite considerable freedoms in the development of policy and, if they proved their worth, de Gaulle was happy to leave them in place. It was among lesser portfolios that the swapping and changing of posts was rife, reflecting the personalised nature of the Gaullist regime where ministers often found themselves expendable. What lent this the system an aura of stability was the reduced status of parliament which could no longer bring down governments so easily, and whose voice was often ignored by the president. As commentators have pointed out, an unfortunate consequence of this process was that discontent, especially in the social domain, came to be expressed via direct action, helping to explain why the 1968 demonstrations possessed such ferocity.

The aura of stability was further buttressed by de Gaulle's habit of choosing men from outside parliament, thus lending government a non-sectarian appearance, although pressure was subsequently exerted on them to stand for parliament. Among such men appointed to ministerial portfolios, historians (for instance, Serge Berstein) recite a familiar list: Couve himself, initially at the Quai d'Orsay; the Seine Prefect Etienne Pelletier who served as minister of the interior; and the military expert Pierre Messmer who took charge of the army. Technicians, who worked behind the scenes, initiating policy which ministers then had to ratify, included the *conseiller d'état* Robert Janot who briefed on constitutional matters; Roger Goetze, a former inspector of finance, who worked on monetary affairs; and the senior civil servant Jean-Marc Boegner who supervised foreign policy. Recourse to mandarins was not, of course, an innovation. It began during the twilight years of the Third Republic; it persisted during the Occupation; and it was commonplace during the Fourth Republic's enthusiasm for economic planning. As in the past, de Gaulle selected graduates from the *grandes écoles* and the cream of the *grand corps*, but also cherry-picked the *aluminae* of new institutions such as the ENA. Moreover, de Gaulle could call on his allies, not just old hands like Geoffrey de Courcel, and Resistance veterans such as Jacques Foccart, Pierre Lefranc, Olivier Guichard, but those who had first entered politics through the RPF, notably Roberte Poujade, secretary-general of the UNR from January 1968. Those missing from this network of experts, bureaucrats, technicians, loyalists and high-fliers were veteran Fourth Republican politicians who were discredited by their association with the former regime.

While in private de Gaulle might have referred to this system as a monarchy, he was aware that his legitimacy rested on the will of the people and that what the people had given they could easily take away. It was thus necessary for the president to establish direct links with the public in order to drum up personal support which, as Vincent Wright suggests, would confer prestige on his government and lend popular backing for his forays into foreign policy.[8] On one level, this was to be achieved by the electoral process, in particular the resort to universal suffrage in the election of the president. It was further cultivated through referenda although it should be stressed that de Gaulle used this tool sparingly, especially after the resolution of the Algerian crisis. When, in 1969, he called a referendum over proposed changes to

Senate procedures he knew full well that, in the aftermath of 1968, this would become a vote of confidence in his presidency, something he was prepared to risk given his age and exasperation at his people's behaviour.

Beyond referenda, de Gaulle sought to forge links with his compatriots by undertaking extensive tours of France, not so dissimilar from those which Pétain had undertaken during the Occupation. Nor was his attitude to the crowds that different from the marshal's. 'It is necessary to speak to them as children', he confided to Peyrefitte.[9] As Wright observes, he visited every single *département*, together with trips to some 2,500 towns, an exhausting itinerary matched by his frequent journeys abroad where he was a visible sign of French prestige. Such travelling was facilitated, as it was in the case of other world leaders – for instance, Pope Paul VI, the first pope to travel the globe – by developments in air travel, especially the helicopter. De Gaulle had more in common with leaders of an earlier age in his willingness to mix with the people, a phenomenon frowned upon by his security advisers who dubbed these events 'crowd baths'. The public could also watch their 'sovereign' on their television screens, a device de Gaulle used with aplomb just as he had exploited the radio during his wartime exile. Newspaper cartoons frequently depicted the general with a television set for his head.[10] There were some 30 televised address to the nation, brilliantly orchestrated pieces of theatre, each of them deliberately designed to evoke memories of the last, the language deployed suitably ambiguous to avoid giving hostages to fortune. There were also televised press conferences, in which the general spoke for some 40 minutes, without notes, before inviting questions. Not for nothing were these dubbed *conférences à la presse* rather than *conférences de presse*. By contrast, opposition leaders were generally kept off the nation's five million television screens. At times, the situation became farcical. 'In the absence of General de Gaulle there is no political news today,' once announced a presenter when the president was abroad.[11] As the general himself maintained, 'the press was against him, the television was for him.'[12]

Such manipulation was only possible because the state owned the Office de la Radiodiffusion-Télévision Française (ORFT). This transmitted merely one channel until 1964, and there was no commercial competition until 1984–85. Ministers were thus unashamed in their vetting of coverage. On taking over as information minister in 1962, Peyrefitte recalls discovering a series of buttons on his desk allowing him to assemble, at his choosing, the heads of the principal media services.[13] Such manipulation was further facilitated through the Sevice des Liasions Interministérielles pour l'Information (SLII) set up in 1964. For their part, journalists were prepared to censor themselves knowing they faced the sack if they refused. As Julian Jackson suggests, the danger of this interference was a trend towards 'illiberalism'.[14] France's security forces, whose numbers swelled under de Gaulle, exploited the lack of news coverage to perpetrate all manner of misdeeds. It is doubtful whether the brutality with which the police crushed the Algerian demonstration of 17 October 1961 could have been covered up without the news black out imposed by the ORTF. The other unintended consequence of state control was rising public frustration with the regime. The fact that de Gaulle was forced into a second ballot in 1965 has frequently been attributed to the coverage of opposition personalities, the first occasion the people had opportunity to weigh up such men.[15] In 1968, anger at the government's monopolisation of television news was central to the demonstrations of that year. So contagious were the May events that ORTF staff were inevitably drawn into the maw of the protests, but many journalists found they were out of a job after the barricades had been dismantled.

The remaining means by which de Gaulle sought to reach out to his people was through a political party, the UNR, created in 1958 and comprising veterans of both the Free French and the RPF. Except that the UNR was not supposed to be a political party. In conscious imitation of the ill-fated RPF, this new organisation avoided the word 'party' in its title as it had no wish to be associated with sectarianism. As we have stressed, Gaullism aspired to be embodiment of national union, whereas parties were regarded as mere pressure groups. Moreover, surmises Berstein, were parties not driven by an uncontrollable urge to seize the reins of power when their real duty was to serve, not control, the state?[16]

Such concepts explain several peculiar characteristics of the UNR. De Gaulle himself was not a member; nor were most of his ministers, although we now know that the general vetted all UNR candidates before election.[17] At election time, the UNR was expected to subsume its identity, working as part of a broader Gaullist coalition of forces: the Association pour la Cinquième République (ACR), established in 1962; and the Comité d'Action pour la Cinquième République (CACR), set up in 1967. Less attention was paid to local and municipal elections where the UNR performed with only moderate success. Membership itself, said to comprise 35,000 in 1960 and 62,000 in 1962, was deliberately restricted, not least for fear of OAS entryism. An especially warm welcome was accorded to businessmen and high-ranking civil servants who were regarded as symbols of French modernism and progressivism, although this system of patronage soon smacked of corruption. In a fictional setting, it is fitting that the detective novelist Patricia Highsmith depicted the father-in-law of her anti-hero, Tom Ripley, as the head of a large chemical firm and a member of the Gaullist party. Only in 1967 did the UNR attempt to extend its base, confusingly changing its name in 1967 to the Union des Démocrates pour la Cinquième République (UDVe) and in June 1968 to the Union pour la Défense de la République (UDR). (In December 1962, it had stood as the Union pour la Nouvelle République-Union Démocratique du Travail). Supporters themselves came from a variety of political backgrounds; social republicans (for instance, Jacques Chaban-Delmas); extreme rightists (Colonel Thomazo); Christian Democrats (Edmond Michelet); and technocrats (Albin Calandon). Yet, despite such variety, discipline was regarded as everything, and decision-making was a decidedly autocratic process. In 1960 Soustelle was severely rebuked for his independence of spirit. So it was that the UNR presented itself as a highly-disciplined, centralist, elitist, modern-looking and supposedly non-sectarian body whose *raison d'être* was to serve the nation.

Historians agree that, in essence, the UNR was a political party much like any other in that it was designed to get the people out at election, a task at which it became extremely skilled. The UNR, together with its electoral partners, secured 20.3 per cent of the votes in the November 1958 elections, 35.5 per cent in November 1962, 37.7 per cent in March 1967, and 44.5 per cent in June 1968, when the party won 296 seats out of 487 in the National Assembly, thanks to a conservative backlash against the May events. Not for nothing did a cartoon in *Le Canard Enchaîné* depict the Chamber as one full of little men in képis with big noses.[18] In other respects, too, the UNR possessed all the hallmarks of a party. It was expected to serve the government, or more especially the president, tasks which, as Jonathan Watson has shown, created the kind of personal rivalries, jealousies and bickering found in all political organisations.[19] A further irony lay in the fact that the UNR sought to emulate the old Radical Party which had held sway during the Third Republic. According to Chaban-Delmas, the two were the same in their avoidance of extremes, in their advocacy of a meritocracy, in their ability to feel the pulsebeat of the people, and in their search for consensus. While the Radical Party had undoubtedly once fulfilled such functions, those with longer memories recalled that in the 1930s it had come to symbolise, however unfairly, the 'republic of pals', doing deals with smaller parties in parliament, and struggling to provide direction both at home and overseas. Surely these were the very things of which de Gaulle disapproved? If anything, the Radical Party was more honest in its assertion of centrist policies. Although the UNR claimed to stand above the right-left divide, through its rejection of Marxism, through its championing of a strong executive, and through its calls for obedience within public life, it 'clearly lay to the right'.[20]

Towards a Two-Party System

Because of the UNR's domination of the political stage, together with its advocacy of right-wing policies, commentators (for instance, Vincent Wright) have questioned whether the Fifth Republic did away with the 'régime des partis', that is 'the multi-party system' characteristic of French political life since the Third Republic', replacing this with a bi-polar one in which highly-organised coalitions on right and left com-manded the electoral and political system.[21] Occasionally, this process is termed *bipolarisation* and is commonly explained with reference to two factors. First, as Peter Morris writes, the importance of the presidency as the supreme political 'prize' and the adoption of a two-round electoral system encouraged parties to cooperate with another 'before and after – as well as during – election campaigns', something rare before 1958.[22] Second, he continues, the political, social and economic landscape was changing. Before 1958, the meat-and-drink issues for politicians were such things as the competing claims of town and countryside, the place of religion within national life, the future of the empire and the work-ings of the constitution. In the 1960s, such matters counted for less in a country which was increasingly urbanised, secularised and reconciled both to the events of 1958 and decolonisation. There was, instead, a need for politicians to meet the expectations of a new town-based and increasingly youthful electorate, abandoning the stale battle-cries of pre-vious generations. It is thus claimed that these underlying changes forced both parties and voters into two broadly distinct camps of left and right as arguments ensued over how the products of economic pros-perity could be best distributed.

That France was experiencing rapid social and economic change cannot be doubted (see below), although whether these transformations percolated sufficiently through the political system so as to produce *bipolarisation* is debatable. While a two-bloc system was gaining ground and would arrive in the late 1970s, French politics under de Gaulle continued to possess a byzantine quality, with larger parties still dependent on smaller ones. It would be more accurate to state that a 'dominant party system' emerged during the 1960s in which the Gaullist movement, reliant on Giscardian support for a parliamentary majority, commanded political life, although it should be stressed that the Gaullists were only dominant compared to what France had known before.[23]

As Berstein asserts, it was the very success of Gaullism that transformed the nature of right-wing politics, ensuing the dominance of the UNR.[24] On the margins, the extreme right struggled to recover from the failures of Pierre Poujade and the suppression of the OAS and, until the emergence of the Front National (FN) in the 1970s, coalesced around such fringe groupings as the Association pour Défendre la Mémoire du Maréchal Pétain (ADMP). In the mainstream, the success of the UNR spelt disaster for the Conseil National des Indépendants et Paysans (CNIP) which, it will be recalled, had been the key conservative player in the Fourth Republic, and whose condition in the Fifth has been neatly summarised by Berstein. Bitterly divided by the Algerian war, increasingly old in its representation, undermined by the death of one of its most famous names in the shape of Paul Reynaud, hamstrung by the timidity of its other famous name, Antoine Pinay, who was reluctant to challenge de Gaulle on the electoral stage, and hopelessly divided by the 1962 referendum – the CNIP was soon in tatters. A group of moderate independent republicans also congregated in the Fédération des Républicains-Indépendants (RI) (1962) under the leadership of Valéry Giscard d'Estaing, an aristocratic technocrat who was dismissed as finance minister in 1966. In an attempt to produce blue water between itself and the UNR, the RI championed a political programme that was pro-European, liberal and centrist. Giscard encapsulated this attitude towards de Gaulle in the famous phrase 'yes, but', a phrase that apparently drew a sharp retort from the general.[25] As historians have stressed, and as the president himself was aware, the RI was never more than a convenient shelter for conservatives who sought to advance their careers without becoming part of the Gaullist party. At election time they could be depended upon to join forces with the UNR, and the latter begrudgingly relied on their support in parliament.

The success of the UNR also created problems at the centre, hitherto dominated by the Radicals and the Mouvement Républicain Populaire

(MRP). Both performed badly in the 1962 elections. The Radicals were too associated with the backstairs deals of the Fourth Republic and were rooted in a society of artisans, small-scale producers and peasants that was fast disappearing. Much of their leadership was also dead. As to the MRP, its appeal had been dented by the 1959 Debré law granting generous state subsidies to Catholic schools and it, too, struggled to maintain an electoral base in a France that was becoming ever more secularised. Undaunted, several centrists aspired to the creation of a 'Third Force' coalition, similar to that which had defended the Fourth Republic against the Gaullists and Communists, which would go on to win the presidency. This meant doing business with the socialist left which was to create problems. As we shall see, thought turned to the Socialist mayor of Marseille, Gaston Defferre, who hoped to rally the centre in a Kennedy-style campaign. This caused anxieties within the MRP and many of their potential allies, and he withdrew his candidature. Moderates subsequently rallied round the Christian Democrat Jean Lecanuet who did sufficiently well in the 1965 presidential elections for the MRP to subsume its identity in the Centre Démocrate, where it rubbed shoulders with former Radicals and non-Giscardian independents.

It remains to consider the left. Outside of the Communist Party, this was in such disarray that in the early 1960s political scientists were already writing the obituary of French socialism. Membership of the Section Française de l'Internationale Ouvrière (SFIO), recounts Wright, was down from 335,000 in 1944 to 80,000 in 1962. Women, he continues, were almost absent from its ranks, as were young people; many party newspapers had folded; and the share of its vote in November 1962 was a mere 12.6 per cent. In the eyes of voters, the party was intimately associated with the discredited politics of the Fourth Republic, while the unreconstructed Marxism of its leader Guy Mollet seemed to belong to another world, especially as the Social Democratic Party (SPD) in West Germany was moving towards an abandonment of Marxism. Within the party itself, there were continuing divisions over what position to adopt towards de Gaulle, and there was indignation among the rank-and-file at the way in which SFIO bosses from the industrial heartlands of the Nord-Pas-de-Calais monopolised the party apparatus. The result was further infighting. In 1958, dissidents broke away to found the Parti Socialiste Autonome (PSA) which reemerged as the Parti Socialiste Unifié (PSU). Never mustering much popular support, yet including some famous names such as Mendès-France, this argued that the ideals of socialism had been betrayed by Mollet's pusillanimous response to de Gaulle and that it was time for French socialism to call upon its revolutionary heritage.

In this situation, attempts to arrest the decline of Socialism emerged outside of party cadres. Reflecting the emergence of an expanding *bourgeoisie*, comprising university lecturers, technicians, bureaucrats, white-collar workers and trade-union officials, France in the early 1960s was awash with so-called *sociétés de pensée*, in essence political salons, which self-consciously aped those clubs which had flourished during the eighteenth-century Enlightenment. In the words of Mitterrand himself, the left at this stage was not a 'tired old thing, peopled with old fogeys futilely reciting their beads in front of dusty altars'; there were instead the clubs full of 'fresh ideas'.[26] As listed by Gildea and Berstein, they comprised Citoyens 60, which grouped together Catholic youth leaders; the Lyon-based Cercle Toqueville, which favoured economic modernisers; Club Jean Moulin, named after the famous resister and fronted by his former secretary Daniel Cordier; and the Ligue pour le Combat Républicain, whose leading light was Mitterrand. Together with the venerable Club des Jacobins, founded in 1951 by Charles Hernu, in 1964 Mitterrand established an umbrella organisation, the Convention des Institutions Républicaines (CIR). While these organisations liked to claim they were apolitical, in the sense that were free of party ties, as Gildea declares, the 'political clubs were nothing if not political', and, with the presidential elections of 1965 looming, thoughts naturally turned to how the left could best exploit the new system of 'direct universal suffrage' to oust de Gaulle.[27] Paradoxically, as Arnaud Teyssier remarks, this also meant acknowledging the legitimacy of the 1958 settlement which Mitterrand had earlier described as a 'permanent coup d'état'.[28]

Crudely speaking, two alternatives emerged. The first originated out of an article of 1963 in the new political weekly *L'Express*, which enjoyed close links with Club Jean Moulin. Drawing on Theodore White's recently translated *The Making of the President*, which told the story of the recent Kennedy campaign from the primaries to the Oval Office, the journal drew up a profile of 'Monsieur X', the perfect candidate to run for president. He was expected to be 'un homme nouveau', selected from outside the usual political circles, alive to the possibilities of new technology, in tune with the aspirations of the burgeoning middle classes, unhampered by ideological baggage, aware of social realities, and able to persuade enough Frenchmen, as had Kennedy, 'that their vague concerns were justified enough to require a change in leadership.'[29] When it transpired that *L'Express*, together with a number of the clubs, was thinking of Defferre, who had also been the hope of the centre, enthusiasm waned and consensus evaporated. It was at this stage that a second left-wing alternative emerged in the shape of Mitterrand who now announced his candidacy. Brushing aside Lecanuet, the eventual candidate of the centre, he built on his support in the CIR to found the avowedly left-wing Fédération de la Gauche Démocratique et Socialiste (FGDS), which drew together the non-Communist left (Radicals, the SFIO and the PSU). Mitterrand subsequently ran de Gaulle close in the 1965 elections, and two years later the FGDS performed well enough in the legislative elections to indicate that socialism was on the road to recovery.

There remained the PCF, which ever since its inception in 1920, had retained a sectarian and pro-Soviet posture, reluctant to partake in *bourgeois* politics. On the eve of the Fifth Republic, it seemed in no hurry to shake off this image even though this had resulted in a series of unpopular policies. In 1956, it refused to condemn the USSR's crushing of the Hungarian uprising and balked at Khrushchev's denunciation of Stalinism; it was a vehement critic of Anglo-French intervention at Suez while its attitude to the Algerian war smacked of opportunism; and, in 1958, it again went against public opinion by condemning de Gaulle. It did, however, hang on to its core support. Historians and political scientists (Wright again) have since credited this survival to the forces of *Italianisation*, that is an opening up of the PCF's hitherto secret party machinery in the manner of its Italian counterpart, and *deRussification*, a policy which entailed a gradual distancing from the USSR. Both developments were aided by the death of the unreconstructed Marxist leader Maurice Thorez in 1964 and his replacement by the forward looking René Waldeck Rochet. So it was that, outside the UNR, the Parti Communiste Français (PCF) appeared the healthiest of all parties. To consolidate this influence, the PCF even shed some its sectarianism, supporting Mitterrand's presidential candidacy in 1965 and later working alongside the FGDS in the 1967 legislative elections.

While the PCF was not to be sidelined in the way de Gaulle had hoped, this does not fundamentally alter the broad picture of a 'dominant party system' in the 1960s. As will be seen, it was in the late 1970s that *bipolarisation* was achieved.[30] As Alistair Cole writes, the 1978 parliamentary elections threw light on the new party system which had been evolving, in essence a *quadrille bipolaire*: 'four parties of roughly equal political strength divided voter preferences evenly between left and right coalitions.'[31] These parties, continues Cole, were the Communists and the recently created Parti Socialiste (PS) on the left, and the neo-Gaullist Rassemblement pour la République (RPR) and the liberal conservative Union pour la Démocratie Française (UDF) on the right. Whether *bipolarisation* survived the Mitterrand years is another point of contention especially given the decline of the far left and the rise of the far right. Although it remains possible to speak in very general terms of left and right, behind these labels exists an exceedingly complex party system comprising six 'broad families', to which can be added various marginal groupings. As Cole concludes these groups comprise 'the Communist left (PCF), the Socialist/centre left (PS), the Greens, the centre-right UDF, the central right (RPR) and the extreme right (FN).'[32] To this day, the party system in France continues to undergo a slow transformation whose outcome is hazardous to predict.

The Trente Glorieuses: Winners and Losers

Whereas de Gaulle had previously indicated little interest in economics, on his return to power he understood how a vibrant industrial and social base was essential both for the success of domestic policy and for his bid for *grandeur* abroad. On many occasions, he thus underscored the importance of modernisation, notably during the presidential elections of December 1965. How critical he personally was in promoting prosperity is a matter of debate; since the late 1940s the French economy had been displaying several vibrant shoots of recovery and, in any case, the general was largely inarticulate when it came to economics. Nonetheless, during the period 1959–70 annual growth, as measured in Gross Domestic Product (GDP), rose faster than at any other time in the country's history reaching an average annual rate of 5.8 per cent. For this decade at least, France caught up and outstripped its competitors; Japan alone managed a healthier performance. Alongside these statistics, industrial productivity grew, new structures were put into place, investment rose, overseas trade flourished, agriculture became leaner and more efficient, consumerism thrived, a baby-boom (begun during the Vichy years) was sustained and a new vocabulary (marketing, management, *la réclame*) entered the French language.[33] When the bad times resurfaced, as they did during the world oil-crisis in the 1970s, economists looked back on the 1950s and 60s as a halcyon age. According to Jean Fourastié, a leading light in the planning revolution, the period

1946–1975 had constituted the *trente glorieuses*, a phrase which has become commonplace in describing the French economy at this time.[34]

Not that there is any consensus over the causes and nature of these transformations. It has been argued that France was merely making up for time sacrificed during the Depression years of the 1930s and the Nazi Occupation, reverting to patterns of development evident in the 1920s. Another explanation has credited growth to the general recovery of Europe during the 1950s, stressing the importance of US money provided through Marshall Aid and the boost provided by the early steps towards European integration. Credit has also been attributed to the successive devaluations of the *franc* in the 1950s which made French industries more competitive. The other way in which the state facilitated growth was, of course, through economic planning which was all the rage in the 1950s and which continued until the early 1970s. Yet another approach has counselled caution, stressing that the 1960s were not necessarily such a golden age, bringing with them the associated problems of inflation, US infiltration of business and an imbalance in the distribution of riches. If any consensus emerges out of these debates it is that there is no *one* single causal explanation of French growth in the 1960s, and that, as Vinen states, it is virtually impossible to distinguish between 'cause and effect.'[35] In this situation, perhaps the best that can be ventured is a general description of the principal changes that overcame the economy, together with an assessment of the ways in which these rebounded on society.

In discussing the *trente glorieuses* it is customary to begin with the phenomenon of state planning which is credited with the modernising of industry yet, as historians have pointed out (Vinen again) the greatest changes overcame agriculture. While the France of the 1930s was not without its forward-looking enterprises, especially in the Nord, Paris basin and the Centre, as Eugen Weber writes, most rural families owned a small holding, 'often without running water and electricity', and remained rooted to traditional farming methods.[36] After the Second World War, this sleepy parochial world, which had changed so little since Emile Guillaumin's 1904 novel *La Vie d'un simple*, underwent a massive jolt. On the one hand, agriculture's importance in the overall economy declined, reflecting the new found power of the commercial tertiary sector: in 1946, it represented 17 per cent of GDP; in 1973, its share was a mere 5 per cent. On the other hand, performance was much healthier, as the figures cited by Kenneth Mouré illustrate. Between 1950 and 1990, agricultural output rose by 200 per cent; productivity per man hour in agriculture grew by approximately 7 per cent per annum, in comparison to 5.3 per cent in industry; and France became the world's second largest exporter of agricultural goods.[37] The corollary to these changes was a dramatic fall in the rural work force leading some commentators to speak of 'la fin des paysans'.[38] Whereas some six million tilled the fields in 1950, only one million remained by 1990, the surplus entering industry and, most critically, the service sector. A futher dimension to this transformation was the disappearance of peasant homes: it is calculated there were some five million villages in 1954, a mere two million some 20 years later.

How did agriculture become leaner and fitter? Planning was undoubtedly a factor. As well as providing credit, the Monnet Plan of 1947 was especially important in boosting mechanisation. There were 20,000 tractors in 1946; 137,000 in 1950; 558,000 in 1958; and over one million by 1965. No longer were oxen pulling a plough a common sight in French fields. Among the peasantry, the tractor was an 'obsession', a status symbol, much as there had been a 'cult of the tractor', and even a 'Song of the Tractor', in the Soviet Union of the 1930s.[39] More generally, the state was eager to modernise French farming so that it could compete on the world market. The Farming Orientation Law of 1960 rejected price support as a policy for sustaining agricultural production, put pressure on old farmers to retire and facilitated the consolidation of small peasant landholdings into larger units although it should be stressed that medium-to-small size farms remained the norm. There was also a vogue for science. The widespread use of fertilizers, the introduction of new crops, the application of new technology and the expansion of agricultural training were all outward signs of change. Significantly, the *pieds noirs*, eager to eke out a living, proved highly responsive to these new ways, although their success was often resented by others, especially in Corsica where they became the victims of popular violence.

Without doubt, the modernisation of agriculture created tensions among the rural world. As Gildea outlines, this conflict took place on several different levels: generational; institutional; and regional.[40] In generational terms, older peasant-style farmers, so-called *vieux plocs*, resented their youthful counterparts, self-appointed modernisers, who came armed with diplomas and better training and who found a champion in the young farmers' leader Michel Debatisse whose book *La Révolution silencieuse, le combat des paysans* of 1963 advocated wholesale modernisation. In the institutional sphere tension arose as these forward-thinking farmers, often congregated in the Catholic Jeunesse Agricole Chrétienne

(JAC), worked to infiltrate existing institutions, notably the young farmers' movement, the Cercle National des Jeunes Agriculteurs (CNJA), together with the key union, the Fédération Nationale des Syndicats d'Exploitants Agricoles (FNSEA). And, regionally, anger grew against the commercially-minded wheat farmers, rich *céréaliers* and *better-aviers*, congregated in the Paris basin and the Nord, who dominated the FNSEA.

As Gildea continues, not only were these big cereal-producers resented by land-hungry modernisers of the CNJA, chiefly located in western France, the Rhône and Languedoc, they were also disliked by the older peasant farmers of the Pyrenees, Alps and Massif Central who looked back with nostalgia to the protectionist ways of the Third Republic. In 1959, such peasants flocked to the Communist-leaning Mouvement de Défense des Exploitants Familiaux (MDEF). As to the modernisers of the CNJA, they expressed their frustration at the tardiness of government to implement the Farming Orientation Law, by dumping produce and blocking the highways with their tractors. Paris was forced to respond. Yet further pressure was thus put on older farmers to retire and the so-called SAFER organisations (Sociétés d'Aménagement Foncier et d'Etablissement Rural) were inaugurated. These semi-public bodies purchased farm land whenever it came up for sale, so as to ward off speculators and facilitated the creation of the co-operatives favoured by the CNJA. In 1962 French agriculture received a further boost when the EEC provided subsidies through the Common Agricultural Policy (CAP), a form of economic protectionism designed to shield France from the economic muscle of West Germany. The fact that France tenaciously clung on to CAP subsidies was an acknowledgement of social and political realities. As several historians have pointed out, while farmers are no longer such an influential group within French society, governments ignore the concerns of this vocal interest group at their peril.

Within the industrial sector, the story was also one of innovation confounding the long-held notion that, beyond the countryside, France was a country of artisans and small-scale producers, grouped together in small self-financing enterprises. Whereas industry's share of GDP had been a paltry 20 per cent in the 1950s, 20 years later this stood at a third. Productivity also increased as did the profitability rates of most companies. Moreover, such growth was apparent both in the so-called staple industries such as iron, steel and coal, and in 'newer' activities, for instance chemicals, motor cars and telecommunications. Especially noticeable were the transformations within French energy. Before 1940, France had depended heavily on coal, yet this had struggled to provide the nation's power, and there was concern that France's main coalfields in the Nord-Pas-de-Calais were vulnerable to German invasion. These worries had already led the nation to experiment with hydroelectricty in the late 1930s. These ventures were now taken a stage further as huge dams were built in mountainous areas, areas once free of industry. Likewise, the landscape of the rural south-west was transformed by the discovery of natural gas in the early 1950s. Oil, however, became the principal source of French energy, largely because it was cheap and plentiful. It was not to be cheap and cheerful. Serious problems arose in the 1970s when problems in the Middle East hiked up prices. Oil inflation interrupted another feature of earlier French expansion: high investment rates. Between 1960 and 1974, investment increased at a rate of 7.7 per cent per annum; only Japan and West Germany managed better. Statistics for trade were a further source of pride. In the period 1959–1974, the volume of French trade increased by nearly 11 per cent year. During the same period, records Gildea, exports as a proportion of GDP rose from 10 per cent to over 17 per cent, the overwhelming proportion of these going to fellow European Economic Community (EEC) states, rather than to overseas possessions belonging to the so-called *franc* zone.[41]

Explanations of growth are manifold and mirror the more general explanations of the *trente glorieuses*. Some experts have even studied these reasons hoping to find an elixir which will cure the recent sluggishness of the economy so that the whole experiment can be reenacted. It is generally agreed, however, that the key stimulus to industrial growth was state planning. This was, of course, initiated by the Fourth Republic. In 1946 Jean Monnet, a cognac merchant who had spent the war years in New York and Washington where he had been a vital element in Roosevelt's 'Victory Program', took over the newly-created Commissariat Général du Plan (CGP), a small assembly of some 40 experts armed with few formal powers but infused with tremendous enthusiasm and sense of public service. Eschewing the highly-directed *planisme* favoured by Vichy and opposed to the collectivist solution favoured by the left, Monnet's first plan was able to exploit Marshall Aid and the recent nationalisation of the key deposit banks to promote reconstruction. The results were promising tackling many of the problems bequeathed by dislocation of the war years. GDP rose by 39 per cent in the period 1946–52; staple industries flourished; roads and railways, in a pitiful state since the Occupation, were regenerated; and new institutions such as the Institut National de la

Statistique et des Etudes Economiques (INSEE) were set up to co-ordinate future state intervention.

A second plan of 1952–57, framed in the frosty environment of the Cold War in which the Communists railed against the government, concentrated on the needs of management, improving technology and stressing productivity levels. The third plan, primarily the work of the former liberal economist Jacques Rueff, aimed at the long-term prosperity desired by de Gaulle. This sought to attack inflation by curbing public sector pay increases, reducing the welfare budget, devaluing the *franc* and looking to Europe. The Fourth and Fifth Plans (1962–65 and 1966–70 respectively) marked a further shift in emphasis, this time setting targets for new industries, among them computers, petroleum industries and telecommunications, which were hailed as 'national champions'. The desire to present a modern image of France to the world also led to ambitious projects, for instance the building of the supersonic aeroplane Concorde, and the construction of a new airport at Roissy to the north of Paris, later named after de Gaulle. There was even a Sixth Plan (1971–75), recognised as far less significant, which slashed government aid to public industries in the hope that they would emulate their private counterparts. There were a further four plans – 1976–80, 1981–85, 1984–88 and 1989–92 – but these were increasingly irrelevant.[42]

Planning on this scale was possible for several reasons. It helped that France possessed the centralised structures of the so-called Jacobin state which made government intervention that much easier. The First Plan also borrowed much from the ground work of the Pétain regime, although the priorities and philosophy of the latter was very different. Planning further benefited from the wish to build anew in the Liberation and would also have been difficult without the widescale nationalisations that took place in 1944–46. While some firms, for instance Renault, were appropriated as punishment for wartime collaboration, other take-overs, notably in the banking and in the energy sector, were prompted purely by economic reasons, thus allowing the state to exert far greater direction over the economy overall, although it would be a mistake to believe that planning was a well-oiled, trouble-free operation. US money, as already noted, was also vital, as was the initial cooperativeness of the French left. Perhaps of greater importance in the longer-term was the support of elites, not merely the graduates of the ENA, but the leaders of industry themselves, many of whom were congregated in the employers' organisation the Conseil National du Patronat Français

(CNPF). Naturally suspicious of state intervention, which smacked of a left-wing Jacobin tradition, they were reassured by the fact that all the plans were infused with a strong capitalist ethos.

Just as in agriculture, it would be wrong to believe that all of French industry had been overhauled and that small businesses had disappeared. While France witnessed a merger-madness, the so-called 'national champions', for instance Péchiney-Ugine-Kuhlmann, the aluminium manufacturer, did not match their foreign counterparts. Renault was the nation's largest enterprise, yet came twenty-second in the global league table. As Berstein writes, by the early 1970s, some 1,500 companies were responsible for some 90 per cent of French trade. A further 45,000 units, he adds, had no overseas trade whatsoever.[43] The new emphasis on planning and on the tertiary sector of the economy (banking, insurance, computers) had, however, resulted in a reshaping of society, especially within the traditional ruling elites, often referred to collectively as the *bourgeoisie*. Traditionally, this had comprised the captains of industry, often belonging to family dynasties such as the textile giant run by the venerable Marcel Boussac; financial occupations, including stockbrokers; the liberal professions, among them doctors, lawyers and academics; well-placed bureaucrats; and holders of large real estate, the great landowners. These were now joined by a new group, essentially senior managers, who moved effortlessly from the civil service into both nationalised and private firms and whose numbers more or less doubled from 477,467 in 1954 to 806,600 in 1968. In the words of one contemporary, a member of this class was 'a product of the Paris of government, of higher education, of competitive exams, of company boards, a world in itself which has no use for family tradition and in which it is every man for himself.'[44] For some, this new meritocracy was the realisation of the dream cherished by the Third Republic of an open elite, based on talent, although sociological studies have shown that a majority of the *cadres* were drawn from the traditional ruling families who would once have been called the *notables*.

Below the *cadres*, there emerged a new salaried middle class. Whereas previously the middling ranks of society had been dominated by prosperous farmers, small businessmen and local civil servants, the expansion of the tertiary sector saw the proliferation of 'white-collar workers' and middle management, who comprised anywhere between a third and a two-fifths of the salaried classes. Some 704,196 strong in 1954, the numbers of these *cadres moyens* had risen to 1,197,360 by 1968. These were an aspirant middle-class, almost exclusively urban-based, anxious to distinguish themselves from the workers, and desirous to take advantage of a new consumer lifestyle. Many were the sons and daughters of artisans, peasants and small shopkeepers, keen to better themselves and forge a different path to that of their parents, although it should be stressed that the majority were still the offspring of middle managers. Social mobility might have been a part of the *trente glorieuses*, yet there remained a glass ceiling ensuring that it was exceedingly difficult to join the elites.

There remained the working class. Always a heterogeneous group, this underwent even greater splintering. On the decline were those belonging to the older industries such as iron, coal, steel, textiles and the railways, subject to the processes of rationalisation of the 1960s, and the victims of retrenchment a decade later. Whereas France boasted some 330,000 miners in 1947, some 70,000 were laid off in the next eight years; some 30 years later, a mere 33,000 dug for coal.[45] The numbers of the working class overall, however, did not fall but grew slightly, from approximately seven million in the late 1950s to just under eight million by the mid-1970s, reflecting the advent of new technology and the shrinkage of the rural workforce. It further comprised women and immigrants who, for the most part, lived in the sprawling urban developments that were becoming a feature of most French cities. It was also a working class that tended to be less skilled than previously, reflecting the changes in large factories where automation was commonplace. No doubt employers prayed that this fresh breed of workers would be less militant than in the past, and there was indeed a crisis in direction on the part of trade union organisations in the 1960s. While the Communist-led Confédération Générale des Travail (CGT), some 1.5 million strong, still saw itself as the vanguard of the proletariat, the religious-minded Confédération Française des Travailleurs Chrétiens (CFTC), with its 800,000 members, aspired to a new social order based on Catholic social doctrines. In 1964, a majority of elements within the latter body (perhaps 700,000) broke away to found the non-confessional Socialist-leaning Confédération Française et Démocratique du Travail (CFDT). Initially moderate, this was the most successful at recruiting among the new working classes and, in May 1968, proved far more militant than the CGT.

Such militancy was evidence that not everyone had benefited from the riches of the *trente glorieuses*, in particular the consumer revolution that it helped produce. This new affluence was evidenced in the fact that average French families now spent less on food and more on housing and domestic products, a trend especially marked in the cities. Whereas in 1956 the outlay of a typical working-class family per annum was 4,083 *francs* on food and 3,993 *francs* on other products, by 1969 out-goings on food were 8,274 *francs* as opposed to 12,242 *francs* on non-food items. Another outward manifestation of consumerism was the acquisition of televisions, some five million in 1965 compared to one million a decade previously. Motor cars were also important. Richard Kuisel recalls that at the end of the 1950s one of the most popular films was *La belle américaine*, not a paean to some screen goddess, but an homage to a car manufactured by General Motors.[46] In 1946, the Renault 4 CV was all the rage; then came the Citröen 2CV, its shiny contours unveiled in showrooms in 1955. By 1970, nearly three-quarters of French families possessed an automobile, a trend that created traffic problems in the major cities. The one commodity which the French were slow to acquire, ironic given the later zest for communications, was the telephone. Much to the embarrassment of a government which prided itself on embracing new technology, in 1964 there were 12 phones to every 100 inhabitants, the same proportion as for Switzerland in 1935. Moreover, it took up to 14 months for a phone to be installed.[47]

There remained, however, the possibility of getting away from the pressures of modern living by taking a holiday. By the early 1970s, some three fifths of the population took vacations. Traditionally, the French had been reticent travellers. As Carteret wrote in 1893, for much of the nineteenth century 'Frenchmen went from one end of Europe to the other end without a word of complaint when Napoleon ordered them to, but the shortest trip in the stagecoach filled them with doubts and fears.'[48] The railways had opened seaside resorts to the middle classes from the 1850s onwards; the paid holidays of the Popular Front had created accessibility for the working classes in the 1930s; in the post-1945 years, popular tourism was facilitated by Club Méditerranée. Founded in 1950 by the Belgian sportsman Gerard Blitz, and nurtured by Gilbert Trigano, the son of Algerian Jews and a Communist resister who became a skilled 'adman', this established sites throughout southern Europe, especially Majorca, and embraced a very different philosophy to that initially favoured by Butlins in Britain, which also attempted to bring leisure to the people. Club Med sites were not camps but 'villages' where holiday-makers escaped the drudgery of daily life and could slough off the austerity of the war years. By purchasing their drinks with beads (kept around the neck or wrist), vacationers could even forget, albeit momentarily, the reality of money. Rather than red-coats the staff were known as *Gentils Organisateurs* (GOs) and their visitors *Gentils Membres* (GMs), although some GOs occasionally resembled Vichy's GMs – *Gardes Mobiles*. This did not detract, however, from Club Med's 'ultimate goal of the care of the self and its recuperation through play, relaxation and pleasure.'[49] The fortunes of Club Med would go into decline in the 1980s, abandoned by a new generation who sought their pleasures elsewhere and who had plenty of travel firms to choose from. It was a sign of the times when Philippe Bourguignon, the Euro Disney executive, was appointed head in 1998 with the task of turning round Club Med's fortunes, something he has done, largely by focusing on family needs.

This consumer revolution was not merely a reflection of economic growth. It also owed much to the growing Americanisation of French culture. This had always been a source of unease. Before 1940, industrialists had often admired the dynamism of American production techniques, typified by Fordism, but intellectuals such as Georges Duhamel had feared the advance of an unmitigated materialism and had stressed the superiority of French culture, making a rare exception for those US Black jazz musicians who made Paris their base and who were respected as outcasts of American society.[50] In 1958, Louis Malle employed a heroin-soaked Miles Davis to produce the haunting music to his film, *Ascenseur pour l'échafaud*. These ambivalent attitudes towards the US had persisted after 1945 and were nowhere better demonstrated in the arguments that surrounded the sale of Coca-Cola in France, which hitherto had only been on sale at selected tourist spots. Many in big business were for; intellectuals were divided; those in the Communist Party were wholly against this intrusion of US capitalism, as were wine growers and fruit merchants who feared that the sales of their own product would suffer. Fantastic rumours circulated, including one that Coca-Cola intended to turn the front of Notre Dame cathedral into a huge advertising board similar to that in Piccadilly Circus, London.[51] Yet because of its reliance on US money, the French government ruled that Coca-Cola could indeed be sold, beginning a steady infiltration of American life leading, in 1979, to the establishment of McDonalds in Paris, and the adoption of English terms in popular speech, the phenomenon known as *franglais*.

The Catholic Church was another party troubled by the creeping influence of Americanisation, but its declining hold over the population undeniably facilitated consumerism. Already, with the growth of urbanisation and industrialisation, France in the 1930s had been described as a *pays de mission* ('missionary country'), not that these two forces automatically equalled secularisation. Nonetheless, the slippage in the levels

of religious practice was irreversible, something revealed in the pioneer-
ing studies of the religious sociologists Gabriel Le Bras and Fernand
Boulard conducted in the late 1940s.[52] Adult attendance at mass, on a
weekly basis, tumbled from approximately one quarter of the population
in 1960 to under 15 per cent by 1970, a worrying trend even noticeable
in traditionally pious areas such as Britanny.[53] There was also a crisis in
recruitment of clergy. There were some 40,000 priests in the 1960s, yet a
mere 27,000 two decades later. In 1984 there were a mere 13 ordina-
tions. This though is not to believe that France has turned its back
wholly on Catholicism. Historians have since spoken of the emergence
of the 'occasional conformist', one who no longer regularly attends services on a Sunday, or even Easter, but who may partake in the rituals of
baptism, marriage and burial, although even here observance of the
sacraments has dropped sharply. Undoubtedly, however, this type of
believer is one who has chosen which of the Church's doctrines to obey,
often ignoring its warnings on the use of contraception and the dangers
of materialism.

Perhaps this spread of consumerism was understandable as people
struggled to break free of wartime austerity. It was an urge further
enhanced by societal changes, most obviously the growing influence of
women, to whom much advertising was directed.[54] This was the heyday
of such magazines as *Elle, Marie-Claire, Nous Deux, Confidences* and *Marie-
France* which trumpeted the use of labour-saving devices in the kitchen:
during the period 1954–70, those homes owning a washing-machine
rose from 8 per cent to 55 per cent. Not that the *trente glorieuses* were a
liberating period for women in other respects: they have been labelled
the *trente laborieuses*. The so-called 'second sex' still suffered legal restrictions. Before 1964, women could not open a bank account or possess a
passport without their husband's permission; and it was not until laws of
1975 and 1979 that women gained (theoretical) equality in the divorce
courts and workplace. As to sexual freedoms, change was also late
coming. Despite a growing liberalisation in attitudes, the outmoded law
of 1920, severely restricting contraception, was abolished only in 1967,
and contraception was not generally available until 1974; and abortion
was not made legal until 1975, a move prompted by public disgust at the
infamous Bobigny affair in which a 16-year old girl from the Paris
suburbs was prosecuted for having an illegal termination following a
rape. Outside the courtroom, feminist chanted, 'l'Angleterre pour
les riches, la prison pour les pauvres', an allusion to abortion on
demand which had been legalised in Britain in 1967.[55] And in political

and institutional domains women were conspicuous by their absence. During the 1960s, a mere 5.2 per cent of the staff of the Conseil d'Etat were women and a paltry 6.5 per cent of the Cour des Comptes. Among *haut fonctionnaires*, historians regularly recite a dispiriting roll call: the first female entrant to the Polytechnique was not until 1972 (she later passed out first!); the first woman to be elected to the Académie Française (Marguerite Yourcenar) was in 1980; and it took Giscard to promote women to ministerial positions, notably Simone Veil in charge of the Health portfolio, although as late as 1988 a mere 33 women were elected to the National Assembly. In 1973, a mere 6.7 per cent of parliamentary candidates were women, the majority belonging to the Communist Party. As gender historians emphasise, women might have been granted the vote in 1944 yet, in the relationship between the sexes, the playing field was decidedly uneven.[56]

Institutional barriers and social pressures to marry and have children were undoubtedly obstacles in the way of further freedoms, together with a deep-rooted male chauvinism. As John Ardagh writes this was nurtured by traditional Catholic attitudes and a Latin *machismo* which saw women primarily as wives and mothers.[57] Yet it must be stressed that women themselves were slow to challenge these attitudes. In 1949 Simone de Beauvoir published her renowned feminist manifesto *Le Deuxième Sexe,* yet this had little impact outside of intellectual circles, and jarred with the image being presented to women in such publications as *Elle.* So it was that French feminism remained on the fringes of French politics, represented by Marie-Andrée Weill-Hallé, a young doctor who in 1956 inaugurated what became the Mouvement Français pour le Planning Familial (MFPL) which struggled to make contraception freely available, and the Mouvement Démocratique Féminin (MDF), set up eight years later by Marie-Thérèse Eyquem which enjoyed close links with Mitterrand's CIR. As we shall see, French feminism would have to wait until the upheavals of May 1968 before it made any real headway.

Whether the frailties of the women's movement and the active discrimination against the 'second sex' accounts for another significant feature of the *trente glorieuses* – the baby boom – remains a moot point. Nevertheless, this was a period of massive demographic growth which contrasted markedly with the stagnation of the interwar years. During the period 1946–75, the population grew from 40.5 million to over 52.7 million. This growth partly reflected a fall in death rates yet historians stress that a rise in the birth rate was the more crucial. In the 1960s, the birth rate averaged 18 per cent which contrasted favourably with the

15 per cent managed during the years 1935–45. In part, France was making up for lost time. In 1945, as men returned from prisoner-of-war camps and the hated compulsory work service in Germany, the Service du Travail Obligatoire (STO), the heartwarming rejoining of families inevitably produced more children. It may even be that, in the liberating atmosphere of the *après-guerre*, young couples reacted against the Malthusian spirit of their parents, who had often limited themselves to one or two children, by embarking on larger families of three or more. Significantly, those with bigger families tended to be among the higher reaches of society, and such couples were clearly anxious to reap the rewards of the new prosperity whose end did not seem in sight. In this respect, it is telling that birth rates were not especially high in poorer regions such as the Auvergne and Limousin. Vichy legislation also made an impact. Not only did the regime extend Daladier's 1939 *Code de la Famille*, providing substantial welfare for fathers of big families, it also improved post-natal care. Something Vichy had not welcomed was the presence of foreigners within society, yet in the Liberation period governments deliberately encouraged immigration as a means to offset a labour shortage. Statistics record 1.7 million foreigners in France in 1946; this figure had doubled by 1975. While many came from neighbouring European states, Italy, Belgium, and the Iberian Peninsula, whose growth rates could not match those of France, an ever-increasing number hailed from North Africa.

This growing population had, of course, to be educated (see next chapter) and housed. This became an urgent priority in the postwar years, especially as one-in-four buildings had been razed in 1940–44. As Ardagh recounts, this meant a reversal in government policy which had long neglected accommodation and which had been happy to leave on the statute books the archaic law of August 1914 on rent increases, designed to protect soldiers from grasping landlords, but one which had discouraged property developers.[58] By the early 1950s, France was still a long way behind Britain and West Germany in the construction of new homes, and it was calculated that over a third of the urban population lived in cramped circumstances. Particularly badly off were those immigrants and non-skilled workers who were congregated in the so-called *bidonvilles*, shanty towns constructed out of cardboard and tin, on the outskirts of Paris and other large cities. Matters had, however, reached a head and government responded with the *Habitations à Loyer Modéré* (HLMs), essentially council flats, erected by local authorities in conjunction with the state. Some 400,000 of these were being constructed by the

1960s, yet conditions in these new breeze blocks could not be said to be good, and they remained beyond the means of the very poor, especially foreign workers and the unskilled. The HLMs were brutally satirised in Jean-Luc Godard's futuristic film *Alphaville*, which likened them to agents of government indoctrination, and more recently have figured in Thomas Gilou's 1995 film *Raï*.[59] Many were centred in what were known as *Zones d'Urbaniser à Priorité* (ZUPs), priority urbanisation zones. Just as London acquired its densely-populated areas of cheap housing in Slough, Basildon and Luton, so too Paris acquired satellite towns in the shape of Bagnolet, Créteil, and Sarcelles. Inevitably these centres lacked the necessary infrastructures yet they were at least some that were linked to the centre of Paris and the *métro* with the high-speed *Réseau Express Régional* (RER), a regional rail network opened in 1969 and now extending to EuroDisney. So it was that in 1968 two-thirds of the French population came to live in towns in contrast to just over half in 1946.

More urban, more modern, more prosperous, far less rural, less backward-looking, less insular – France's economy and society were undoubtedly changing in the 1950s and 60s, although the pace of change was not everywhere the same, and nor did the forces of change act in harmony. Whether the years 1946 to 1975 were truly a golden age will thus remain a contentious issue, yet there was a shared belief among the French people that the nation was embracing the modern world. The problem was that not everyone was benefiting from the *trente glorieuses*. The *cadres* might have gained, as did elements within the salaried middle class, yet there were plenty who were disgruntled: young female workers; immigrant labourers; small-scale and medium-size rural producers; students in overcrowded lecture halls; small businessmen eased out by state planning; workers in the older industries; and even those in the burgeoning tertiary sector who were unhappy at the slow rise in the standard of living. Indeed, it should not be forgotten that the 1960s remained a period of violent demonstrations. In June 1961 peasants, angered at enforced modernisation, occupied the sous-préfecture at Morlaix, a protest that soon spread to the whole of Brittany. That same year miners at Decazeville protested at the forced closure of pits. The scale of their protests was nothing compared to the widespread strikes in the Nord-Pas-de-Calais two years later. While de Gaulle's own popularity might have remained high, opinion polls constantly revealed that the discontented outnumbered the contented when it came to economic issues. It was the general's hope that *grandeur* abroad would offset something of this dissatisfaction. In the event, this was not to be.

The Politics of Grandeur

While de Gaulle was too skilled a statesman merely to use his foreign policy as a way to assuage domestic discontent, as Philip Cerny has stressed, it was a domestic consideration that remained at the fount of his thinking on international affairs: the nation-state.[60] For de Gaulle this was everything. Its interests came before all others, both at home and abroad. Whereas at home, the state was threatened by sectarian factions, abroad it was challenged by competing nations, something painfully revealed by Hitler's invasion in 1940. It was thus essential that France should pursue an uncompromising policy of *realpolitik* so that it was capable of standing up for itself in a hostile world, a world where self-interest predominated over ideology. De Gaulle was always contemptuous of ideologically-driven foreign policies, whether the liberalism of the USA, or the communism of the USSR, believing that such ideologies were a smokescreen for power politics. This explains why he referred to the Soviet Union as Russia, or the 'eternal Russia'; he referred to the USA less flatteringly as 'les Etats-soi-disants unis' ('the so-called United States').[61]

From this attachment to the state emerged another trait in Gaullist foreign policy: the pursuit of *grandeur*. At root, this meant asserting the autonomy of France – an ability to act in the international arena without the prior approval of others, notably the USA, a country always suspect in de Gaulle's eyes following his traumatic relationship with Roosevelt during the Second World War. It was this quest for independence that often lent a surreal quality to French foreign policy when the nation appeared to be living in the past and defying the realities of the new world order that had emerged out of 1945. In this regard, the most blatant episode was his speech in Canada in 1967 when he proclaimed, 'Vive le Québec libre' – almost certainly an unscripted remark, but a long-held sentiment. Inevitably this conjured up images of an eighteenth and nineteenth-century past in which French power had really counted, even on this side of the globe. What is striking is that, despite many setbacks overseas, de Gaulle established the contours of a French foreign policy that remained broadly constant ever since his death.

The quest for *grandeur* and the assertion of the needs of the French state were immediately apparent in the policies which de Gaulle pursued in respect to the empire. In the wake of Indo-China and Algeria, he recognised the folly of attempting to defy the aspirations of Third World nationalism; France had no need of its own Vietnam. Yet for France to give up its empire altogether was to sacrifice the nation's greatness and to relinquish an opportunity to influence events in different parts of the globe.

So it was that in the referendum of September 1958 France's colonies were presented with three options. It will be recalled that they could choose between becoming a part of France itself, as fully-fledged departments, of becoming autonomous states within a French Community (a structure similar to the British Commonwealth), or of breaking away from France altogether, thereby relinquishing any assistance from the 'mother' country. In the event, only Guinea opted for this last possibility, but it was not long before others, Senegal, Sudan and Madagascar, sought to detach themselves. This led to a series of agreements in 1960 in which Paris granted independence to these former colonies without them losing all of their links with the Community. This precedent soon had other states lining up to sign similar agreements, among them Cameroon, Togo, Dahomey, Ivory Coast, Upper Volta, Niger, Mauritania, the Central African Republic, Congo, Chad, Gabon and Mauritius. In effect, the bilateral arrangements agreed with these nations meant the end of the French Community which failed to acquire a life of its own.

De Gaulle ensured, however, that independence did not mean the end of French influence. The future of former colonies, especially in Africa, was closely monitored by his faithful ally, Jacques Foccart. As Dalloz relates, France retained military bases in many of these areas; French troops came to the assistance of various regimes in trouble, notably president Tombalbaye of Chad in 1968; French officials were on hand to advise and administer; behind the scenes, French secret services practised their skulduggery; aid was provided so long as France received valuable raw materials in return; an African *franc* was instigated, linked to its counterpart on the metropole; and French influence was even extended to the former Belgian colonies of Zaire, Rwanda and Burundi.[62] Within international relations, Paris happily sided with its former possessions, but expected them to dance to France's tune in the United Nations (UN), especially if there were votes to be won against either the USA or the USSR. It was a form of neo-colonialism, prolonged by the Pompidou and Giscard regimes, never properly acknowledged by the French themselves, and never entirely abandoned by the Socialists in the 1980s.[63] As we shall see, it ensured that France propped up some particularly unpleasant African dictatorships. It was also a form of neo-imperialism supported by the so-called DOM-TOMs (Départements d'Outre Mer Territoires d'Outre Mer), those areas such as Martinique, Guadeloupe, Guyana, New Caledonia, and Réunion, which were ruled directly by Paris and which were denied a vote in the 1958 referendum. While certain of these – notably New Caledonia in the 1980s and 90s, where there was a conflict between French settlers and Melanesian Kalaks – proved extremely troublesome, their retention kept alive the notion of France as a great power.

Such status had, of course, been called into question by the new bipolar world, dominated by the USA and the USSR, that emerged out of the Second World War. De Gaulle bitterly resented the manner in which this new global order restricted his country's freedom of movement, and strove for the creation of a more malleable international framework in which French interests would not be tied to those of the superpowers. Haunted by this so-called 'Yalta Syndrome', he thus sought to distance Paris from Washington, and looked to build some understanding with Russia, using this as a bulwark against American influence. As Nicholas Wahl recalls, for de Gaulle international politics were like communicating jars in a physics laboratory. For the level of French and European power to rise, the general observed, it was first necessary for American power to fall.[64]

As to the USA, de Gaulle was doubly indebted to the Americans: for having expelled the Germans in 1944 and for having supported the western democracies through Marshall Aid and the North Atlantic Treaty Organisation (NATO). At root, however, he considered that the USA was essentially looking after its own economic and strategic interests: it was, he declared, an expansionist power,[65] and there no disguising his dislike of Yankee materialism. Given his faith in the nation state, together with the pursuit of *grandeur*, it was thus unacceptable that France should not be able to act independently of the USA, in particular through the possession of nuclear weapons, which were as much an outward symbol of power as they were weapons of mass destruction. 'A great state which does not possess them while others have them', he pronounced, 'does not command its own destiny.'[66] He was thus especially galled that Britain had acquired its own nuclear capability and was angered that Washington wanted to establish Intermediate Range Ballistic Missiles (IRBMs) on French soil. Desperate to be part of the nuclear club, he proposed a council comprising the USA, Britain and France, which would determine the deployment of atomic weapons, together with the pooling of technical know-how. When in 1959 President Eisenhower rubbished this suggestion, de Gaulle withdrew the

French Mediterranean fleet from the NATO command structure and embarked on the acquisition of the bomb. It was joked at the time that the best France could aspire to was a *bombinette*, yet the first atomic device detonated in the Sahara in February 1960 was dramatic enough, and signalled France's determination to achieve nuclear independence. If anything this desire had been hardened by the explosion of the first Soviet bomb in 1949, which raised the frightening prospect of Washington contemplating the destruction of western Europe in order to protect American soil. As Julian Jackson asserts, the subsequent shift in American strategic policy, from one of 'massive retaliation' to one of 'flexible response' was, in de Gaulle's eyes, further evidence of the USA's unreliability, and seemingly supported the increasingly hard line he had adopted towards the Americans.[67] His veto of British entry into the EEC in 1963 was, in part, because of his pique at Anglo-American cooperation over Polaris. In that same conference he rejected President Kennedy's proposal of a Multilateral Nuclear Force (MLF) envisaging three-way cooperation between London, Paris and Washington on the grounds that France could never permit others to have a say in the use of its weapons, a different standpoint from that he had taken in 1958 when he had been desperate to become part of the nuclear club.

Through its development of *Mirage* bombers and the submarine *Redoubtable* France went on in the 1960s to develop its nuclear capabilities, and when it was objected that these were a huge drain on the budget and could never be as plentiful in number as those belonging to the superpowers, the response was the same: given the destructive potential of these weapons, in a nuclear war the French *force de frappe* was just as much of a deterrent as that of the American arsenal which might well sacrifice European soil to protect US cities. It was this quest for independence that, in March 1966, led France to withdraw from the integrated NATO command structure, something accomplished a year later. Meanwhile, France attempted to assert its independence of the USA in other spheres. In 1963 the government tried to prevent General Electric's takeover of the French computer firm Bull, just one of many American French acquisitions at that time; in financial affairs, de Gaulle ordered the Banque de France to build up huge gold reserves to combat the Yankee dollar, which acted as *the* international reserve currency; and French officialdom frowned on the Americanisation of national life. As Richard Kuisel writes, 'De Gaulle was unique among West European nations in resisting American investment during the 1960s.'[68] To add insult to injury, de Gaulle undertook a series of foreign policy initiatives which clearly irked Washington. Historians (for instance, Jackson) recite a familiar list of provocations. In 1964, he recognised the People's Republic of China; that same year, in Latin America, he denounced US influence; in 1966 he condemned the escalation of the Vietnamese war; in 1967 he made his famous declaration in Canada; and in the Middle East he lent support to the Arab states as opposed to Israel, in 1967 expressing sympathy with Egypt in the Six-Day War and in 1969 selling arms to the military regime recently created by the coup d'état of Colonel Gadaffy in Libya.

While this seeming anti-Americanism often went down well with the French public which remained distinctly ambivalent towards the USA – Jean-Jacques Servan-Schreiber's 1967 volume *Le Défi Américain* was a huge bestseller – it seemed to many outside observers a futile policy which cast France as a difficult player on the international stage. It was undoubtedly a policy which sacrificed much American goodwill and denied French firms much-needed US investments which simply went elsewhere. Yet it should be recognised that there were limits to de Gaulle's defiance. France belonged to the free world, and remained a part of the NATO alliance in which it was obliged to defend fellow members should they be attacked. At crunch moments, for instance when the Russians erected the Berlin Wall in 1961 and threatened to station missiles on Cuban soil, thus threatening world war, de Gaulle stood firm alongside Kennedy, a man he admired. His successor Johnson was dismissed as a Radical of the Third and Fourth Republics – a 'cowboy Radical'![69]

While de Gaulle had no truck with communism, and despised the PCF for subordinating itself to Moscow, as the Soviet Union was a part of Europe, it had to be accommodated. In any case, he asserted, there were several long-standing links with France.[70] Its Bolshevism was, in his mind, only a passing ideological fancy, cloaking *raison d'état*. After the Cuban Missile Crisis, he also felt that a Soviet invasion of Western Europe was less likely. So it was that he sought some measure of détente, organising a series of high-level exchanges of officials between Moscow and Paris, culminating in de Gaulle's own visit to Russia in 1966. Further visits to eastern Europe ensued in 1967, yet these resulted in little other than expressions of mutual goodwill, a tolerance of French spies in East Germany and a series of bilateral trade negotiations, although the overall volume of French trade to the USSR was a third of that it enjoyed with Belgium. In August 1968, the uncompromising ideology of Communism displayed itself in full when the USSR marched into

Czechoslovakia, discouraging any further goodwill gestures. Indeed, as Robert Paxton observes, at such moments of crisis, when the Soviets let slip the mask of civilisation, among Western leaders de Gaulle was their most ferocious critic.[71]

The other means by which de Gaulle hoped that France could escape the strictures of a bi-polar world was through Europe. Here, it is necessary to stress that his conception of Europe was very different to that of the founders of European integration. A believer in the nation state, he had no time for the supranationalism espoused by Robert Schuman and Jean Monnet. Nor did he have time for the Atlanticism of others, which would have cemented closer links with both the USA and Great Britain. Rather he wished to see a culturally, economically and militarily independent Europe, a so-called 'third force', which would mediate between the two superpowers. This, though, did not mean the surrender of any form of national sovereignty on the part of EEC members; it would instead be a *Europe des états*, and one which acknowledged the preeminence of France.

To pursue this goal, in 1961 the Gaullist loyalist Christian Fouchet presented the European Commission with a plan for future cooperation. This envisaged some measure of collaboration of EEC states in the formulation of foreign policy, and various 'confederal, functional bodies to make common policies by unanimous agreement'.[72] It was obvious, however, that this project was designed to stymie any developments towards a supranational Europe, and clearly had in mind the exclusion of Great Britain. For these reasons, Fouchet could not carry the Belgians and Dutch who remained committed to greater political integration. Angered at their refusal, in May 1962 de Gaulle delivered one of his most famous speeches in which he said the only option possible was 'a Europe of countries', for 'Dante, Goethe, Chateaubriand would not have served Europe very well if they had been stateless, men thinking and writing in some form of integrated Esperanto or Volapük'. At the famous press conference in January the following year, he gave concrete expression to these views by unilaterally vetoing the entry of Great Britain into the EEC, despite the fact that complicated negotiations for its entry had been going on since 1961, and had reached a near breakthrough.

De Gaulle's reasons for using the veto were threefold. First, he claimed Britain was historically a maritime nation whose commitment to free trade and industry would undermine the unity of a Continent, protectionist in instinct and heavily reliant on agriculture. Second, he saw

Britain as being the catspaw of the USA, a view reinforced by the ways in which London and Washington had cooperated over the nuclear programme. Finally, he felt that Britain's inclusion would threaten his plans for a Franco-German reconciliation. It should not though be necessarily believed that de Gaulle envisaged Britain's permanent exclusion. To Peyrefitte, he observed that the UK would eventually become a member when its links to the empire were much reduced and when its government was headed by young conservatives of a different generation to Churchill and Macmillan, a forecast not so wide of the mark.[73]

Contemptuous of Britain, de Gaulle actively courted Bonn so that the West German foreign policy could be kept in check. To this end, he cultivated excellent relations with the German Chancellor Adenauer and, in 1963, achieved a Franco-German Friendship treaty which led to a high measure of cultural cooperation. There was, however, a flaw in de Gaulle's thinking. As many commentators stress, he failed to recognise that West Germany was far more pro-American than other West European states even Great Britain. Consequently, West Germany did not accept the subordinate position de Gaulle had envisaged, meaning that French initiatives in Europe became ever more a series of blusters, culminating in the 1965 crisis when Paris threatened the whole European project, demanding a restructuring of the Community's institutions and the implementation of generous CAP subsidies. That France ultimately got part of what it wanted – the right of an individual country to veto a decision affecting all of the others, the last vestigial outcome of the Fouchet Plan – chimed in well with de Gaulle's ideals, and halted European integration in a supranational sense for some 15 years.

The policy of *grandeur* often degenerated into threats, tawdry dealings and unnecessary crises, and it is not difficult to see why de Gaulle's foreign policy has been so severely criticised. As Douglas Johnson wrote in an influential article of 1966, ultimately France could not challenge the realities of the bi-polar world; his snubs of the USA seemed childish and provocative; his courting of the USSR produced no real dividends; the failure of the Fouchet Plan merely exacerbated European divisions; West Germany had its own mind; and the links with empire degenerated into a form of neo-colonialism.[74] It is perhaps only with the historian's privileged benefit of hindsight that we can see de Gaulle was prescient in his beliefs, as Jackson has remarked. NATO would indeed eventually result in Europe being brought increasingly into the American orbit, with the placing of cruise missiles on British and German soil in the 1980s.[75] By refusing to become a US arsenal, France also escaped the surge of Anti-American sentiment which was commonplace elsewhere on the Continent. As de Gaulle further forecast, the Anglo-American friendship would disrupt European integration. Nor did bi-polarity prove a permanent fixture of international relations. And, in the Middle East, Israeli expansion into the West Bank seemed to vindicate France's position in the Six-Day War. Most crucially, writes Jackson, France under de Gaulle had been seen to be a key player in overseas affairs, a country which demanded to be noticed and which was not afraid to speak its voice, even if there was little it could actually accomplish. Whether de Gaulle was successful in carrying his public with him is another matter. While his forays abroad often played well at home, there was a feeling that his regime was more bothered about the world than it was about France.

Conclusion: Worrying Portents

As well as overseeing an expansion in the number of televisions, the 1960s also witnessed the ever-increasing use of opinion polls. These revealed that, apart from a dip at the time of the miners' strike in 1963, levels of satisfaction with de Gaulle were continuously high, standing at over 50 per cent. Yet while the president could take satisfaction in the fact that France seemed to be a modern, forward-looking country, when asked about their material lot French men and women gave a very different answer. Given his mastery of the political scene immediately after 1962, de Gaulle could afford to discount these grumblings, yet the 1965 presidential elections indicated that a credible opposition was at long last developing, something further illustrated in the 1967 elections when the UNR was run close by Mitterrand. None of this made the 1968 demonstrations inevitable, but it helps explain why they acquired such a dynamism.

Chapter 4: La Contestation: *1968*

Armed with the privileged benefit of hindsight, historians often like to embarrass contemporaries for their want of anticipation. 1968 is one of those occasions. At the beginning of that tumultuous year, few predicted what momentous events lay around the corner. De Gaulle himself remarked that he greeted the year with 'serenity'. Early indicators seemed to justify his complacency. Writing in *Le Monde* on 15 March, Pierre Viansson-Ponté observed, 'What presently characterises our public life is "ennui".'[1] So it was that, on 2 May, prime minister Pompidou jetted off for an official trip to Afghanistan and Iran confident in the knowledge that he had left the house secure. Only the previous day, the traditional May Day celebrations had passed off without incident. Admittedly in 1966 the *Bulletin du Club Moulin* had forewarned of trouble on university campuses and there had been student demonstrations aplenty in 1967 and early '68.[2] Yet these were eclipsed by those in Italy, Germany and USA. The influential journal *L'Express* doubted whether French students had it in them emulate their foreign counterparts.[3] Events, beginning on 2 May at the new campus of Nanterre to the north-west of Paris, proved commentators wrong. Within days the revolt spread to the Sorbonne and regional universities; it was soon joined by the workers.

Out of nothing, a widespread social and economic crisis erupted which threatened the state itself. In an echo of the *exode* of 1940, when workers fleeing the German advance made for those holiday resorts they had known as part of the Popular Front paid holidays, by late May 1968 the *bourgeoisie*, recalling their winter breaks in Geneva, Lausanne and Berne, were queuing at the Swiss border to place their savings in bank deposits.[4] In another echo of 1940, Edouard Balladur recalls how one civil servant at the Matignon had to be restrained from creating a pyre of government papers as had happened outside the Quai d'Orsay shortly before the Germans arrived to seize the capital.[5]

Conscious of historical parallels, de Gaulle was all too aware of the similarities between 1940 and 1968, especially the way in which the state had seemingly 'disappeared'.[6] For their part, historians have not been sure of the overall importance of the May *événements* and, until recently, the exploration of this momentous year was primarily a concern of sociologists.[7] One of the most notable of these was Alan Touraine, himself a sociology lecturer at Nanterre and a first-hand witness to events, who interpreted them as a struggle between a fast developing society, rapidly assimilating a new culture born of economic change, and a state apparatus, slow to adapt and all too ready to retreat into its authoritarian instincts.[8] Certainly the participants themselves believed they were making history. One book by André Quattrochi and Tom Nairn, which appeared that year, was entitled the *The Beginning of the End*, a reference to the imminent collapse of *bourgeois* society.[9] In London, the left-wing activist Tariq Ali, who had already travelled to Prague and Hanoi in the quest for revolution, was especially keen to join the student protesters until he received an anonymous call from a middle-aged man in a phone box (undoubtedly a Home Office official) warning him that, should he travel to France, he was in danger of breaking a five-year injunction to stay in UK and would not be allowed back into the country. Against his better judgement, he stayed.[10]

Those who did partake in the Paris events also came to have regrets, believing that they had allowed a wonderful occasion to pass them by. In their view, 1968 was a *révolution manquée*, let down in particular by the organised left in the shape of the PCF and CGT which had been caught off-guard by the spontaneity of the protests. As early as 3 May, the Communist leader Georges Marchais outlined the official line by questioning how the student leaders, the 'sons of the *bourgeois*, contemptuous of those students of working-class origin,' could teach the workers anything about revolution?[11] And, in any case, how could a revolution be mobilised without the leadership of the party *cadres*?

This remained the Communist position throughout, the invective against the student leaders matched only by the vitriol of the right. 'Students, these youngsters? Young guttersnipes, fit for the remand home, if not for a court of summary jurisdiction, rather than for university,' announced the right-wing daily *Le Figaro*.[12] While more sensationalist right-wing commentators believed the protests were part of an international conspiracy – in much the same was as early nineteenth-century conservatives such as the Austrian chancellor Metternich had believed in the existence of a revolutionary committee ready to topple the established order – a more measured assessment came from Raymond Aron. A professor of sociology at the Sorbonne, a regular contributor to *Le Figaro*, and an exile journalist in Britain during the Nazi Occupation, his book on 1968, *La Révolution introuvable*, published that very year, portrayed the protests as 'a pyschodrama'. 'The French', he wrote, 'always magnify their revolutions in retrospect into great festivals, during which they experience all that they are normally deprived of, and so they have the feeling that they are achieving their aspirations, even if only in a waking dream.' From this perspective, the students were 'role-playing' – pelting police cars with stones was safer than driving fast cars, Aron concluded.[13] The slogans of the time tended to reflect this viewpoint – 'the dream is reality'; 'be realistic, demand the impossible'; 'I am a Marxist, Groucho tendency'.[14] It is perhaps best that a veil is drawn over other psychological explanations of 1968, for instance the notion that the students were caught in a warped Oedipus complex, compelled to kill their father in the shape of de Gaulle.[15]

It has since become commonplace to dismiss the 1968 protests, at least those in France, as being little more than 'a psychodrama'. This, though, is to overlook their real significance. As Arthur Marwick argues, the *événéments* are best seen as protests for 'personal liberation' which would lead to a flowering of a whole series of bodies agitating for women's rights, ecological change and homosexual equality.[16] These movements proved far more influential in changing the political landscape than the ideas of those 'intellectuals' who had previously assumed an elevated place in French society.[17] Additionally, a *génération '68* would grow up to occupy positions of power. While we need to be careful when speaking about those generations involved in the May events (see below), these men and women adopted a fresh approach to traditional issues. In this sense, 1968 was a harbinger of change. The writing was on the wall for the days of the authoritarian state. A more pluralist society, less ready to tell its citizens what was good for them, beckoned. As one of the slogans of the day put it, 1968 was all about 'getting the state off the backs of the people.'[18]

Viewed from this perspective, an explanation of 1968 is that much more tangible. This was one of those rare episodes in history when a series of seemingly unconnected trends came to the surface in dramatic fashion, the drama exacerbated by the inept handling of the situation by government. Put simply, the structures of the French state, modern-looking yet still heavily influenced by traditional values dating back to the previous century, were out of kilter with a society fed by the consumer boom and cultural innovations of the post-1945 world. This 'lack of symmetry', as Berstein puts it, was all the more serious because de Gaulle's authority was more wounded by the challenges of 1965 and 1967 than was realised at the time.[19] It was something which the general himself did not properly understand, and helps explain why he was caught out by 1968. Whether he later understood the true importance of that year is also questionable, but he at least retained some of his instinctive feel for politics, which enabled him to overcome the crisis, albeit with considerable help from Pompidou. Within a year, de Gaulle had resigned, frustrated at the behaviour of his compatriots. The one consolation he could take with him was that the Fifth Republic had survived yet again.

The Student Protest

Any understanding of 1968 must begin with an appreciation of the student protests, together with an awareness that the turmoil in the universities was not a phenomenon unique to France. Students at the University of Tokyo, at the London School of Economics, at the University of Berkeley in California and at the University of Columbia in New York, to name but some of the most celebrated institutions, partook in a world-wide phenomenon of protest. It was, however, in France that the student movement was most conspicuous. As will be seen, this was partly because of the changes that had taken place within the university system there. It was also due to the importance the French had traditionally attached to intellectuals.

Despite having an extremely ambivalent attitude towards intellectuals, it was de Gaulle himself who acknowledged their role – and their responsibilities. 'An intellectual is not less but more than another', he reflected. 'He is an inciter. He is a leader in the strongest sense.'[20] Such a viewpoint had been shaped by his reading of French history. As Jeremy Jennings relates, the eighteenth century had been the era of the Enlightenment when so-called *philosophes*, such as Voltaire and Diderot, readily questioned the world of privilege which underpinned *ancien régime* society; the nineteenth century was the turn of the *savant*, for instance Comte and Michelet, who specialised in specific areas of study, such as history and science; and, at the turn of the twentieth century, emerged the *intellectuels*.[21] The miscarriage of justice, in which the unfortunate Captain Alfred Dreyfus was wrongly accused and imprisoned for selling military secrets to the Germans, prompted a series of writers, among them Emile Zola, Charles Péguy, Anatole France and Marcel Proust, to enter the political arena.[22] Ever since, intellectuals have prided themselves on shaping national debate,[23] although they have often discussed among themselves as to how far they should throw themselves into partisan debate, lest they lost their independence.[24]

The Liberation of 1944 only emboldened the claims of the *intellectuals*, or *les intellos* as they are popularly known. This confidence was especially marked among left-wing writers. Their counterparts on the right were discredited by their support for Vichy. This self-assurance also stemmed from the fact that such left-leaning writers as Jean-Paul Sartre, Paul Eluard, Louis Aragon and Paul Langevin had been at the forefront of the intellectual resistance to Nazism and were reluctant to relinquish that *engagement*, especially since the politicians of the Fourth Republic appeared incapable of defending the freedoms that had been won at such cost.[25]

Initially, postwar French intellectual life revolved around the so-called existentialists fronted by Sartre and Simone de Beauvoir who frequented the fashionable cafés and jazz clubs of the Left Bank in Paris and who published regularly in the influential journal *Les Temps Modernes*. Taking its cue from such diverse philosophers as Kierkegaard, Nietzsche, Husserl and Heidegger, existentialism argued that events only took on their true meaning after they had taken place, and asserted that these happenings were not in any sense part of a pre-ordained plan. It has been succinctly defined as a materialist philosophy that emphasises individual choice, which often boils down to a struggle to overcome a work-a-day existence. Yet, despite its all-pervading influence in the immediate post-war years, existentialism was not without its critics, notably Albert Camus, Raymond Aron and Maurice Merleau-Ponty, all of whom disliked its pro-Soviet bias. Not that Sartre's ideas always chimed well with Communism. While he was impressed by what he saw during his visit to the USSR in 1954, Sartre was never a wholehearted supporter of the PCF and was disconcerted by Marxist didactics and its championing of collectivism. The brutal crushing by Russian tanks of the Hungarian uprising in 1956 forced a major rethink in his attitude towards the Soviet alternative.

The year 1956 was a thus a crucial year in shaping what has been the termed the 'New Left', or *gauchisme*. This was the name given to those ideologues whose dissatisfaction with the USSR led them to articulate a different set of principles to orthodox Marxism, and it was their ideals which would be prominent in 1968. It is the historian Robert Gildea who has disentangled the many different strands of this typically amorphous movement.[26] There was first, he writes, the review *Socialisme ou barbarie*, the brainchild of the Greek Communist Cornelius Castoriadis and the French Trotskyist Claude Lefort. In its brief lifetime (1949–65), this journal berated the bureaucracy of the USSR and vaunted the demo-cratic decision-making of workers' councils which had originated in the Russian soviets and which had reappeared in 1956 Hungary. These councils would again be emulated in 1968 as the student leader, the red-haired Daniel Cohn-Bendit, 'Dany la rouge', articulated the notion of *autogestion*, drawing heavily on *Socialisme ou barbarie* for inspiration. A second element in the New Left, continues Gildea, sprang from the work of the Henri Lefebvre. A professor of sociology at Nanterre, his *Critique de la vie quotidienne* (1947–81) drew on Marx's 'early, humanistic writings' to condemn the 'alienation' that was a fundamental part of capitalist society. Lefebvre looked instead to a wholesale revolution – in political, economic, social, and sexual life – so that humankind could achieve self-fulfilment. It was a dream that ensured his banishment from the PCF, but earned him the admiration of the self-styled Situationist Movement. Founded in 1957, and prominent at the University of Strasbourg, this displayed parallels with Dadaism and surrealism in its criticisms of convention and work-a-day existence, and in its champi-oning of imagination and spontaneity. These themes underscored the 1967 film *Société du Spectacle* of director Guy Debord, who also edited the short-lived *L'internationale situationiste*. In common with the so-called Yippies in the USA, the French situationists sought, in the words of David Caute, 'a playful society in which individual self-expression would replace the solemn masks worn by those trapped in the pro-ductive process', and they did not hesitate to mock those earnest and purse-lipped leftists who sought to re-enact 1917.[27] Situationism also had links with the third strand of the New Left, identified by Gildea, the anarchist wing which congregated in the Union des Groupes Anarchistes Communistes (UGAC), whose review *Noir et rouge* drew on the writings of Bakunin to expound a particular form of anarcho-Marxism that appealed to Cohn-Bendit and his supporters but which alienated traditional Communists.

More conventional in its approach was the fourth element of the New Left – that fronted by the Marxist professor Louis Althusser. Through his analysis of Marxism, especially the role of revolutionary elites, he inadvertently focused attention on Mao-Tse-Tung's Communist China regarded by many idealists, among them Régis Debray, as an alternative model of Communism in action. 'President Mao is the Lenin of our epoch', declared one group of students.[28] Drawing inspiration from the Algerian war of independence, this interest in the Third World (*tiersmondisme*) soon took in Castro's Cuba, the Palestinian struggle against Israel and, inevitably, Vietnam. In Tony Judt's opinion, this support for these revolutionary causes was a means by which left-wingers distanced themselves from the USSR without ever having to take on board the past behaviour of the Soviet Union.[29] Whatever the case, 1968 was awash with Maoist committees which fulminated against capitalism and US imperialism in the Far East, although it should be noted that among the young at least there was no widespread rejection of a new American culture typified by blue jeans, rock and roll and long hair.

Althusser had no part in these initiatives, and remained, in many senses, an orthodox Marxist, his ideas informing the new fad among French intellectuals, that of structuralism. Championed by the likes of the anthropologist Claude Lévi-Strauss, the literary critic Roland Barthes, the psychoanalyst Jacques Lacan and the philosopher Michel Foucault, this ventured that all aspects of human activity, whether they be sociology, science or linguistics, were subject to a series of structural constraints. In the mind of Foucault, it was thus the responsibility of the intellectual, not to act as some kind of visionary, but to develop the *outils*, or tools of analysis, that could define the ways in which institutions, for instance prisons, schools and hospitals, exerted a grip on society.[30] This rather bleak concept of the world, bound by unseen structures, had little space for humanism, creativity and individualism, and it is little surprise that the structuralists were heavily criticised by the students in the *mêlée* of May 68.

An instinctive mistrust of authority in all its guises (whether de Gaulle, the state, university rectors or the leadership of the PCF), a distaste at the war the USA was fighting in Vietnam, a rejection of consumerism (although this was riddled with ambivalence as students embraced a culture of Levis and rock records), a willingness to experiment with new forms of representation, a desire to combine political and artistic life, the wish to build a new society – these were just some of the ingredients that would go into making 1968 a tumultuous year. Yet it should not be believed that all students were enamoured of the New Left. As Julian Jackson has underscored, May 1968 was made by 'two distinct generations'.[31] The first was that of the student leaders – Cohn Bendit, born in 1945 and Alain Geismar, born in 1939 – men who had been 'politicised' by the founding of the Fifth Republic, the assertion of Gaullist hegemony and the fighting in North Africa. A similar point is made by Kristin Ross: for this generation the 'war in Algeria provided the background noise of their childhood, whose adolescence and adulthood coincided with the massacres of hundreds of Algerian workers at the hands of Papon's police on 17 October 1961, with Charonne and the near daily attacks of the OAS.'[32] Not only had these figures been politicised by the Algerian war, when they had become disillusioned with the leadership of the PCF, as Jackson adds it was also likely that they had attended the most prestigious of French institutions of higher education, namely the ENA or Ecole Normale Supérieure (ENS), where there existed a rarefied academic atmosphere, absent in most other branches of education. It was here, in the cafés, bistros, bookshops and libraries of the Left Bank in Paris, that *gauchisme* flourished.

As Jackson continues, beneath this elite was the second generation of 68 – the mass of students, generally ten years younger, who knew little about de Gaulle and even less about Algeria and the foundations of the Fifth Republic. That the student body in 1960s France was becoming increasingly apathetic towards politics is borne out by the sharp drop in membership of the Union Nationale des Etudiants de France (UNEF), some 100,000 strong in 1962, at the time of the Algerian war, yet maybe possessing only 30,000 members by 1967, despite the overall growth in numbers at university.[33] Among those who remained, hyper political squabbles prevailed, spilling out into several splinter groups, notably the Union des Jeunes Communistes Marxistes-Leninistes (UJCML) and the Comité de Liaison des Etudiants Révolutionnaires (CLER). It has sometimes been said of those who stayed out of politics that they were the 'generation of Lennon' as opposed to Lenin, yet at least Lennon had been a mountebank revolutionary. The concerns of the majority of students of the 1960s were not so far removed from the preoccupations of the young couple described in Perec's novel, *Things*. Frequently pursuing the inferior two-year degree courses introduced by the Fouchet Plan of 1966, they wanted a share in the new consumer boom sweeping through society and could ill afford to drop out of the careers they hoped awaited them. It is frequently pointed out that one of the common demands of 1968 was not American withdrawal from Vietnam, but the right of male students to visit female halls of residence. Incidentally girls could visit the boys, but only if they were over 21 and had their parents' written consent!

That said French students had very real grievances about their working and living conditions. At the root of these problems was the enormous growth in the university sector which had resulted from the postwar baby boom and legislation of 1959 increasing the numbers staying on at secondary schools to take the *baccalauréat*, the school-leaving certificate that opened the doors of higher education, although this examination was a fiendish obstacle to cross.[34] There were some 200,000 in the university system in 1960; eight years later, this had more than doubled. Government had attempted to meet these problems through a restructuring of higher education in 1966, introducing different cycles of study. The numbers of lecturers, however, were not increased, leaving universities increasingly reliant on part-timers and non-tenured staff who became prominent in the lecturers' union the Syndicat National de l'Enseignement Supérieur (SNESup) of Geismer which, in 1968, agitated alongside the UNEF. Full-time senior staff almost invariably lived in Paris, regardless of where in the provinces they worked. They were known as 'turbo-profs', still a familiar sight on the Train de Grande Vitesse (TGV) today, commuting to far-flung universities in France, cramming all their teaching into one or two days, and then rapidly retreating back to the capital to pursue their own researches. Nor had enough money gone into the construction of new buildings and halls of residence, although most French students still tended to live at home. It was said that many students attended less popular courses simply in order to get a seat in the lecture theatre instead of perching on window sills or listening outside in corridors. Inevitably, the courses themselves had not been overhauled to meet demand. These might have worked when student numbers were small and there was some inter-personal contact between undergraduates and their professors. Such lecture series proved hopelessly inadequate and old-fashioned when dispensed to the multitude. Ultimately the highly centralised university system proved incapable of initiating syllabus reform, allowing problems to fester.

Historians agree that it was little surprise that the student protests should have originated at the new campus at Nanterre to the north-west of Paris. Established in 1963–4 to ease the demand for places at the Sorbonne, the half-built Nanterre resembled the stark and functional architecture of a HLM rather than an institution of higher learning. In the words of Robert Merle, it was a 'ville-usine, ville-dortoir, ville univer-sitaire'.[35] Touraine remarked that 'he liked Nanterre not for what it was, but for what it was not, for showing clearly the nature of the French uni-versity system, unmasked by historical associations, unmitigated by prox-imity to life in the Latin Quarter.'[36] Students, their numbers ever rising, were less sanguine at being so isolated from the libraries and cultural centres to be found in Paris. The home to some 2,000 undergraduates at its creation, by 1968 15,000 were congregated in the concrete dormito-ries and lecture halls, and another 10,000 were expected the year after, all of them reliant on an irregular suburban rail service to return them to Paris, an essential journey as many of the facilities, such as the newly-erected swimming pool, were only available if students possessed the necessary documentation issued at the Sorbonne.[37]

The swimming pool had already been the focal point of ugly scenes at the start of 1968 when Cohn Bendit interrupted the opening ceremony performed by François Missoffe, the Minister of Youth, berating the gov-ernment's man for saying nothing about the sexual problems encoun-tered by the young. 'With your looks, no wonder you have problems', was Missoffe's reply, suggesting Cohn Bendit took a swim to cool off.[38] It was an unfortunate quip. While facilities at Naneterre were slightly better than many other new universities, it housed a large contingent of sociology students who, through their intellectual discipline, took a genuine interest in the world, even though Cohn-Bendt denounced soci-ology as an American import designed to uphold the capitalist system. Whatever the case, students at Nanterre were less concerned with gaining the keys to the women's sleeping quarters, focusing instead on Vietnam and protests against *bourgeois* society more generally. It was here that Godard set part of his 1967 film *La Chinoise* which focused on a group of Maoist undergraduates. Under the skilful leadership of Cohn-Bendit and Alain Krivine, on 22 March more militant students known as the *enragés* took over the Senate buildings. So originated the Movement of 22 March, an echo of the Movement of 27 July of Fidel Castro, which attempted to convert undergraduates into fully-fledged revolutionaries who would work to tear down the university system, itself a particular expression of capitalist society, and replace this with a classless society, based on creative, cultural and sexual freedoms.

Hierarchy still existed, however, in the shape of Pierre Grappin, the dean of Nanterre, a Resistance veteran who had escaped from a Nazi concentration camp. Despite his left-wing leanings, he was so aghast at the regular teach-ins on the American imperialism and the attacks on students by right-wing ruffians spoiling for a fight, that on 2 May he ordered the closure of the campus.

The following day, Nanterre *gauchistes* arrived in the centre of Paris to occupy the courtyard at the Sorbonne whereupon they transformed what had been a localised protest into a national event. On the request of the rector, some 500 heavily-equipped police belonging to the para-military Compagnies Républicaines de Sécurité (CRS) assembled at the gates and that night started bundling the protestors into the back of police vans. It was an unwise move. The protesters were quickly joined not only by militants but by some 2,000 student sympathisers. 'CRS, SS', became the chant, although this had already been heard three days earlier before the CRS were sent in.[39] A greater irony was that this branch of the police force had been founded at the Liberation to root out Vichy sympathisers, and had included Communists until there was a purge in 1947. For a long time after 1968, in the minds of the left, the CRS were synonymous with a new fascism. Even passers-by, oblivious to the origins and nature of the protest, were shocked at police tactics which involved the use of *matraques* (batons)[40] and tear-gas. One motorist who dared express his indignation found himself dragged out of his car by the CRS to be punched in the face. Some 80 police were injured, but this was as nothing compared to the hundreds of students and civilians, unwittingly caught up in the fighting, nursing bruised bones, poisoned lungs and temporary blindness brought on by the use of CB gas. Some 590 were behind bars. The scale of this violence caused outrage beyond Paris and, in the period 3–11 May, the student protests gathered in pace, spreading in particular to Strasbourg, the site of Situationist protests in 1967, and taking in the support of politically motivated *lycéens*, secondary school pupils, who looked with horror at what might await them after gaining the *bac*. The more politically aware had already begun to mobilise in the Comités d'Action Lycéens (CALs).

The student demonstrations culminated with the so-called 'night of the barricades' of 10–11 May when police and students, maybe 30,000 in number, clashed head-on: tear-gas, grenade guns and truncheons versus stones and improvised Molotov cocktails. Barricades were erected, the first occasion they had been seen in Paris since the Liberation, and once again ordinary passers-by were caught up in the events as tear-gas filtered down into the *métro*. Remarkably no lives were lost, although ulti-mately the May events would leave eight dead: a bystander at a Paris demonstration on 24 May, a hapless police commissioner crushed by a runaway lorry, and 6 workers, killed by police.[41] For some historians, these casualty figures illustrate that the CRS was more tolerant of students, whose middle-class parents occupied positions of authority, than it was of the working classes who were deemed more threatening. A reading of *Le Livre Noir des Journées de Mai*, a recital of police brutality published shortly afterwards by the highly influential Editions du Seuil, which itself evolved out of the firmament of the 1960s, suggests there was little such calculation in the behaviour of the forces of law and order.

When on the evening of 11 May Pompidou returned from his overseas visit to Iran and Afghanistan, he immediately recognised that the police action had been over-zealous, awakening public support for the students. To pour oil and troubled waters, he thus ordered the reeopening of the Sorbonne – closed since 5 May, only the second time in its seven hundred year history, the other occasion being the student protests against the Nazis in 1940 – and promised the release of students arrested on 2 May. Rather like one of those sassy student slogans, sprayed on the walls of Paris, it was too little and too much. It was too much in that the Sorbonne immediately became an open forum for student debates which were also conducted at the Odéon theatre in the Latin Quarter. It was too little in that trade unionists, initially apprehensive at the protests, ordered a demonstration against police brutality to take place on 13 May culminating in the Place Denfert Rochereau. The next phase of the events, a social crisis, had begun.

The Social Crisis

Although the demonstration of 13 May was hugely impressive, bringing together some 800,000 participants, it was the extension of the student protests to the working classes that made the 1968 events in France exceptional in the western world. It also made them that more dangerous. The participation of the workers had always been a goal of the *enragés* and they made their first real contact with the proletariat when, on 13 May, they marched to Boulogne-Billancourt in the northern outstretches of Paris, the home of the enormous Renault plant, a site of worker militancy ever since the improvised strikes of the Popular Front in 1936. The first strikes proper in 1968 took place on 14 May at Renault-Cléon outside of Rouen (followed shortly by other Renault depots at Flins and Le Mans) and at the Sud-Aviation factory in Nantes where the manager, Duvochel and his staff were placed under house arrest and subjected to revolutionary songs blaring from loudspeakers. Within eight days some ten million workers, without any direction from their union bosses, were involved in improvised strikes on a scale far greater than those witnessed in 1936.[42] As Berstein stresses, they were also distinctive in that they were not confined to any particular economic sector, but affected private and public enterprises, white collar and blue collar, new technologies and staple goods, big firms and little firms, town and countryside.[43] Some unusual areas of national life were caught up in the downing of tools. The prestigious film festival held at Cannes had to be abandoned after the influential directors Godard and François Truffaut urged their colleagues to strike. There emerged shortly afterwards an 'Estates General of the French Cinema' which set out to capture the atmosphere of 1968 through photographs of graffiti and short films of the demonstrations, today invaluable primary sources. Other incongruous strikes included the nude dancers of the Folies Bergères downing their boas. In certain rural areas peasants, who could not have inhabited a more different world to that occupied by workers and students, began to obstruct the highways with their tractors and ploughs.

How had a student protest – originating out of the militancy of a few, who had skilfully played on the generalised discontents of a majority – turn into a social crisis? Part of the answer lies in the breakdown of government reporting controls – ORTF staff were soon on strike – which facilitated public sympathy for the students. In his eye-witness accounts of 1968, the American writer Hans Köning recalls how independent media organisations such as Radio Luxembourg and Europe One gave vivid and uncensored descriptions of police violence which left only the most 'determined law and order person' unmoved.[44] Another side to the answer lies in the general sense of economic dissatisfaction that had been developing since the miners' strike of 1963. It was becoming clear that not everyone was going to benefit from the *trente glorieuses* which were, in any case, drawing to a close. The economic slowdown of 1967 was indeed a warning that the good times might be near an end. More fundamentally, there existed within the workplace a similar sentiment to that which existed within the lecture hall – workers and students felt that they were entrusted with little responsibility and were expected to display unblinking obedience towards hierarchy. In sum, they had become dehumanised by working practices. This dissatisfaction was inevitably expressed against those managers who expected their charges to meet new production rates without protest. Yet it also extended to the leaders of the CGT who had not done enough to modernise relations between capital and labour and who seemed to collude too easily with the system. This explains why the experiments of *autogestion*, new forms of social organisation and worker participation, were so eagerly experimented with on the shop floor. For their part, CGT leaders and PCF bosses, used to the beer-and-baguettes approach to industrial relations, were angered that they could not control the very people whose very interests they claimed to represent. This explains why the Catholic-orientated CFDT, which had originated out of the CFTC, proved more effective in harnessing the 1968 protests. Conscious of the alienation which was part and parcel of working-class life, and alive to the lack of spirituality in its members' day-to-day drudgery, the CFDT decried the loss of human nobility. Its struggle was for qualitative changes that were dismissed as overly idealistic by the hard-nosed CGT .

Given the unprecedented scale of these protests and the way in which the workers had seemingly jettisoned the services of their traditional representatives to side with the intellectuals, the impression grew that France was on the verge of revolution. Yet with the benefit of hindsight it may be seen that the country was some way off from emulating its insurrectionary past. The alliance between workers and intellectuals undoubtedly marked a shared rejection of an authoritarian society, yet their 'alliance' was no more than one of convenience, and class differences were never that far beneath the surface. As one metal-worker put it, 'We keep apart from the students but we don't criticise one another.'[45] Nor were the leaders of the CGT and PCF going to relinquish their grip over the workers without a fight. They constantly attempted to rein in the more enthusiastic of the protestors and soon earned the scorn of the student leaders who denounced them as 'Stalinist filth'. If they had thrown their whole-hearted support behind the strikes and sit-ins, the government might have been facing a far more serious conflagration. Pompidou, who had taken to reading *L'Huma* very carefully, was also relieved at the Communist position. This sense of reassurance might have enabled government to have recovered its nerve, although this was never a smooth operation.[46] In the event, recovery owed as much to the prime minister Pompidou as it did to de Gaulle.

The Political Response

Several of his biographers have puzzled over de Gaulle's behaviour in 1968. Although a firm believer in authority, throughout his career he had made a point of questioning hierarchy. Did he not, then, possess even a smidgen of empathy for the students in the battle with their superiors? Additionally, as a devout Catholic, had he not decried the dehumanising nature of modern society, most recently after the presidential elections of 1965? Moreover, was he not a man who thrived on crisis? Previously it had brought the best out of him, illustrating his qualities of brinkmanship and zest for the dramatic. This time his qualities seemed to have vanished. Was it his advanced years? 'Old age is a shipwreck' he had said of Pétain, yet in 1968 he too was almost an octogenarian. This is not to believe that his mental facilities had deserted him, but something was undoubtedly missing. He can perhaps be forgiven for not understanding why the protests had first erupted, yet he must surely be blamed for misjudging their potential. On 14 May, only a day after the enormous demonstration in the Place Denfert-Rochereau, he left France for a state visit to Romania, only to have to cut short his trip four days later. Even on his return, he still seemed unaware of the crisis swirling around him; and his initial, pusillanimous, response only made matters worse, not better.

This reply was in the political domain. Addressing his ministers on 18 May, he snorted, 'la réforme, oui; la chienlit, non.' As commentators remark, the phrase is virtually untranslatable. We now know that de Gaulle had used it before in respect of those self-serving politicians who he held in contempt – in fact, the etymology of the phrase originates in the eighteenth century.[47] 'Chienlit' may perhaps be translated as 'chaos', yet it was an allusion to the students as 'shit in the bed'. Such resort to the language of the barrack-room was a further indicator that the general had yet to wake up to the true nature of the problem, and no concrete measures followed. The next move was his television speech of 24 May in which he promised a referendum so as to strengthen presidential power which would then be used to facilitate greater openness in government ('la participation'), powers he hardly needed. As noted, de Gaulle used his broadcasts sparingly, and usually to good effect, witness that of 18 June 1940 and those on Algeria of 29 January 1960 (although the one five days earlier had flopped) and 23 April 1961. On 24 May 1968, he did not come over as a man in charge of the situation, but a mere mortal struggling for way out. As several historians have pointed out, for the first time in his career de Gaulle seemed an anachronism; he himself apparently said he was 'à côté de la plaque'. Whereas in the past, he had stirred the passions of his compatriots, both for and against, in May 1968 he was looked upon as an irrelevance, just one part of the capitalist state that was rapidly disintegrating. Pompidou himself put it best when on 11 May he quipped, 'General de Gaulle? He no longer exists.'[48]

The marginalisation of de Gaulle appeared to be further confirmed on 25 May when Pompidou drew together trade union representatives and bosses at the Ministry of Labour buildings in the rue de Grenelle. After some 30 hours of negotiations, in which Pompidou found the traditional leaders of the CGT far easier to manage than those of the newly-formed CFDT who put the emphasis on 'qualitative demands' such as the desirability of a shorter working week, there emerged the so-called *Accords de Grenelle.*[49] This agreement, relates Bridgford, spoke of the desirability of the following: a rise in the minimum wage, known as the SMIG, by 60 *centimes* to 3 *francs* per hour, in effect an overall increase of 35 per cent; staggered pay awards in the public sector amounting to a ten per cent rise overall; a fall in social security contributions; the reduction of the working week by at least one or two hours; the accrediting of local trade union representatives; and the granting of half-pay during strikes.[50] It was not enough. Expectations had soared and the workers were not going to be bought off by vague promises of a traditional kind.

At this stage of the May crisis, it thus looked as though the government had run out of options. Reopening the Sorbonne had simply encouraged the protestors; the actions of the CRS merely triggered public support for the students; ministers were visibly scared; traditional social bargaining had failed to tackle the underlying questions that had paralysed the nation; and de Gaulle's skills in a crisis seemed to have deserted him. The only solution on offer seemed to be that of Mitterrand's FGDS which called for the creation of a provisional government, headed by the veteran politician Mendès-France, which would carry the ship of state safely into the constitutional harbour of fresh presidential and national elections. As the PCF was lukewarm on this idea, this proposal never had any real chance of success.

As the state's power slipped inexorably into the streets, de Gaulle recovered his appetite for political theatre. In the manner of the English detective novelist Agatha Christie who had disappeared for a weekend, on 29 May de Gaulle vanished. It was initially thought he had merely quit for Colombey, but it was soon apparent that this was not the case. Not even Pompidou seemed to know where the general had gone. Wild stories were soon circulating: the general had committed suicide; he was mustering troops on France's borders in much the manner of Louis XVI in his ill-fated Flight to Varennes; he was now living as an exile abroad, just as he had done in June 1940. In fact, he had flown to Baden-Baden, the German holiday resort favoured by the French aristocracy in the mid-nineteenth century when Paris became too hot. Now a French para-trooper base, it was also the home of the loyal General Massu who had stood alongside de Gaulle both in the Second World War and in Algeria. On 30 May, the president reappeared in Paris where he presided over the Council of Ministers that afternoon.

The episode in Germany has led to much sleuthing. Both Massu and Pompidou, keen to present themselves in the best possible light, have suggested that the president, overcome by depression, had panicked, and that it was they who restored his self-belief. It has also been specu-lated whether de Gaulle was attempting to enlist the support of Massu's troops so as to forestall a repetition of the Paris Commune of 1871. De Gaulle's supporters, notably his son-in-law General de Boissieu, have pre-sented a more sympathetic picture.[51] In their eyes, the flight to Baden-Baden was another of his pieces of political theatre, a master stroke which allowed his country the opportunity to see the folly of its ways.

Drawing on the authoritative accounts of François Goguel and Jean Lacouture, among others, it is the British historian Julian Jackson who has put together the most persuasive interpretation of 29 May.[52] That de Gaulle was downhearted, and overcome with tiredness, seems in little doubt. He had displayed such characteristics previously.[53] Yet, as in the past, he was not a quitter. If he had once thought of throwing in the towel, possibly after the speech of 24 May, by the 29th he appeared to have overcome that despondency. Although never quite the master tact-ician as portrayed by de Boissieu, as Jackson argues he had nonetheless recovered a sense of purpose and was again ready to contemplate the kind of spectacular political manoeuvre that had served him well in the past. Away from Paris, and safe from any possible Communist attack on the Elysée, he thus created a moment of drama, in which the French people were forced to stare into the abyss; he could then re-emerge as the man of the moment, a figure of stability amid the chaos. This aura of authority was evident in his speech to the nation on the afternoon of 30 May. Unlike the broadcast of six days earlier, there was no effort to respond to the social aspirations of the protesters; instead de Gaulle emphasised the primacy of the state. If this was not upheld, France would be plunged into revolution in which the only winners would be the Communists. On the back of this threat, he announced the follow-ing: the postponement of the referendum he had earlier announced, his resolve to stay in office, his preparedness to use whatever powers were needed to keep order, and the calling of fresh elections for the National Assembly the following month.

It was a remarkable piece of brinkmanship and could easily have backfired. That it worked owed much to the massive pro-Gaullist demonstration of that same evening. This was 500,000 strong, smart jacketed and orderly rather than the denim and violence of only a few days ago. Naturally it was presented by government spin-doctors as a spontaneous rallying of support; in truth, it had been planned long in advance. Whatever the case, *bourgeois* Paris on the march seemed to sap something of the confidence of the protesters who had previously believed the streets belonged to them. More crucially, as Berstein suggests, de Gaulle had posited the resolution of the crisis in the conventional institutional structures of elections, away from the surrealism of the Odéon and the uncertain world of *autogestion*. There at long last seemed a way out, something which a majority had been looking for. In this sense, de Gaulle had caught the changing mood of the nation. People generally were becoming fed up with spontaneous strikes, the disruption to their daily lives, the inability to get to work on time, the non-delivery of the post and the resort to violence. It was such sentiments, in essence a conservative backlash, that gave the president's party an overwhelming victory in the June elections. Running under the banner of the Union pour la Défense de la République (UDR), the Gaullists won 293 seats, while the Independent Republicans mustered 61; the left was trounced. The Communists were down 39 seats to 34, while Mitterrand's FGDS lost 64 deputies, its share reduced to 57. For the next decade the extreme left would indulge in its favourite sport – fighting among itself – while mainstream socialism underwent a painful process of recovery.

De Gaulle should not, however, be allowed to take all the credit for bringing an end to the May explosion. As the historian of Gaullism Jean Charlot argues, Pompidou was also very influential. While he is frequently criticised for the reopening of the Sorbonne on 11 May, he was fully aware of the dangers inherent in the excessive use of force, and realised the need to let the violence expend itself, even if he took the precaution of having the army to hand.[54] If de Gaulle had had his way – and had brought in the tanks, the *gendarmerie*, the *Gardes Mobiles* from the provinces, reservists – who knows how the situation would have evolved.[55] There would surely have been more deaths. The Place Denfert-Rochereau would have all too resembled Wenceslas Square in Czechoslovakia where Soviet machine guns extinguished the Prague Spring. It should also be remembered that de Gaulle's other attempt to solve the crisis on 24 May was hamfisted. Although his disappearance was a master stroke, it should not be forgotten that the idea of dissolving parliament and temporarily abandoning the referendum was Pompidou's. In this sense, as Charlot concludes, 'the crisis of May 68 was indeed settled thanks to a joint initiative' on the part of president and prime minister.[56]

1968: A Balance Sheet

In the aftermath of the June elections, it almost seemed as though the events of the previous month had never happened – 'a bad trip' in which only imagination had run riot, not that French students, unlike their counterparts in American and Britain, were especially interested in drugs. 'Elusive May' is one observation about 1968.[57] De Gaulle called the events 'insaisissables'. Much though had changed, something which de Gaulle himself acknowledged. Buoyed by his huge majority in parliament and various polls revealing that his personal popularity was as large as ever, he felt the confidence to push ahead with his own agenda. On one level, this involved the removal of Pompidou, who was physically exhausted, and his replacement by the technocrat Couve de Murville. Officially, the explanation was that Pompidou had served his time and lacked the populist and reformist touch that was now needed, although Couve was much renowned for his aloofness. In truth, de Gaulle had long been wanting to get rid of Pompidou, probably since autumn 1966 (thanks to the slow pace of social legislation), and was now angered that, in the midst of the crisis, Pompidou had proved more than his equal.[58] This challenged the very basis of the Gaullian concept of the constitution in which the prime minister was expected to play a subservient role to the president. While de Gaulle tried to soften the blow by speaking of his former colleague as being in the 'reserve of the Republic', the 'deputy of the Cantal', as he was also addressed, was bitterly disappointed, something which he could not hide in his memoirs. In truth, of the two men de Gaulle was the most vulnerable from a psychological point of view. He never truly got over the 1968 events, still bemused and troubled that the nation could behave as irresponsibly as it did. For his part, Pompidou drew confidence from his handling of the crisis and the fact that many now looked to him as the general's successor, despite allusions to Couve as a potential president.[59] This was especially true of those UDR deputies elected on the tide of fear in June 1968. They had little truck with the progressive reforms which de Gaulle was intent on introducing, and quickly recognised that their future rested with Pompidou.

Those reforms were most evident within the educational domain. Under the watchful eye of the minister, Edgar Faure, the outdated and autocratic government of universities was dismantled so as to make them more accountable to the people who worked in them: teaching staff, administrators and students. The old 23 universities, hopelessly over-crowded, were now split up into 76 new entities; for instance, the University of Paris was divided into 'Paris 1', 'Paris 2', and so on. The syl-labus was also overhauled to allow the introduction of new courses, per-mitting universities the right to set their own examinations. And many of the petty restrictions that had blighted students' lives, notably the access to halls of residence, were abolished. As Antoine Prost relates, similar reforms took place in the *écoles* and *lycées* of the secondary sector: dress codes were relaxed; smoking was permitted; punishments were relaxed; the timetable was reduced; and administration was democratised.[60] As is the way in the highly structuralised world of education, many of these reforms took time to percolate through the system and were often delib-erately held up by conservative professors. Disappointingly, the most serious problem – that of overcrowding – was not addressed, meaning that many of the discomforts which had sparked the 1968 protests con-tinued. In the 1970s, French students never quite lost their zest for protest although this did not match the scale of 1968.

Within the workplace, the *Accords de Grenelle* brought about shorter hours and pay rises, although these increases were made more or less worthless by the endemic inflation that blighted the 1970s. There were also attempts to improve labour-capital relations resulting in broader trade union representation and greater collective bargaining. None-theless, this did not stop the number of strikes, already on the up before 1967, from rising. In part, this militancy reflected the new-found influence of the CFDT which had pushed aside the CGT and PCF. It also reflected a continuing idealism. Hopes had been raised in 1968 and they could not easily be allayed, even if industrial relations were still in the dark ages. When in 1973 the employees of the watch-making firm, Lip, in Besançon attempted to put *autogestion* into practice by reclaiming their factory which had gone bankrupt, they discovered themselves on charges of theft. Notwithstanding this episode, for a long time after 1968 both employers and *bourgeoisie* had a real fear of the working classes and did not dare impose real austerity measures, although strikes were still broken up in an ugly fashion. As we shall see in the ensuing chapter, Giscard's economic policy was characterised by 'stop go' – the radical Barre plans, which involved wages freezes, were often moderated in the name of political expediency. Real austerity measures would not be pushed until the Juppé plans of 1995–97.

Ultimately, both workers and students wished to have their share of the consumer society, something increasingly elusive with the ending of the *trente glorieuses*. In this respect, it is sometime argued that 1968 prefigured the rampant individualism of the 1980s, the emergence of 'yuppies' rather than 'yippies'. This, though, is to be overly cynical. As David Hanley and Pat Kerr point out, it ignores that fact that the 1980s economy was far more sophisticated than the 'low-tech, labour intensive economy' of 20 years earlier.[61] It also overlooks the fact that many *soixante-huitards* never relinquished their idealism; for instance, former student leader Serge July distinguished himself in 1973 by setting up *Libération*, a left-wing newspaper which was instrumental in helping Mitterrand into power in 1981.

Indeed, not all of the idealism of the May events would curdle, although it is not always easy to identify direct links between 1968 and its cultural impact. For some that year lifted the lid on several movements which had largely been hidden from public view. Primarily concerned with issues relating to the individual – gay rights, feminism, ecology and nuclear disarmament – this interpretation lends support to the notion that the 1968 protests are best seen as movements of 'personal liberation.'[62] In a wide-ranging analysis of western industrial society, Ronald Inglehart has shown how, in the aftermath of 1968, the young, unencumbered with vested interests in the status quo, were especially prepared to embrace these radical ideologies.[63] Within France itself, this was especially noticeable among young gays and lesbians. For them, 1968 was a platform on which to launch successive protests, which eventually achieved some measure of success in the 1980s.[64]

It was, though, the feminist movement which drew most inspiration from 1968. Already making its presence felt before the explosion in the universities, it will be recalled that the efforts of a small number of feminists, gathered in such fringe bodies as the Mouvement Démocratique Féminin (MDF), had been held up by a variety of factors: a deep-rooted male chauvinism, societal institutions (such as marriage), pressure to conform, institutional barriers, religious prejudice and an unwillingness on the part of women themselves to challenge the status quo. After 1968, French feminism possessed a greater confidence. As de Beauvoir reflected in 1984, 'I believe that militant feminism grew directly from the '68 demonstrations, that properly feminist attitudes arose when women discovered that the men of '68 did not treat them as equals. Men made speeches, but women typed them.'[65] This militancy was soon apparent. In late autumn 1970, female activists stormed the so-called Estates General being organised at Versailles by the glossy fashion magazine *Elle*. Here, they urged that women should pay less attention to such things as make-up and beauty, and shun the traditional role allocated to them. The next year the infamous *Manifeste des salopes* (The Tarts' manifesto), appeared, signed by the likes of Catherine Deneuve and François Sagan who made known they had undergone illegal abortions. As Clare Duchen relates, 1973 saw the forming of the Psychanalyse et Politique, an offshoot of the Mouvement de Libération des Femmes (MLF) which highlighted the unconscious ways in which men exploited women, undertaking a vigorous campaign against pornography, notably the sado-masochistic film *Histoire d'O*.[66] Enjoying support from magazines such as *Le Nouvel Observateur*, rather than *Marie-Claire*, playing on the sympathies of the left broadly defined, and drawing public support after the so-called Bobigny case (see above), the women's movement succeeded in improving the availability of contraception, and in 1975 abortion was legalised, although availability was still constrained. More fundamentally, despite legislation in 1972, equal pay and equal rights at work were not yet within the grasp of women despite the fact that, the 'second sex' comprised half the working population and dominated such professions as typing, nursing, and primary school teaching.

It is tempting to speculate whether further reform would have been forthcoming if de Gaulle had continued in office after 1969. As we have noted, after the June 1968 elections he recovered something of his confidence and appeared happy to indulge those reformist instincts which had always been a part of his political psychology. He famously quipped, 'Here is a PSF (right-wing) chamber with which I will make a PSU (left-wing) policy'. It was too little too late. His health was failing; and old age, which he had always feared, enveloped him in a general despondency. He was also in hock to a deeply conservative parliament and had to contend with Pompidou, who was increasingly viewed as the leader-in-waiting. For his part, the 'deputy for the Cantal' declared that he was ready to run for office, when there was an election, although he tactfully added that he was not in a hurry. It was partially in an attempt to undermine his rival that de Gaulle sought to reinforce the bonds between president and people by conducting the referendum promised in 1968. In this the electorate was asked to approve some highly complex reforms to both the Senate and to regional authorities. To many it seemed a highly unnecessary of piece of business, and the results were a rejection of de Gaulle's schemes (52.4 per cent voted 'non'). As soon as the results became clear, and all the indicators before the vote on 27 April 1969 pointed to a government defeat, the president was impatient to leave office. Despite his authoritarian leanings, de Gaulle always respected the will of the people, as expressed through universal suffrage, and on 28 April announced his resignation. Eighteen months later he was dead.

Conclusion: Durability

If 1968 had exposed the frailty of de Gaulle, the year had also demonstrated the durability of the Fifth Republic. Ever since its founding in 1958, the survival and evolution of the regime appeared to depend largely on de Gaulle himself. 1968 proved otherwise. The regime had overcome a tremendous test and emerged confident, albeit a little bruised and bewildered. Critically, it had managed to stifle its critics on the extremes. Through its behaviour in 1968, the Communist Party indicated that it was prepared to work within the institutional structures; indeed, the PCF was just as terrified as the *bourgeoisie* at the behaviour of the workers. The far right, less influential but noisy nonetheless, had also rallied to the support of the regime, if not to de Gaulle himself, who could not be forgiven for his behaviour over Algeria. This was to be fortunate for Pompidou. But he also made his own luck. Over the next five years, he was to show that he was his own man with his own ideas. 'Historic Gaullism', it is often said, died in 1968 to give way to the development of Gaullism more broadly defined, and it is to the ensuing history of the Fifth Republic that we must now turn.

Chapter 5: La Confiance: *Pompidou and Giscard, 1969–81*

Throughout the 1970s, French political life was punctuated by a series of doubts. In April 1969, the question on everyone's lips was whether the Fifth Republic would survive the resignation of de Gaulle. As Jean-Jacques Becker observes, the regime had been so closely identified with its maker that it was difficult to envisage life without him.[1] The immediate answer was provided by the election of Pompidou as president: a Gaullist to take charge of a Gaullist creation. At his premature death in 1974, the issue was whether the Republic could cope with the presidency of a non-Gaullist in the shape of Giscard Valéry d'Estaing, and again the answer was yes, just as it was in 1981 when he was supplanted by the socialist François Mitterrand. On both these occasions, however, it should be stressed that the future was never seriously in doubt as the two men had more or less come to accept the broad institutional framework as established in the 1958–62 period, even if they were uncomfortable with some of the particulars. It will be recalled that Mitterrand had effectively acknowledged the legitimacy of the Gaullist achievement by standing for the presidency in 1965. So it was that France possessed a political settlement that was no longer dependent on its founder, but one which could develop a momentum of its own. This, though, is not to say that the 1970s were an especially happy time for France. The Pompidou presidency was largely disappointing. While the constitutional settlement was safeguarded, notably the primacy of the presidency, internal problems and ill-health prevented him from realising his dream of modernisation. Giscard offered greater promise, attempting progressive measures which sought to undercut some of the inequalities that had contributed to the

116

1968 protests. In the event, these proved disappointing: a series of factors combined to restrain the reforming impulse, notably a growing caution on the part of the president himself. It was a further misfortune for Giscard that his term of office coincided with the 1970s oil crises which emasculated the economy, plunging France into a trough of high unemployment, corrosive inflation and retrenchment.

Pompidou: Legitimation and Disintegration

In 1969, it was Giscard's hope that the regime would be able to prove its robustness by turning to a 'candidate of appeasement', who would soothe over the troubles bequeathed by the May events and by the general's departure. No doubt he was also thinking of a person who would boost the standing of his own party, the Independents. Yet the man he had in mind, Antoine Pinay, was reluctant to put himself forward and was hardly up to the job. No such scruples beset Georges Pompidou who quickly announced his candidature, a move approved by the Gaullists which had no other obvious heir-apparent. His subsequent elevation to the Elysée seemed effortless, facilitated by his own charisma (he was a superb television performer), the fact that he was not de Gaulle (something he kept repeating whenever interviewed), his promises of stability, his pledge to open a dialogue with others (save the Communists) and the disarray of his opponents. The principal challenger on the right was the centrist politician Alain Poher who had been acting president since de Gaulle's departure. Although early opinion polls indicated a groundswell of support for Poher, he was unable to build on this. He looked dull compared to Pompidou and lacked his rival's Gaullist associations. It was not overlooked, at least among the UDR members, that he had mobilised a 'rebellion of notables' in the April 1969 referendum, campaigning for a 'no' vote.[2] Among centrist deputies, Poher could look to unwavering supports, notably Duhamel, but others were bought off by Pompidou's pledge to facilitate greater European integration. Finally, Pompidou was assisted by the splintering of the left, which was in disagreement over the legacy of 1968. No fewer than four left-wing contenders entered the ring: Alain Krivine, for the Trotskyist Ligue Communiste; Michel Rocard for the PSU; Gaston Defferre who stood for the Socialists in place of Mitterrand, widely blamed for the electoral reverses in the parliamentary elections the previous year; and Jacque Duclos who fought an invigorating campaign for the PCF. Duclos came third in the first round, marginally behind Poher.

With the left largely abstaining in the second ballot, arguing that the choice was between a 'blanc bonnet et bonnet blanc', Pompidou scored 58.2 per cent of the vote as opposed to 41.8 per cent for Poher. Not even de Gaulle had performed so well in the run-off of the 1965 contest. All looked rosy for the future. Not only had the president achieved a healthy mandate, he could also look to the support of the Chamber elected in June 1968 which, it will be recalled, had returned a large right-wing majority. Outwardly, too, the regime oozed confidence, eventually agreeing to erect the enormous skyscraper, the Tour Montparnasse, on the left-bank of Paris. And at the pulse-beat of the regime, Pompidou himself looked forward to governing on his own without having to look over his shoulder to see what de Gaulle was doing. In truth, as Berstein and Rioux argue, his concept of government differed little from that of his mentor: a 'strong state', steered by a strong president, with a strong economy, which would achieve modernisation at home and independence from the superpowers abroad. If this was accomplished, Pompidou predicted that historians would write not about him, but of his achievements.[3] Historians have subsequently mentioned his name aplenty, as an important figure in the legitimation of the Fifth Republic unquestionably, but ultimately as a politician whose legacy remains ambivalent. His commitment to modernisation cannot be doubted, but it was thwarted by the many problems he encountered and, ultimately, by his failing health.

On coming to office, Pompidou's initial difficulty was the legacy of his predecessor. The fact that he was not de Gaulle had helped him during the campaign itself, but he appreciated that once in office comparisons would inevitably be drawn. Whereas de Gaulle emanated from a minor aristocratic family in Lille, Pompidou was the son of a school teacher, based in Albi. As Philip Thody recalls, when de Gaulle first met his future prime minister, he murmured condescendingly, 'Georges Pompidou, originaire de Montboudif', an illusion to the remote village where Pompidou had been born, although he never grew up there.[4] Whereas de Gaulle, the Verdun veteran, became renowned for his opinions on modern warfare, enjoying the patronage of Paul Reynaud, Pompidou disliked his military service and was handicapped by his poor vision, although this did not stop him from becoming a *sous-lieutenant*. On 18 June 1940, de Gaulle had launched his 'call to honour' becoming the unquestioned leader of the French Resistance overseas; it is believed

Pompidou heard of this broadcast some four days later, yet continued teaching at the Lycée Henri IV in Paris throughout the Occupation. It is frequently recalled that, on one occasion, he rebuked a pupil for removing the portrait of marshal Pétain from the wall, although it is accepted that he had no liking for Vichy. It is less well known that he read his pupils extracts from Vercors' resistance novel, *Le Silence de la Mer*, and even distributed clandestine tracts.[5] The fact that Pompidou was never one of the 'clan Gaulliste', that is those men who dared to quit France for resistance in London and the empire, nonetheless irked UDR leaders. After the war, he pursued his career as a financier in the Banque Rothschild, while developing a close relationship with de Gaulle, serving on his staff during the RPF years, joining the president's entourage in 1958 and acting as an unofficial negotiator with the FLN. It was his skills as an administrator, accountant, listener, confidant and good communicator that endeared him to the general. It was a patronage that naturally gave rise to jealousy. There is little doubt that, in 1969, it was Gaullists who hoped to smear Pompidou by implicating him in the murder of Stephan Markevich, a shady character, almost straight out of a Maigret novel, who had served as a bodyguard to the actor Alain Delon.

There was, then, always something begrudging in the attitude of the UDR towards Pompidou, a recalcitrance that soon became apparent in parliament. On the one hand, he had to contend with the suspicions of traditional or so-called 'historic' Gaullists who had followed the general since 1940 and who were well aware of de Gaulle's doubts about his most likely successor. For all his charm, Pompidou could not inspire like the general. On the other, the new president had to get along with those conservatives, strengthened by the backlash to 1968, and grouped around the party's secretary-general René Tomasini, who was suspicious of reform and of his prime minister, Jacques Chaban-Delmas. A former resister and onetime member of the Radical Party, a membership he had combined with the RPF, Chaban-Delmas had not relinquished his progressive enthusiasms. In a famous speech of 16 September 1969, infused with Kennedyesque phrases, he set out his vision of a 'new society', a France committed to modernisation, social inclusiveness and political reconciliation with the moderate left. This not only alarmed conservatives, who also felt it too critical of the Gaullist legacy, it also disheartened those historic Gaullists from whose ranks he had come, not that they had ever entirely trusted him. He was too marked by 'the spirit of the Fourth.'[6] 'Chaban, that's the Fourth!', had grumbled the Gaullist politician Battesti in 1958. 'That's the symbol of all we have fought against.'[7]

Gradually all sides of the UDR began to feel that Chaban was not one of them, and that he devoted too much time in the chamber to wooing centrists and Independents, who were more amenable to his plans for reform. Even Pompidou, himself a moderniser and indulgent of Chaban,[8] tired of his plans for a 'new society', perhaps fearing these might steal his own thunder and undermine the elevated role of the presidency. Nor did it help that Chaban had been accused of tax fraud. In 1972, Pompidou replaced him with the cautious Pierre Messmer, another former resister, who was more acceptable to all sides of the UDR. As Andrew Knapp observes, in Pompidou's eyes Messmer was ideal in that he was unscathed by scandal, was a loyal devotee of de Gaulle, and had no real power base on which he could mount a challenge to the president.[9] Although this was an assertion of the Gaullist principle of presidential ascendancy, there was no hiding the fact that Pompidou was having to interfere in party politics far more than his predecessor. Nor did it help matters that Giscard, who served as finance minister, was not afraid to speak his mind, on the look-out to strengthen his own presidential credentials and the standing of the Independents who he wished to make 'the majority party of government'.[10]

Pompidou's troubles in parliament were compounded by the declining fortunes of the Gaullist party which, it will be recalled, had in June 1968 retitled itself the Union des Démocrates pour la République (UDR). At its peak during the 1960s, this had dominated political clientage and parliament in much the same way the Radicals had dominated the institutions of the Third Republic, although as Vincent Wright observes this is not to deny that there were fundamental differences between the two parties.[11] In the parliamentary elections of 1973, the first signs of UDR vulnerability became evident when it and its coalition partners' share of seats fell from 372 to 276 of the 490 available. This effectively meant that it no longer controlled parliament as it had done in the 1960s. It was a decline not difficult to comprehend.[12] No longer could the party bask in the glory of its founder; no longer did it speak with a clear voice, something illustrated by the conflicting objectives of Chaban and Messmer; no longer did it seem to possess a discipline, as personality disputes took centre stage; no longer could it claim to be unlike other parties as successive scandals, largely revolving around property deals, became public; and no longer did it seem to be in rhythm with social developments, especially after some of the fears raised by 1968 had been allayed. As Wright has remarked, 'the electoral base of Gaullism was not only becoming smaller, it was also becoming socially more conservative: it was older, more rural, more female and more Catholic.'[13] Something of this decline seemed to be mirrored in Pompidou himself who suffered from Waldenström's disease, a type of cancer. While this news was kept away from the public, from 1972 onwards the signs of ill health were all too visible, notably a puffiness caused by growing doses of cortisone; no-one believed the increasingly desperate press briefs which attributed the president's many public absences to the flu and piles. As Mitterrand reflected, 'I found it repugnant to look at the bloated television reports, or to try to make wild medical guesses about what the changed look about his eyes meant.'[14] Privately, Pompidou himself displayed immense physical and mental courage, but outwardly he seemed to be dying a very public death. His eventual demise on 2 April 1974 was a welcome release from excruciating pain.

For all Chaban's talk of a 'new society', it is generally agreed that Pompidou's presidency was not a period of major social and economic change. Admittedly there was modest reform: state controls on the media were relaxed; industries were grouped together in oligopolies, even though small to medium sized firms still predominated; public transport was granted greater autonomy; a Ministry for the Protection of Nature and the Environment was established; the minimum wage was overhauled to become the *Salaire Minimum Interprofessionnel de Croissance* (SMIC); social benefits were raised; many workers were in future to be paid on a monthly rather than a weekly basis; urban planning was trumpeted; and the powers of local government were enhanced. However, none of this legislation was sufficient to overcome the 'blocked society' which Chaban had complained of. None of this legislation would have looked out of place under de Gaulle, especially in the wake of 1968, and it is noticeable that concessions to big business and property developers continued. To be fair to Pompidou, something of his freedom of manoeuvre was limited by the end of the *trente glorieuses*, the conservative nature of the Chamber, the power of big business and his own failing health. Yet there was always an ambivalence in his own attitudes towards economic and social reform, an ambiguity which may have acted as a break on further liberalisation. On one level, he was a genuine moderniser, believing in technology, the coming together of industrial enterprises and the building of a new urban environment which reflected the dynamism of a new France. On another, he never entirely relinquished his peasant background which inculcated a caution, a faith in traditional conservative values and a dislike of the world that had emerged out of the 1960s. It is difficult to avoid the conclusion that his overall aim was to make the cake bigger so that it could be distributed without ever calling into question existing social relationships and hierachies.

Within foreign policy Pompidou was at least loyal to de Gaulle's legacy. Anxious to break up the bi-polar world dominated by the USA and the USSR, he sought to assert France's independence at every opportunity. This resulted in a refusal to participate in the Strategic Arms Limitation Talks (SALT); the pursuit of an ambitious Mediterranean policy which favoured Algeria, Morocco and the newly created regime of Colonel Gaddafi in Libya; and repeated snubs to Israel which led to French support for Egypt in the Yom Kippur war of 1973. At the same while, Pompidou seemed indulgent of the USSR, despite the crushing of the Czech uprising only two years previously. After his visit to Moscow in October 1970, he arranged for the Soviet and French foreign ministers to meet 'on a regular basis (in theory twice a year) which gave the French the sensation that their country was a world player', even though the reality was very different, something which Pompidou acknowledged more readily than de Gaulle.[15] Where Pompidou did break with his predecessor was in his attitude towards the EEC. Although no subscriber to the federal ideal, he considered that there was no alternative but to facilitate the extension of the EEC, in particular by accepting Britain's long-delayed entry. Not only would the UK's involvement offset American economic power, it would also provide a bulwark against West Germany which, under the chancellorship of the Social Democrat Willy Brandt, was displaying far too much independence, throwing its considerable financial weight throughout Europe, and pursuing overtures of *Ostpolitik* with the East. To this end, in 1972 Pompidou held a referendum on the entry of Denmark, Ireland and the UK to the EEC (narrowly won) thus paving the way for British membership the following year.

Notwithstanding differences over the EEC, Pompidou's presidency was to all extents and purposes an addendum to that of de Gaulle's. In this sense, his principal achievement was to have ensured a smooth hand-over of power after the general's death, a process that undeniably strengthened the Fifth Republic's institutions. Elsewhere, he had remained loyal to the general's interpretation of the constitution, privileging the presidency over the premiership, witness the replacement of Chaban by Messmer, and he had used this concept to pursue a foreign policy largely of his own making. As before, this remained very firmly the president's *domaine réservé*. Within social and economic policy,

Pompidou promised much but his early death stymied real progress. He had hoped that he would leave France industrially strengthened, a real player on the global markets. That further change came over the economy cannot be doubted, as shall be seen below, all but too often the president was a mere bystander, his powers weakened by the strength of big business and his own failing health. After summer 1972, there was little that his government initiated in this area, and it was unfortunate for his legacy that around this time the *trente glorieuses* came to a close, a development he could not have prevented. It was thus left to his successor to pick up the pieces and show what the Fifth Republic could accomplish in the hands of a non-Gaullist.

Giscard d'Estaing: From Liberalism to Monarchism, 1974–1981

While Pompidou's ill health was widely bruited in political circles, his death still came as a shock to the Gaullist party which struggled to rally round Chaban–Delmas as its presidential candidate. Chaban's former ministerial colleague Jacques Chirac was especially sceptical and led 43 rebellious UDR deputies into the Giscard camp. He claimed this was for the good of France as to let the uncharismatic Chaban to go un-challenged was to invite a left-wing victory. It is more likely Chirac was paving the way for his uncontested leadership of the Gaullists. Whatever the case, this spectacular display of disloyalty, coupled with public dissat-isfaction with the so-called *Etat-UDR*, ensured that Chaban came a poor third in the first round of voting, scoring 15.1 per cent as opposed to 32.6 per cent for Giscard and 43.25 per cent for Mitterrand who suc-ceeded in rallying large sections of the left (see below), including the Communists who voted for him, just as in 1965. The run-off proved to be a close thing, Giscard winning the presidency by the slimmest of margins: 50.8 per cent to Mitterrand's 49.2 per cent. Ultimately, Giscard had run a slicker (and very American-style) campaign, performing well on television and displaying a feel for France's conservative instincts through his slogan 'change without risk'.

The first non-Gaullist president of the Fifth Republic was every part the technocrat. Born in 1926 into a comfortable middle-class family, which boasted rather dubious aristocratic origins, Giscard studied at the Lycée Louis-le-Grand, the ENA and the Ecole Polytechnique, taking time out in 1944 to serve as a volunteer soldier in the Liberation of France, ensuring that he had a good war record. Blessed with a sharp intellect, he had climbed to the high echelons of the civil service, served under Edgar Faure, before being elected in 1956 deputy for the Pûy-de-Dôme, a seat vacated for him by his grandfather. Born to rule, he readily accepted a post as finance minister under de Gaulle but, even before his dismissal in 1966, he was canny enough to establish a distance between himself and Gaullism, and sought his own political base through the RI. He also had reservations about Pompidou, especially over his handling of the May events, but in 1969 he knew not to stand against the general's successor, recognising that he lacked the wherewithal to launch a successful campaign. It will be recalled that he had tried to hide behind the candidature of Pinay. It was an astute piece of gamesmanship and facilitated his return to government as minister of finance, a portfolio he held until 1974.

On election to the presidency, Giscard proclaimed that he wished to rule France in a conciliatory fashion, building consensus and soothing over the wounds opened by 1968. This objective ran through his political style, his choice of ministers and his philosophy, although in each area the image was often different from the reality.

In terms of style, like other French politicians, Giscard sought to emulate Kennedy, presenting himself as a visionary in tune with his compatriots yet, as de Gaulle reputedly observed, 'Giscard's problem is the people'.[16] Not so much a Kennedy, he resembled the Orleanist king Louis Philippe (1830–48), at root an aristocrat not always at ease with change, who had been misleadingly called a 'citizen king' simply because he adopted *bourgeois* dress and put his own coals on to the fire. As with Louis Philippe, appearances were deceptive. On his inauguration, Giscard favoured a lounge suit over a morning coat; he made a virtue of the fact that he played the accordion; and solicited invitations to dine with French families, events that were subsequently given much publicity. Yet it was not long before Giscard's lack of a common touch and vaulting vanity shone through. This was a man who insisted on his aristocratic roots, however dubious, who enjoyed big-game hunting, shooting rare beasts such as lions and elephants, and who rarely trusted his advisers.

In his choice of ministers, Giscard again promised a consensual style breaking up the so-called the *Etat-UDR* by assembling a cabinet of broad political views. This was more or less a necessity given that his power base in the Chamber was so slender. He was though brave to appoint Simone Veil as minister of health, the first woman to occupy a truly important portfolio. He also turned to Chirac as his prime minister; this was in thanks for the part he had played in supporting Giscard's campaign and a sop to Gaullist opinion. Once in the Elysée, Giscard ran a tight ship. Each of his ministers was intimately watched by his pal and ally, the interior minister Prince Michel Poniatowski, who unlike the president could boast true blue blood, and who was all too ready to play the part of Guizot, the manipulative first minister of Louis Philippe. A special watch was kept on Chirac, especially after he took charge of the UDR in December 1974. It was widely known that the ambitious Chirac had his own aspirations for the Elysée. In 1976, he used the pretext of a cabinet reshuffle to resign, the first premier under the Fifth Republic to do so on his own volition, so that he could prepare for the forthcoming presidential campaign. To this end, he relaunched the UDR as the Rassemblement pour la République (RPR). His replacement at the Matignon was former Brussels commissioner and economics professor Raymond Barre. An unelected official, sharing the same centrist philosophy as the president, it was anticipated that Barre would prove a more malleable ally, as indeed proved the case.

Giscard's philosophy, if it merits such a grandiose term, was given shape in his *La Démocratie française*, a slim and abstract volume published in 1976,[17] which lent itself easily to satire.[18] No great work of originality, it rehearsed several themes he had long held dear: the ability of a people to improve their lot so long as they did not succumb to the weaknesses of human nature; the embracing of change so as to reduce inequalities; a belief in social betterment; a renunciation of Marxism; the accomplishment of a social market economy; an advocacy of a pluralistic society in which institutions such as trade unions and companies would work in harmony with a centralised state apparatus; and a championing of the virtues of consensual politics.

And, to begin with, it seemed that Giscard was loyal to this vision. As John Frears summarises, in youth affairs legislation of 5 July 1974 granted the vote to 18 year olds, bringing France into line with most other Western democracies. The rights of young people were also bolstered by the Haby law of 11 July 1975, so-called after the minister of education, which implemented the comprehensive principle into state education and shook up the notoriously rigid secondary school syllabuses so as to provide greater vocational training. In social maters, the value of pensions was raised, the retirement age was reduced to 60 years, and a series of welfare measures were adopted to help the physically disabled. Within the world of broadcasting, on 17 August 1974, the monolithic ORTF was at last disassembled, divided into seven different organisations, including Radio-France, TF1, Antenne 2 and FR3. This was supposedly an attempt to promote commercialisation and broadcasting independence; in truth, government censorship continued unabated. Censorship even persisted after the creation of a new Ministry of Culture and Communication in 1978. At least something of the centralised state apparatus was diluted by legislation in 1975 which endowed Paris with an elected mayor; in the meantime, Giscard used his extensive powers as president to put a stop to the random construction of skyscrapers and modern buildings, the so-called *gigantisme urbain*, that looked set to disfigure the capital's skyline. As Frears continues, a 220 metre-tall tower had been planned for the Place d'Italie while a motorway had been envisaged for the left-bank of the Seine, similar to what had already been built on the right.[19] Within the suburbs, the dismantling of the *bidonvilles* was stepped up while outside of the towns measures were adopted in 1977 to protect moun-tainous areas, which were in danger of being turned into one big ski resort. Yet perhaps the most significant reforms were those augmenting civil liberties. Cinema censorship was abolished; legal aid was enhanced; prisons were reformed; and women's rights extended. On 4 December 1974, pharmacies were permitted to sell contraceptives; on 17 January 1975 the so-called Veil Law made abortion legal during the initial ten weeks of pregnancy; and, on 11 July 1975, the notoriously misogynistic rules governing divorce were relaxed.

There were, however, limits to these liberalising impulses and, after the first couple of years of the Giscard presidency, reform dried up. Proposals for the abolition of the death penalty – France retained the guillotine – were quietly dropped, much to the dismay of liberal opinion represented by such opinion-forming journals as *L'Express*, and the dra-conian penal code remained largely intact.[20] It would take Mitterrand's first minister of Justice Robert Badinter to abolish the death penalty, something in which he took great pride.[21] Although the powers of the Constitutional Council were enhanced, the reduction of the presidential term from seven to five years was not enacted. Especially disappointing were the economic measures. There was no real attempt to overhaul the tax system, with the result that indirect taxes still hit the poor hardest. Nor were there any sustained attempts to augment workers' rights. Poniatowski, as minister of interior, did not hesitate to authorise the use of police dogs to clear factory sit-ins, and demonstrations were often broken up in an ugly fashion. Anti-nuclear protests at Aléria, Bastia and Creys-Malville in July 1977 resulted in fatalities after the police charged in. This though paled in comparison to the strong-arm tactics used to put down the Corsican movement for independence.

So it was that the Giscard presidency moved from being liberal and reformist during its first two years of existence to being cautious and conservative for much of the remainder. There was talk of change; little was effected. As *Le Point* of 12 May 1980 reflected, during Giscard's *septennat* there had been a 'contrast between lucid analysis and insufficient action.'[22] Why was this? To begin with, it should be remembered that early reforms were essentially crowd-pleasing initiatives. It further helped that they cost little and did not alienate any vested interests. Perhaps the bravest reform was that legalising abortion, when Giscard, as on other occasions, had to rely on opposition votes to see the measure through. This points to a further break on his reforming impulse. He was always confronted with a conservative-minded Chamber, and it must be remembered that his own Independents only numbered 60 or so deputies. Thus he was always having to build cross-party support, even after 1978 when he created a new coalition of like-minded centrist parties in the UDF. Drawing together the Independents, who had confusingly retitled themselves the Parti Républicain (PR) in 1977, the Centre des Démocrates Sociaux (CDS), the Centre Démocratie et Progrès (CDP), the Parti Social Démocrate (PSD) and a smattering of right-leaning Radicals, this mélange of interests was an obvious platform on which to build for the 1981 presidential elections. It was also a means of combating the relaunched RPR Gaullist party of Chirac, who had become the first elected major of Paris in March 1977. It was, indeed, Chirac who constituted an additional break on Giscard. As prime minister, he was not in sympathy with many of the legislative proposals he was asked to introduce into parliament; by 1976, these disagreements were becoming uncontainable, another factor that prompted Chirac's resignation that year. As already observed, Barre was chosen as a facilitator who would do what he was told. This assertion of presidential primacy did not produce a renewal of the liberalising drive, thanks to yet another obstacle: Giscard himself. Ultimately it must be questioned how far he was prepared to change the country he governed. As the journalist Jonathan Fenby has acutely observed, 'The president was like one of those eighteenth-century aristocrats who played with all the most advanced ideas about changing society, who set up model farms and chatted with Voltaire and felt good envisaging a new enlightenment – but who were never really ready to challenge the society which had bred them.'[23] Mitterrand summed up the president very astutely when he noted in his diary, 'Giscard is there to conserve.'[24]

The final factor that restrained Giscardian reform was the end of the *trente glorieuses*. Although there are good grounds for believing that the lengthy period of postwar expansion was already coming to an end – growing inflation and rising unemployment were the tell-tale signs – the world recession of the 1970s speeded the process along. Economists agree that this was prompted by two factors. The first was the decision of those Middle East nations, gathered together in Organisation of Petroleum Exporting Countries (OPEC), to increase the price of oil. Angered at their failure in the Arab-Israeli war of 1973, this was a piece of economic warfare designed to hurt the economies of the pro-Jewish states, although they might not have imagined that their actions would lead to such a steep rise. Given that post-war economic recovery in the Western world had relied extensively on cheap petroleum, especially in the automobile and plastics industries, the effects of this hike (a fourfold increase) were disastrous. France, hardly pro-Israeli, was nonetheless vulnerable as the nation imported 75 per cent of its oil, chiefly from Algeria, Iraq, Saudi Arabia, and Nigeria. A balance of trade deficit, which had always seemed likely in the 1960s, had it not been for the income provided by tourism and agricultural products, soon followed, accompanied by appropriately labelled 'stagflation' – a spiralling inflation rate of 14 per cent, over double the levels in the USA and West Germany. The revolution in Iran toppling the Shah and inaugurating the Islamist regime of Ayotollah Khomeini in 1979, only exacerbated the situation sparking off further rises in the price of so-called 'black gold'. In 1981 the cost of a barrel of oil was $32; nine years earlier, it had been $2.16.

Oil, however, was not the sole cause of the world recession. US financial policy, it is agreed, also played its part. Exhausted by the costs of the Vietnam War and the expensive domestic welfare schemes inherited from the 1960s, in August 1971 the US president, Richard Nixon, untied the dollar from gold. This effectively put an end to the system, established in 1944 at Bretton Woods, whereby European currencies were officially linked to the dollar. The steadiness provided by that system had done much to rebuild the shattered economies of Europe – its abandonment plunged the money markets into confusion and exacerbated the more general effects of the oil crises.

Historians generally agree that the impact of the recession put into relief the on-going frailties of the French economy, notably the relatively small size of French businesses. Both Pompidou and Giscard had encouraged the merger of industries to form large-scale enterprises: in chemicals Rhône-Poulenc took Pechiney, Saint-Gobain and Naphtachimie; in electronics a number of firms were taken over by Thomson-Brandt; and in steel, Usinor and Sidelor dominated. Impressive though these 'national champions' were, they were still small compared to their foreign counterparts, and consequently struggled in a period of cut-throat international competition. As to smaller and medium-sized enter-prises, which still dominated the French economy, they too fared badly in an unfavourable climate of cheap imports from abroad and rising inflation at home. Economists agree that the uncompetitive nature of French industry, both large and small, was further compounded by the comparatively steep price of labour, a problem exacerbated by the *de Grenelle Accords* (real wages grew by some 35 per cent in the period 1969–73) and the SMIC, although it must be stressed that the latter only benefited around one million workers who otherwise would have pos-sessed no real safety net. There was, however, a more general concern about the increasing amounts France was spending on its social welfare budgets. Together with spiralling labour costs, observes Gildea, this cut into investment rates which had already begun to falter in the 1960s.[25]

How did the recession manifest itself? The first indicator was a down-turn in growth rate. Figures cited by Forbes and Hewlett show that for much of the 1960s, this had hovered around six per cent per annum, compared to 4.4 per cent in West Germany and 3.2 per cent in the UK. In 1973, French GDP fell to under three per cent in 1973; and plunged into negative figures in 1975 at –0.3 per cent. For the first half of the 1980s, growth was just over one per cent, recovering to over three per cent by 1991.[26] The second indicator was a trade deficit. During the con-sumer boom of the 1960s, France had begun to suck in many manufac-tured goods from abroad yet, as already mentioned, income produced by tourism and agriculture kept France in the black. That was no longer possible after the oil crises which left the nation 14,000 million francs in the red. Through an aggressive exports policy, some limited improve-ment was effected, although France also began to exploit the morally dubious benefits of the arms trade: this grew from 4,800,000F in 1974 to 8,400,000F four years later.

The other problem was, of course, inflation. On the rise since 1969, this stood at just under six per cent for the first three years of the 1970s. The first oil crisis of 1973 sent the figure up to 14 per cent, a figure repeated during the next oil crisis of 1979. During the intervening years, the rate averaged 11 per cent. As to unemployment, this too witnessed a sharp rise. More or less extinguished during the prosperity of the 1960s,

when France had encouraged immigration to make up the labour shortfall, just over 500,000 were out of a job in 1973 (approximately 2.8 per
cent of the working population), a figure that was to reach one million
two years later (7.5 per cent of the working population). The two million
mark would be reached in 1984.

Always excepting Japan, the above problems were depressingly familiar ones in the western world of the 1970s, and were not as serious as in
Italy and the UK. Nonetheless, after the good years of the 1950s and 60s,
they came as a shock to the system, creating a general sense of unease
and reviving uncomfortable memories of the Depression years of the
1930s. Those employed in traditional staple industries such as steel and
coal, concentrated in the Nord and Lorraine, were probably the most
vulnerable. Already the victims of retrenchment, these workers suffered
further as France, in common with other nations, turned to cheaper
imports from abroad. John Ardagh recalls the famous example of the
16,000 steel workers in the town of Longwy, close to the Luxemburg
border, who were thrown out of work in 1978 as government encouraged the closure of inefficient mills.[27] Given that the overall population
of the town was only 80,000, this decision was akin to signing the
region's death warrant and provoked a furious response on the part of
the region's local newspaper *La République Lorraine*. As some 50,000
demonstrated against the cuts in the streets of Metz, there was talk of
Longwy creating its own 'République populaire' conjuring up images of
1968.[28] It will be recalled from the preceding chapter how 1968 haunted
economic policy. This was sufficient for the government to moderate the
closures and to soften the blow by forcing Renault and Peugeot-Citroën
to set up plants in the area. None of this was enough to salvage the local
economy. More pertinently, these developments signalled the nation's
increasing reliance on the tertiary sector, dominated by white-collar
businesses such as computers. It was unfortunate that this development
should also have been accompanied by a further reduction in the size of
the rural workforce. It will be recalled that during the *trente glorieuses*,
there had been a trend towards the amalgamation of small farms into
larger units, improving efficiency and agricultural production, albeit at
the price of rural unemployment. During the 1970s the efficiency drive
was actively encouraged by the Mansholt Plan, approved by the EEC in
1971 but, thanks to stiff rural opposition, not implemented in France
until 1976. Further protests followed, but these could not halt the
decline of farming as an occupation. In 1960, a fifth of the population
had been engaged in agriculture in 1960; this had dropped to a tenth by

1975; by 1990, less than five per cent were employed on the land. As Ardagh writes, it did not help the self-esteem of rural communities that their abandoned farms were bought up by outsiders – either prosperous urbanites looking for weekend retreats or the British middle classes looking for holiday homes in Normandy and the Dordogne.[29]

High unemployment, spiralling inflation, growing inequalities and the spectacle of young lives ruined by recession and poor prospects cried out for a response from the Giscard government, yet this was slow in coming. It will be recalled that he had begun his *septennat* on a high, implementing populist policies on the cheap. By 1976 the crisis could no longer be ignored, especially after the left was visibly benefiting from its impact. In his new prime minister, Raymond Barre, the first non-Gaullist prime minister in the history of the Fifth Republic, Giscard boasted that France had the nation's 'best economist' at its helm. It was even said Barre had been named Raymond after the former Third Republic politician Raymond Poincaré who had rescued France from financial mayhem in the 1920s.[30] Events were not to enhance his reputation for economic competence.

Broadly speaking, Barre's strategy was twofold. First, he demanded that the people should tuck in their belts and brace themselves for some tough measures, what came to be dubbed his *plan d'austerité*, announced on 22 September 1976. This involved wage freezes and cuts in government spending, all designed to curb inflation and thus make French exports more competitive. Second, he aimed at a radical reshuffling of economic structures. This involved the closing down of inefficient businesses, as was the case in Longwy, yet further mergers, the paring down of government subsidies and the abandonment of price controls. No longer would the state prop up ailing concerns, but would privilege the industries of the future such as computers and electronics. The market would take its course. As many commentators have observed, it was a strategy reminiscent of that adopted by Margaret Thatcher in 1980s Britain and was implemented with the same kind of diplomatic tact albeit without quite the same ideological intensity. Commentators have not been slow to compare Norman Tebbit's injunction to the unemployed to get on their bike to seek work with Barre's advice, 'Let them start their own businesses.' Indeed, the immediate effect of the Barre policies was to push up unemployment. This continued to rise partially because of the second oil crisis of 1979 and partially because industry's profits, boosted by the lifting of price controls, were not reinvested. His one success was to keep the *franc* strong, through membership of the European Monetary System (EMS), but this hardly aided exports. Ultimately, Barre's economic policies were self-defeating because they were self-contradictory; the abandonment of price controls, part of Barre's liberalist instinct, sat uncomfortably with a traditional state *dirigisme* which was never truly relinquished.

Unable to do much in the domestic sphere because of economic constraints, worried at the lack of a solid parliamentary base and no longer so enthused at implementing change, from 1976 Giscard focused on 'more traditional presidential interests: foreign policy, European affairs and defence.'[31] This inevitably involved retaining links with the developing world. Outwardly this marked a dilution reversal of the neocolonialism practised by Pompidou and de Gaulle. There was much talk of promoting *Francophonie*, that is a cementing of cultural ties among the French-speaking world, a move which won the support of former colonies, and which helped promote the French tongue in a world where English was increasingly viewed as *the* international language. Foccart, the key minister involved in African affairs, was also dismissed. However, as Verschave has observed, it was business as usual under his successor, and onetime assistant, René Journiac.[32] Hoping to offset American and Russian influence in both Africa and Asia, neocolonialism thus persisted. This meant vetting EEC representatives concerned with the developing world to ensure they were pro-French; the use of African banks to launder the monies of French political parties; the further sponsoring of those Franco-African summits initiated by Pompidou; the extension of French economic interests, especially those of oil companies such as Elf; and support for those Francophile African leaders, even if their human rights records were not without blemish.[33] In 1977 aid was granted to Marshal Sese Seko Mobutu, president of Zaire, the largest French-speaking country on the African continent, in his fight against Congolese rebels who were sponsored by the pro-Soviet regime in Angola; in 1978 similar support was extended to the leader of Chad, Hissan Habré, in his struggle against Libyan-backed guerrillas. Depressingly, French aid was extended to the self-styled emperor of the Central African Republic, Jean-Bedel Bokassa, who liked to call de Gaulle his 'adoptive father' and who showered his friends with gifts of diamonds. French patience ran out only in 1979 when it was revealed that Bokassa had regularly murdered his people, including children, and had routinely indulged in cannibalism; his freezer contained several corpses packed with rice. French troops might have assisted his fall, yet it was Paris that protected him from international justice, setting him up in his own St Helena on the Ivory Coast.

In his relations with the two superpowers, Giscard carried on much in the tradition of de Gaulle and Pompidou. Good personal relations with Brezhnev were highly valued. Giscard also courted US presidents Gerald Ford and Jimmy Carter although there was much that France did which deeply irritated the Americans, especially in the Middle East, where Paris was keen to ease the oil crisis. To this end, France lifted the arms embargo on Middle East countries; the claims, on behalf of the Palestinian Liberation Organisation (PLO), for statehood were officially recognised; good relations were cultivated with two of Israel's most renowned enemies in the shape of Iraq and Egypt; and in 1978 France colluded with the Ayatollah Khomeini rather than lend support to the US-backed Shah of Iran. When in 1979 the Soviet Union invaded Afghanistan, France refused to partake in general sanctions and spurned US-demands to boycott the Olympic Games which were to be held in Moscow the following year. Nonetheless, in one area at least, Giscard was more pro-American than his predecessors, that of defence. A keen supporter of the NATO alliance, France made plain that in the event of a general nuclear war, it would cooperate fully with its western partners even though it remained outside the integrated command structure. In this way, France benefited from American nuclear know-how without sacrificing its claims to be independent and without allowing US missiles to be based on its soil.

As to Europe, Giscard displayed greater ambivalence. On one level, he had little wish to depart from 'the canons of the Gaullist heritage (a strong Europe with weak institutions).'[34] To this end, national governments were given an elevated role in the decision-making process of the newly-formed European Council (1974). On another level, Giscard expressed the vague wish – reminiscent of Napoleon III who had wanted to do 'something' for Italy – that he wished to do 'something' for Europe, even though he was uncertain what.[35] Like a Bonaparte, he was not slow to take any plaudits, whether deserved or not. At the close of his presidency, he prided himself on the enlargement of the community which had overseen the entry of Greece and the former dictatorships of Spain and Portugal. He further took credit for relaunching Franco-German relations, something neglected by Pompidou who had tried to derail the policy of reconciliation with East Germany being pursued by Willy Brandt. To be fair, Giscard enjoyed extremely cordial relations with Brandt's successor Helmut Schmidt. Sharing common purpose, they worked hard for the development of European institutions, for example, the European Council; direct elections to the European parliament (1979); and the setting up of the European Monetary Fund (EMF) (1979). Yet good personal relations with the West German leader could not disguise the so-called 'Euroscelorosis' which had beset the community since the 1960s in which national interests ruled supreme. Arguments, notably over CAP, persisted, revealing Giscard's belief that national interests always came first.

His European initiatives were, however, enough to raise concerns at home, damaging the coalition of forces which supported him in the Assembly. The Gaullists, under Chirac were especially anxious that France was in danger of sacrificing its identity with the result that in the first European elections of 1979 the RPR refused any deal with the UDF, standing instead on a nationalist list headed by former prime minister, Michel Debré. With the benefit of hindsight, it may be seen that these divisions within the right seriously weakened Giscard's reelection bid in1981, yet many other forces conspired against him, not least his public demeanour. It will be recalled that he had always possessed aristocratic pretensions, insisting that on formal events his prime minister should walk three steps behind him; at a famous meeting of the European Council at Strasbourg in June 1979, he dispensed with male gallantry by insisting on being served ahead of Margaret Thatcher, the newly elected British prime minister, who also sat away from him.[36] It was this side to his character – the president who indulged in exotic tastes such as scrambled eggs and truffles or truffles in a soup covered by a pastry shell, although it might be objected these were hardly exotic by French standards – that perturbed public opinion.[37] Especially damaging was the acceptance of a gift of diamonds from Colonel Bokassa, whose abuse of human rights was also becoming widely known. For those keen on historical analogies, the acceptance of this gift seemed eerily reminiscent of the necklace accepted by Marie-Antoinette on the eve of the French Revolution. And, in a way, France was on the eve of another revolution; the election of the first genuine left-wing government since the Popular Front in 1936, and the beginnings of the Mitterrand presidency whose legacy would far outweigh that of Giscard's. For all his talk of reform, for all his desire to appear modern, Giscard had been, in the words of Alistair Cole, the most 'constrained' of the Republic's presidents.[38] Unprepared to rock the boat, lacking a firm political base, opposed by the Gaullists, and buffeted by an economic crisis, his time in office will be remembered as one of transition when the Fifth Republic entered and survived its first non-Gaullist phase. It will additionally be recalled as one in which the non-

Communist left was able to undertake a remarkable recovery in its fortunes, the issue to which we must now turn.

The Recovery of the Left

It had been one of de Gaulle's most cherished aims to push the French left, most critically the Communist party, to the margins. And, at the time of his resignation in 1969, he appeared to have done just that. Whereas the 1960s had seen the flowering of new ideas in the shape of the New Left, 1968 had illustrated that the organised left, in the shape of the Communist and Socialist parties, was incapable of translating popular enthusiasms into political power. Frequently lampooned by the New Left, the Communists' failure to support the student-worker protest and its mealy-mouthed criticism of the USSR's crushing of the Czechoslovakian government that same year alienated potential supporters. The PCF thus seemed to have lost its revolutionary elan, stuck in a Stalinist timewarp, incapable of reinventing itself as it had done in the past. For all the talk of *Italianisation,* that is the acceptance of liberal democracy, the party only partially succeeded in distancing itself from the USSR. It was still the *parti de l'étranger,* an image it has never managed entirely to throw off.[39] In 1974, it suffered a further setback with the French publication of the Russian dissident Alexander Solzhenitsyn's account of the labour camps, *Gulag Archipelago.* As Jeremy Jennings writes, the impact of this book 'was to jolt France overnight into the era of post-Marxism.'[40] As in the aftermath of the 1956 Hungarian uprising, intellectuals, a group generally sympathetic to the Communist ideal, now sought to put clear blue water between themselves and a party which still seemed to listen more to what was said in Moscow than to what was said in France. In 1977–78, two of the most prominent self-titled *nouveaux philosophes* André Glucksmann and Bernard-Henri Lévy, both veterans of 1968, signalled their disillusionment with Marxism, while the eminent historian of the 1789 Revolution François Furet, another onetime Communist, distanced himself from the traditional Marxist interpretations of this most seminal of events.[41] That the PCF was able eventually to recover its influence in the 1970s owed much to efforts of the new party-secretary Georges Marchais who believed that the most effective way ahead was to enter some kind of alliance with the Socialist left. This would prevent the Communists' left-wing cousins from being seduced by those most crafty of suitors, the *bourgeois* centrist parties. As Bell and Criddle suggest, party leaders might also have been thinking to the past and the ways in which such an alliance had benefited the PCF at the time of the Popular Front.[42] Whatever the motivation, the Communists intended that they would emerge as the principal partner in any broad left coalition; they failed to realise that only a Socialist-led alliance had any real chance of success.

That did not seem an unlikely proposition at the start of the 1970s when the Socialist Party (SFIO) was in a truly parlous condition. The party of Jaurès and Blum seemed caught in an irreversible decline. In 1969 Defferre had managed a truly miserable five per cent in the first round vote. As will be recalled from chapter three, membership was down, women and young people were missing from the ranks, the party apparatus (such as newspapers) was in disrepair, no clear ideological programme existed, and a decrepit leadership, fronted by Guy Mollet, general secretary since 1946, appeared wholly fazed by de Gaulle's political manoeuvring. The SFIO seemed to belong to the past, part of the discredited system of the Fourth Republic when, in the periods 1946–51 and 1956–58, it had been the principal party of government. Tellingly, in 1968, the party was largely ignored by both students and workers. Without major surgery, Socialism was in danger of death.

It was to be rescued by a new party secretary, Alain Savary, who took over from Mollet in 1969. At the party congress at Issy-lès-Moulineaux that year, he pointed the way forward by urging the many fragments of the non-Communist left to come together with the SFIO in a new disciplined body. This would eventually emerge at the next party congress in 1971 (these continue to be held on a biennial basis) held at Epinay. Here the united Parti Socialiste (PS) was formally established comprising the following elements, as listed by Vincent Wright: the old members of the SFIO who congregated under the leadership of future prime minister Pierre Mauroy; the supporters of Jean-Pierre Chevènement's Centre d'Etudes de Recherche et d'Education Socialiste (CERES), which championed the Marxist and Jacobin left-wing tradition epitomised by the late-nineteenth socialist Jules Guesde and which later re-titled itself Socialisme et République to denote its liberal-democratic credentials; associates of Mitterrand's CIR; the subscribers to the left-wing clubs founded by Savary and Jean Poperen; and those disparate elements, for instance social Catholics and so-called *soixante-huitards*, who had not formerly belonged to any political grouping.[43] In 1974, the disaffected activists of the PSU, known as Rocardiens after their principal spokesperson Michel Rocard, agreed to throw in their lot with the PS.

Inevitably the bringing together of such kaleidoscopic traditions could not prevent factionalism, especially at congress time, yet in the course of the 1970s the newly-united Socialist Party underwent a veritable renaissance and cemented the *bipolarisation* of politics between left and right which had been evolving since the 1960s. Moreover, the PS was in a position to challenge successfully for the presidency in 1981. Aside from the coming together of the many different factions in the PS, how did this transformation come about?

The first answer often given by political scientists and historians is the leadership offered by François Mitterrand whose own personal fortunes largely mirrored those of the party he came to lead.[44] Born on 16 October 1916 at Jarnac in the Charente, a predominantly rural department in the west of France, he originated from a middle-class Catholic family whose political instincts were typically conservative. Brought up in Catholic schools (*Paris Match* later delighted in publishing a grainy photograph of the socialist president as a Catholic schoolboy) he pursued a traditional path for the sons of the *bourgeoisie* by undertaking his higher education at Paris, where he studied law at the prestigious Ecole Libre des Sciences Politiques. He arrived in the capital just as the left was doing battle with the extreme right-wing leagues fronted by the Croix de Feu, and there is evidence to suggest that the young Mitterrand sympathised with the authoritarian, traditionalist and nationalistic leanings of this extra-parliamentary organisation. By contrast, he indicated little sympathy for Blum's Popular Front, the first Socialist government in France whose work he promised to continue on his election to the presidency in 1981.

In 1940, he displayed great courage in the Battle of France when he was wounded and captured by the Germans. He subsequently undertook several escape attempts before he eventually reached the unoccupied zone of France governed by Marshal Pétain's Vichy regime. As we shall see, his initial sympathy for Pétain, his acceptance of the Vichy medal the *francisque* and his work for the Commissariat Général aux Prisonniers de Guerre (CGPG), together with his earlier associations with the Croix de Feu, came back to haunt him in the 1980s and 90s when France belatedly faced up to its Vichy past, in particular the persecution of the Jews. Yet there was no doubting Mitterrand's resistance record. In 1943 he relinquished his Vichy post to enter the underground network the Mouvement National des Prisonniers et Deportés de Guerre (MNPDG) where he worked under the pseudonym Capitaine Morland, eventually meeting de Gaulle in Algiers, a man he respected but not as the undisputed leader of the Resistance. This ensured that Mitterrand never won the general's patronage.

Eschewing a rightwards political trajectory, in the words of Alistair Cole he evolved into a 'non-Socialist, neo-Radical minister' serving in no fewer than 11 Fourth Republic cabinets.[45] A fierce opponent of de Gaulle in 1958, it will be remembered that he challenged the general for the presidency in 1965, and was influential in attempting to revive the fortunes of the non-Communist left through the CIR. His take-over of the Socialist Party in 1971 thus came late in the day, but the fact that he had stood outside of the cadres of the SFIO proved a benefit in that it lent him an ideological flexibility which proved invaluable in organising the new PS. Although his later actions as president led many to dispute whether he had ever truly been a man of the left – merely an opportunist who had sought power for its own sake – there was no doubting his ambition. Nor was there any doubting his administrative ability. Elected first secretary of the PS on 16 June 1971, he quickly imposed a discipline on the party machine which had proved impossible during the 1960s, undertaking a tour of France to rebuild the party's support.

Under Mitterrand's charismatic leadership the Socialist party strengthened itself in several regards. Membership, which had dropped to 70,000 in 1969 and had all but disappeared in some departments, was nurtured back to health. By 1978, this had risen to 178,000 and would peak at 200,000 during the 1981 presidential campaign.[46] As with the Gaullist UNR of the 1960s, these new supporters emanated from all walks of life. Apart from traditional adherents such as industrial workers, low-paid office staff and shop assistants, the PS won over those groups that had flourished during the *trente glorieuses*, the so-called *groupe centrale*, comprising professionals, white-collar workers, managerial elites and public sector officials. There is even evidence to suggest that the PS won over Catholic support, notably Christian trade unionists, who were attracted to the message of social equality and were no longer alienated by the anticlericalism of the left, although it must be stressed much of this religious-based support stemmed from non-practising Catholics who were disaffected with the traditionalism of their Church. Detailed electoral analysis has indicated that the overwhelming number of practising Catholics still cast their votes for the right. Critically the influx of these incomers, many of whom were young and unaccustomed to political life, replenished the administrative structures of the party from the top down, replacing the ageing stalwarts of the old SFIO. What attracted these recruits was what one political scientist has termed the 'ideological renaissance' of the Socialists, and the vigour with which the party expressed its views. Unlike other European mainstream left-wing parties, such as the German SPD (Social Democratic Party) in the 1970s and the British Labour party in the 1990s which toned down their political discourse in order to make themselves more 'user friendly', the French Socialists embraced daring proposals, interlarding traditional Marxist ideas with plans for *autogestion*, decentralisation, women's freedoms and civil liberties. Not only did this philosophy reflect the ideological eclecticism of French Socialism, it also served to reach out to Communist voters.

It was this appeal to other fellow left-wing parties, notably the Communists, that further contributed to the Socialist revival. On 27 June 1972, the so-called *Common Programme* was agreed between the PS and the PCF. For Marchais, this was an attempt to revive Communist fortunes by dissuading the Socialists from their habit of forming alliances with centrist parties, as had happened after the collapse of tripartism in 1947. For Mitterrand, it was an unpleasant expedient and represented a calculated gamble to overtake the Communists as *the* party of the left, although he was pleasantly surprised at the attitude of the PCF leadership which was so 'gentle' compared to the 1930s: 'no accusations of scoundrel, or reptilian conduct ... no cries of "murderer".'[47] Mitterrand was not fooled, and did not lose sight of the broader goal. While the social democratic ideals of the Socialists had assured them seats in government, he recognised that the PCF had always possessed a clearer identity and thus occupied the moral high ground. This had to be changed.

So the two parties entered into a partnership, each with the intention of outstripping the other. To begin with, relates Bell it appeared that the the PCF had the edge when, in the 1973 parliamentary elections it scored 21.5 per cent of the vote as opposed to 19 per cent for the PS. The tide soon turned. In 1974 Mitterrand ran Giscard close in the second presidential ballot. Subsequent by-elections that autumn saw many traditional right-wing strongholds fall to the PS. As Bell continues, unable to 'find a response', the Communists began 'an open quarrel' with the Socialists.[48] By 1977, the differences between the two parties were so vast that the *Common Programme* was jettisoned. In taking this step, it may also be that the Communist leadership was emboldened by improved PCF showings in the municipal elections earlier that year although, in practice, Communists often had to share power with fellow left-wingers. More crucially, the collapse the *Common Programme* marked the emergence of the Socialists as *the* dominant party on the left.

Despite their ascendancy over the PCF, some six months before the 1981 presidential elections of 1981 a Socialist victory still looked some way off. Opinion polls all indicated that Giscard enjoyed a lead of 20 per cent over Mitterrand. It has since been speculated that the magnitude of this may have encouraged a complacency on the part of the incumbent president who subsequently fought a casual campaign. He seemed oblivious to the damage caused by his autocratic style, the economic downturn which was still biting, the Bokassa diamond scandal, and his rancorous relations with Chirac's Gaullists. Chirac, who came third in the first ballot of 1981, did not forget old scores, and said nothing to his supporters as to how they should vote in the second round. It is calculated that some 15 per cent opted for Mitterrand while another 15 per cent abstained. Befitting its sectarianism, the Communist leadership would dearly have loved Mitterrand to lose, but aware that Communist supporters were going to vote Socialist anyway, Marchais had no choice but to tell party members to behave thus – some 92 per cent rallied to Mitterrand in the second round. It should not be forgotten, however, that Mitterrand had attractions of his own: he was a charismatic, experienced and formidable figure who promised something new. He also presented the electorate with an assured image, something noted by the onetime Giscardian minister Lionel Stoléru.[49] As Le Monde reflected at the start of his second septennat, Mitterrand already had 'stature' aplenty in 1981.[50] Maybe this confidence arose from frequently being called 'Monsieur, le Président'. As Jean Lacouture observes, he had always been a president: president of his circle of students in the 1930s, president of the Union Démocrutique et Socialiste de la Résistance (UDSR), president of the conseil général in the Nièvre, and president of the PS convention at Epinay.[51]

In a reversal of the 1974 result, in 1981 Mitterrand won 51.7 per cent of the votes and Giscard 48.2 per cent. Shortly afterwards, in the June parliamentary elections, the country voted in an overwhelmingly left-wing assembly: the Socialists, together with their allies in the Mouvement des Radicaux de Gauche (MRG), garnered 289 seats; the PCF share fell from 86 to 44; and the combined parties of the right could only muster 155. So began France's so-called 'adventure', the first truly left-wing government the nation had possessed since 1936.

Conclusion: Towards Victory

Whereas the presidency of Giscard constituted a transitional phase in history of the Fifth Republic, Mitterrand's represented another milestone. Although he would withdraw from some of the radical policies implemented during the honeymoon period in office during 1981–83, his term in office proved that the regime was mature enough to accommodate a left-wing government. In this sense, political commentators suggest liberal democracy in France moved closer to the models of Britain and West Germany, which had long seen the alternation of power between right and left, even though it was the right which was more usually in office than out. It also demonstrated that the people of France were ready for change. Both Pompidou and Giscard had tinkered with reform, but had only been prepared to go so far. Notwithstanding Pompidou's ill health, both men were averse to extravagant state funding to implement reform; both lacked a true reforming zeal; both struggled to muster support among the centre-right which was exceedingly fractious for much of the 1970s; and both misjudged the public mood. Giscard was especially hampered by the recession of the second half of the 1970s. The enthusiasms of 1968 had not entirely dissipated, and ultimately needed to be met. In this sense, it could be said that Mitterrand's victory was the revenge of the *soixante huitards*.

Chapter 6: Le Caméléon: *The Mitterrand Presidencies, 1981–1995*

On being elected president on 10 May 1981, Mitterrand announced that his victory belonged 'to the forces of youth, of labour, of creativity, of renewal who have come together in a great national movement for jobs, peace, freedom, themes which were those of my presidential campaign and will remain those of my administration.'[1] Whether such ideals stayed at the heart of his presidency is debatable. After the euphoria of his triumph had elapsed, and the first round of reforms had passed, the shortcomings of the Socialists' economic policy at a time of global recession became apparent, forcing Mitterrand into an astonishing U-turn. In the period 1984–86, his government abandoned Keynesian economics to pursue a strategy of austerity. This might have been successful in curbing inflation, yet it failed to cure the scourge of unemployment, and played badly with the public and the left's natural supporters who believed that the socialist dream had been betrayed. The upshot was the victory of the right in the parliamentary elections of 1986, ushering in the first experience of *cohabitation* in which France was governed by a president of one party (Mitterrand) and the prime minister of another (Chirac). It was something that had always been on the cards, and many doubted whether the constitutional structures would be able to cope, throwing in doubt once again the future of the Fifth Republic. Such doubters need not have worried. Ever the astute politician, Mitterrand acknowledged that the people had voted emphatically for the opposition and he knew not to go against the public will. It is frequently said that he subsequently served as an 'arbiter-president', rarely intervening in domestic affairs, devoting his talents to foreign policy instead. This adroit political manoeuvre not only buttressed the regime; it distanced him from Chirac's disappointing economic measures. It was partially this detachment that secured his reelection in 1988.

This time there would be no repetition of the euphoria that had greeted Mitterrand's elevation in 1981. Nor would the president himself exert as much energy as during his first *septennat*, leaving much decision-making to his prime ministers. In the absence of any sustained reforming zeal and in the presence of growing government corruption, other issues came to the fore. During the early 1990s, several former Vichy officials were belatedly charged with 'crimes against humanity' for their part in the deportation of Jews during the Second World War, forcing the French people to grapple with the legacy of the Nazi Occupation. The increase in the number of immigrants, together with the rise of deeply xenophobic Front National of Jean-Marie Le Pen, further highlighted the issue of race, revealing the limits of cultural assimilation. Paradoxically, however, during the Mitterrand years France lost something of its distinct national characteristics as it came increasingly to resemble its northern European neighbours, the result of Mitterrand's pursuit of further European integration, something which has proved one of his finest achievements. Yet this was not all. Despite the disappointments of his two *septennats*, and these were considerable, commentators generally make the point that France was a much more modern country, economically, socially and culturally, in 1995 than it had been in 1981. As Mitterrand's biographer Alistair Cole observes, this process owed much to the president's ability to operate in a world in which globalisation and interdependence generally reduced the freedom of national governments.[2]

The First Septennat

For Mitterrand, the first year of his presidency constituted a 'state of grace', a moment when he could undertake bold strategic initiatives. There were several reasons for this. To begin with, the electorate was in a euphoric mood having sloughed off the legacy of the Giscard years when the unimaginative policies of deflation and cuts in government spending had masqueraded as economic liberalism. No-one who was in Paris on the night of Mitterrand's victory on 10 May 1981 could forget the sounding of car-horns, the cracking open of champagne bottles, the letting off of firecrackers, the singing and the spontaneous dances in the city's squares. As the president himself reflected, 'I was carried away with victory; we were intoxicated.'[3] Additionally, Mitterrand could afford to be adventurous, confident in the knowledge that he was the most powerful president since de Gaulle. The calling of legislative elections straight after his own victory led to a left-wing landslide, aided by an old-fashioned deal between the Communists and Socialists whereby the two agreed not to run against each other in the second ballot. The PS did spectacularly well, scoring 37.8 per cent in the first round, securing the votes of a wide range of social groups from the working classes, through to middle management, to include elements among business and the professions. With 285 seats out of the available 490, the Socialists, like the Gaullists of 1968–73, had no need for allies in parliament. As Pierre Favier and Michel Martin-Roland remark, this was the first time in the history of the left that it had controlled the presidency, the premiership and the Assembly.[4] For Delors, the scale of the victory was almost an embarrassment. 'This is too much, this is too much', he remarked.[5] Such reservations did not prevent the Socialists from using their political patronage to the full. Two thirds of the *directeurs d'administration centrale* were changed in the period 1981–86. [6]

Mitterrand's confidence not only sprang from the security of this landslide and the use of patronage. In 1981, he was genuinely enthused with the task of reform. His government, he announced, was the natural heir to Blum's Popular Front of 1936 and the successor to the reformist administration of the Liberation. It was his task to complete the work they had initially undertaken. On the night of his election, encountering a tearful Mendès-France, Mitterrand embraced him and remarked, 'Without you all this would not have been possible.'[7] Some days later, at his inauguration, the president proceeded to the Panthéon, the resting place of France's heroes, where he placed red roses besides the graves of Jean Jaurès, the founder of the SFIO, Jean Moulin, the Resistance martyr, and Victor Schoelcher, the abolitionist who, in 1848, had ended slavery in the empire. Mitterrand later emerged from the building to the strains of *La Marseillaise* sung by Pavarotti. That same day, Mitterrand arranged for flowers to be placed by Blum's resting place at Jouy-en-Josas. In the opinion of the journalist Catherine Nay, the president was at this point more or less the reincarnation of the Popular Front leader.[8] Small wonder, many on the right and elements of the *bourgeoisie* were frightened at what these gestures suggested in terms of policy, yet there was nothing really to fear. One cartoon of the day caught the mood perfectly, with a Parisian opening his window and exclaiming,

'My goodness! The president is socialist and the Eiffel tower is still standing!.'[9]

Indeed Mitterrand, while radical, was not hell-bent on revolutionary change, something indicated in his choice of political allies: the traditional socialist and mayor of Lille Pierre Mauroy was appointed to the premiership; the moderate Jacques Delors, author of Chaban's 'New Society' speech, took the reins at Finance; and the former *Monsieur X* Gaston Defferre was put in charge of the Interior. This cabinet proved short-lived thanks to the June legislative elections. Yet the ministry which subsequently emerged continued to embody consensus, including four Communists (a move that troubled the Americans), the onetime Gaullist Michel Jobert and six women, notably Yvette Roudy at the new Ministry of Women's Rights.

Moderate ministers, hand-picked civil servants and a canny president, who was keen not to alienate sections of the electorate unnecessarily, meant that the ensuing reform package was not as daring as some on the left had hoped, yet it still went much further than those adopted by other social-democratic parties in northern Europe, and its achievements deserve to be ranked alongside those of 1946 and 1936. As Alistair Cole writes, the programme, based on the manifesto of the *110 Propositions*, mixed 'classic' left-wing policies in the sphere of social, economic and industrial policy with selective initiatives in other domains such as civil liberties,[10] although overall it lacked cohesion, reflecting the many fingers in the pie.[11] Among those traditional policies came nationalisations. By a law of 11 February 1982, the state took into its charge the following: five key industrial concerns (Compagnie Générale d'Electricité, Saint Gobain, Péchiney-Ugine-Kühlmann, Rhône-Poulenc, Thomson-Brandt); two financial companies (Paribas and Suez); 36 banks; and a host of other smaller enterprises (for instance, CII-Honeywell-Bull, Dassault and Matra).[12] It is calculated that such takeovers massively increased the public sector from one tenth of France's industrial capacity to just over a quarter. The state also had an even greater say in investments and in the allocation of credit. As many commentators have emphasised, Cole especially, these nationalisations were an attempt to keep the Communists on side, yet they also reflected Mitterrand's strange brand of Social Catholicism and Marxist economics which believed that unbridled liberal capitalism only resulted in personal disaffection, social confusion and material inequalities. Such ideological impulses could be further identified in the Loi Auroux of 4 August 1982 which strengthened the say of workers in the running of industries, the augmentation of the SMIC, the extension of paid holidays (both a symbolic and tangible measure), and the introduction of a wealth tax directed at the very well off.

Using the state to loosen the hold of capitalism was accompanied by a law of 2 March 1982 designed to weaken the powers of the state in the localities, a long-held dream of the Socialists as they had reconstructed their party in the 1970s. For Defferre it was a chance to decolonise France, just as France had decolonised Africa.[13] This process of decentralisation redrew the powers of the prefects, to be called *commissaires de la République* (a title soon dropped); devolved policy-making decisions and tax-raising powers to the 96 departmental councils; instituted direct elections to regional councils, hitherto the preserve of local grandees; and debated autonomy for Corsica and the DOM-TOMS which had enthusiastically welcomed the Socialist victory, although they were soon to learn that the Mitterrand was lukewarm in granting real independence. Indeed, it is questionable whether in the long run the Defferre reforms weakened the centralised nature of the Jacobin state. Whatever the case, devolution was warmly applauded as it seemingly brought government closer to the people, building the 'participatory state' without putting into place new and wholly unfathomable institutional structures. The French remain as symbolically committed to the commune, the smallest of local administrative units, as they do to the *baguette*.

The remaining reforms of Mitterrand's 'period of grace' witnessed a veritable modernisation of French society, initiatives which Giscard had promised yet had never delivered. These included the abolition of the death penalty, the dismantling of military courts, the dissolution of the Cour de Sûreté de l'Etat, a Gaullist innovation which had been used to crush Corsican nationalists, the granting of greater freedoms to Corsica itself, the granting of an amnesty to some 130,000 illegal immigrants, and a relaxation on immigration controls and working permits. As France began to approximate more and more its northern European neighbours, artistic and cultural projects came to the fore, reflecting Mitterrand's belief that socialism was 'a choice of civilisation'. The new Culture minister Jack Lang, aptly described as 'un animateur hyperactif'[14], and far more 'serious' and 'ambitious' than any of his predecessors,[15] gave seemingly endless interviews to the media, appearing in articles in between the nudes of the men's magazine *Lui* and the French edition of *Playboy*. Words were translated into policy. Lang championed indigenous French civilization, shunning Anglo-Saxon, or more specifically American influences, boycotting the première of Steven Spielberg's

Raiders of the Lost Arc and denouncing the dangers of the soap opera *Dallas*. In a welter of activities designed to bring the arts to the masses, 'les exclus de la culture', he oversaw the building of concert halls, the construction of opera houses, the pumping of money into libraries, the abandonment of unpopular measures such as the building of a nuclear power plant in rural Britanny, and the jaw-dropping bicentenary celebrations of the 1789 Revolution. Not all of these initiatives were welcomed by a public who, in an age of globalisation, could not withstand outside influences, notably the ever-present currents of Americanisation which blew across the Atlantic. Such winds resulted notably in the building of the EuroDisney theme park outside Paris, although this only became truly popular among the French themselves when it shook off its New World puritanism to serve alcohol alongside fast-food.

In the eyes of public opinion, reflects Cole, the continuing presence of Mauroy as premier was an indicator that Mitterrand was still set on a programme of reformist socialism. In truth, something fundamental had changed, symbolised in the humiliating climbdown on the Savary bill, named after the minister of education Alain Savary. Designed to bring Catholic schools under the aegis of the Ministry of Education, and in the process reduce state subsidies to private establishments, its enemies denounced it as an old-style anticlerical measure. On 24 June, nearly one million people protested against the reform, the biggest demonstration Paris had seen since 1968, a parade of camel hair coats, designer suits and expensive jewellery – in essence, *bourgeois* France on the march. While religious issues were certainly at the heart of the matter, the conspicuous presence of the middle classes – the principal patrons of private education, even though only 20 per cent of them were practising Catholics – suggested that the demonstrations were more a defence of economic interests against socialist intrusions than an assertion of denominational liberty. Cardinal Lustiger of Paris might have called the reform a 'betrayal', but the fact that the bishops themselves were not altogether unhappy with the Savary reforms was a further indicator that religious freedoms were not necessarily at the root of the protests, as was the presence of Chirac who was keen to exploit the affair to the maximum, claiming the Socialists were removing choice in education.[16] Indeed, the protests cost Mitterrand the resignations of both his prime minister and education secretary. Surely but slowly the gloss was wearing off the Socialist experiment, something reflected in the polls. Not only did the PS do badly in the municipal elections of 1983, losing control of over 30 towns with a population over 30,000, it could only muster 20 per cent of the vote in the European elections the following year in contrast to the 43 per cent secured by the RPR-UDF coalition of Simone Veil. Ominously the extreme right-wing party of Jean-Marie Le Pen, to be considered later, was picking up support.

To more perceptive observers, things had started to go wrong as early as 1982 when it became apparent that government economic policy was failing. Although a cultured man, Mitterrand was wanting in his reading of economics. The hope was that Keynesian reflationary policies – increased government spending and much improved salaries – would enhance industrial output and stimulate consumer spending, thus providing a cure for unemployment.[17] It did nothing of the sort. The rise in salaries, most conspicuous among the unskilled who benefited from increased social security payments and a growth in the SMIC, only contributed to a balance of payments crisis as France binged on consumer goods bought from abroad. Moreover, economists stress that the timing was wrong. France was practising Keynesian economics just at the moment when the industrialised world slid into global recession and when its competitors were adopting savage deflationary policies, slashing government budgets, lowering taxes and raising interest rates.

With inflation, unemployment and imports rising, and with government popularity on the down, it is perhaps no surprise that Mitterrand spent much of 1984 on overseas visits, some 30 trips in all and some 70 days away from the metropole. Unpleasant domestic decisions awaited at home. Crudely speaking, the choices confronting Mitterrand were twofold: to continue traditional socialist economics or to pursue the path of austerity mapped out by the G7 Nations meeting at Versailles in June 1982. Given the failed legacy of the Popular Front, which had also been forced to abandon its ambitious public spending plans, weighed heavily with the president, he was reluctant to adopt the latter course. Yet, under the influence of Delors, in June 1982 he oversaw the implementation of price controls, a capping of wage bills and the devaluation of the *franc*, an earlier devaluation the previous year not having done the trick. Increasingly chameleon-like, still the president was reticent in admitting any change of course. After March 1983, commentators concur, the U-turn was obvious.[18] This was forced by France's membership of the EMS. With its neighbours determined on deflationary measures, France had to decide whether to emulate their example or leave the EMS to pursue a protectionist and reflationary path in isolation, the favoured option of the industry minister and dyed-in-the wool socialist Chevènement. Ever the good European, Mitterrand opted to stay in, and reluctantly implemented a series of tough measures, devaluing yet again, cutting back on public expenditure while lowering taxes. Although the president protected internal markets, these moves played badly with the public.[19] The left was disheartened that the government had abandoned its original remit. In Lorraine, workers ransacked the offices of the Socialist party and tore down pictures of the president. The right smugly argued that the answer had been obvious all along and that Mitterrand had dithered.

In truth, the economic dilemmas confronting France in the early 1980s were an illustration of how globalisation left national governments, of whatever political hue, with less and less autonomy, a lesson quickly appreciated by Mitterrand. As will be seen, under his second *septennat* he largely recovered his reputation for economic competence, albeit by innovating little in financial affairs and by keeping a close watch on international trends. Whether in the remaining years of his first term in office he became a fully-fledged economic liberal, in the mould of Margaret Thatcher and Ronald Reagan, as is sometimes argued, is another matter. Mitterrand never wholly embraced the free market – privatisation came late in his reign – and he was alive to the social costs of government cutbacks.[20] Nonetheless, his appointment of the young technocrat and ENA graduate Laurent Fabius as prime minister following the fall of Mauroy in 1984 was an indication of a shift. As *L'Express* observed at the time, never had a prime minister been replaced with someone so different: party man had given way to Epinay man, the old guard for a technocrat, a *bourgeois* for a proletarian.[21] There were further doubts whether Fabius was his own man. 'Mitterrand names himself at the Matignon', quipped *Le Quotidien de Paris*.[22] What gave this period some semblance of cohesion was the rallying cry 'moderniser et rassembler'. In practice this meant the Socialist Party abandoning many of its shibboleths to pursue a modest and somewhat unimaginative economic and social strategy: constrained social reform, the infusion of private money into state concerns and the removal of government subsidies to staple industries which were left to fend for themselves.

Although by 1986 the economy was turning, the electoral damage had been done. Many of the left's natural supporters, never mind the Communists, felt betrayed. The Mitterrand government was also tarnished by the first of many scandals which would dent the Socialists' boasts of probity. In the South Pacific – where France was already struggling to fend off the demands of autonomists in New Caledonia – Australia and New Zealand, together with a range of other states in the region, demanded an end of the Ministry of Defence's decade-long policy of detonating nuclear bombs in French-owned Polynesia. The most recent explosion had been biggest yet, and prompted the environmental pressure group Greenpeace to dispatch its vessel the *Rainbow Warrior* to the area in an attempt to disrupt future testing. Believing that France could behave however it chose in its colonies – one minister comparing the test area to a private bathroom in which one could do as one liked – Paris instructed its secret services to sink the boat, which they duly did on 10 July 1985 in Auckland harbour at the cost of the life of one of the crew. No deaths had been intended, yet the whole episode was one of those botched operations in which the secret services of all countries seem to excel. Equipped with false Swiss passports, knowing nothing of Antipodean culture and making regular cell phone calls to Paris, it was no surprise that the New Zealand police soon made arrests.

Astonishingly both the French establishment and public opinion could not understand the international fuss that ensued, and it was no surprise that an official enquiry headed by the right-winger Bernard Tricot wholly cleared the government. This author remembers clearly reading the headline of *Libération* in the courtyard of the Bibliothèque Nationale: 'Tricot washes whiter than white'. The real indignation was that the government had been found out, largely through the investigative reporting of *L'Express*, *France-Soir* and *Le Monde*.[23] Meanwhile, the two agents arrested by Kiwi police were sentenced to ten years in jail where they apparently wiled away the time reading Victor Hugo and Chateaubriand.[24] Although Chirac later succeeded in releasing the men, at the time Mitterrand was badly damaged and heavily criticised for not keeping a tighter rein on his security operatives. The price was the jettisoning of his Defence Minister and close friend Charles Hernu who was deeply implicated in the affair.

In the broader context of unpopular economic measures, it was hardly the best way in which to prepare for an election, and the ensuing results were widely predictable. They would have been even worse for the Socialists if Mitterrand had not earlier introduced a form of proportional representation which improved the chances of smaller parties, including the FN, and which worked against the interests of the right more generally which remained extremely fractious, divided by personalities and policies. As Mitterrand himself remarked, 'In 1986 I considered that a victory of the RPR and its allies was more dangerous for the country than the election of several deputies for the Front National.'[25] In the event, the PS scored 31.04 per cent of the vote to collect 207 seats (still the third best performance in the party's history); the Communist share dropped to 9.78 per cent and 35 seats, embarrassingly the same number of seats attained by the FN. The 40.98 per cent won by the combined forces of the RPR-UDF, which translated into 288 seats, assured victory for the right, which achieved an overall majority thanks to the support of DOM-TOM deputies. Thus began the Republic's first experience of *cohabitation.*

Under de Gaulle, or even Giscard, *cohabitation* would have spelt disaster. Under Mitterrand this was not to be. He recognised that the voters had spoken and was not prepared to defy their choice. He further appreciated that Chirac, as the head of the RPR-UDF coalition, was an obvious choice as prime minister, and thus avoided appointing some hitherto obscure technocrat who would have scrambled a loose consensus within parliament. Most crucially, he understood that he needed to work constructively with the new government. This did not mean that he became a mere figurehead. The president was determined to see out his seven-year mandate and he was equally resolved to wield political power. As Vincent Wright records, this involved negotiating the composition of the cabinet and the shameless use of political patronage.[26] He naturally asserted his ascendancy within the *domaine réservé,* and did not hesitate to criticise Chirac's domestic policies, notably in July 1986 when faced with privatisation initiatives although ultimately these would go ahead. Indeed, Mitterrand was canny enough to recognise that endless boycotts of his prime minister's policies would test the constitution to the limits and make him unpopular with the electorate. As a result, Chirac was able to pursue his economic agenda. This involved a watering down of state *dirigisme* whereby the Ministry of Finance was able to control prices, at least in certain sectors. He also embarked on a highly ambitious privatisation programme, much more extensive than that initiated by Margaret Thatcher in the UK. No fewer than 65 companies were to be offered up for sale, an auction expected to bring in some 200 billion *francs,* although much of the capital raised went into propping up ailing state firms such as Air France. In the event, the glass company St-Gobain was sold off, along with Havas, TF1, the arms/electronics firm Matra and a handful of banks. Further sales were postponed because of the 1987 shares crash on Wall Street, and were then ruled out by the Socialist victory a year later. Privatisations would not resume until Balludur's premiership in 1993.[27]

Given the tension over domestic policies, *cohabitation* was inevitably an uncomfortable experience for both sides; *cohabitension* was how

Le Canard Enchaîné described it. Yet it proved popular with the increasing number of voters who despaired of partisan politics. More crucially, government continued to function. In this way, Mitterrand skilfully recrafted his role, presenting himself as an arbiter whose task was to serve the interests of the nation, an image enhanced by his many overseas trips when he was regarded as the embodiment of France. The legend of Tonton Mitterrand ('Uncle Mitterrand') soon developed. In truth, Mitterrand was just as much of a politician as his rival but, in standing back from the hurly-burly of the political life, he seemed to have rediscovered something of his social Catholic roots: a belief that the affairs of the nation were best served by consensus as opposed to sectarian politicking. By contrast, Chirac was viewed as the archetypal shifty politician, his image further tarnished by his aggressive policies which came at a high social cost. Students were alienated by the restrictions placed on higher education; workers were upset by changes to unemployment law which made it easier for employers to carry out redundancies; and immigrants balked at enhanced police powers to arrest purported illegal aliens, a move resulting in the expulsion of 101 Malians by chartered jet in October 1986.

Because of Chirac's uncompromising style, in 1988 the surprise, relates Cole, was not that Mitterrand should have won the presidential elections. (It should also be added that Chirac was unpopular with the centre right which had also been courted by Raymond Barre.) The real puzzle was why Mitterrand should have stood again at the age of 72. One very strong possibility is that he had embraced the Gaullist concept of the president as a virtual monarch, and could not bear to relinquish office. He certainly had no wish to hand over the reins of power to Rocard who was becoming increasingly popular and who had been a potential rival in 1981. Nor did he wish to give way to the hated Chirac. A more charitable explanation is that his decision to stand again was dictated by this belated search for consensus. Another sympathetic interpretation is to believe that the president wished to pursue his European mission. During *cohabitation*, he had devoted much time to EEC matters and was determined to promote greater integration (see below). Whatever the case, his political instincts had not deserted him. Within five days of his reelection, he dissolved the right-dominated Assembly and announced fresh elections which the Socialist duly won. Once again the glitz of the president rubbed off on his party even though the margin of victory was nowhere near as great as in 1981.

The Second Septennat

For the sake of clarity, Mitterrand's second *septennat* may be divided into four phases, each one delineated by his choice of prime ministers. Initially the premiership was entrusted to Rocard, who was indeed deeply irritated that Mitterrand had decided to stand for a second term, thus dashing his own tilt at the Elysée. The president appreciated, however, that Rocard was popular, not just among fellow Socialists, but with the electorate as a whole. It was a wise choice. No sectarian socialist, Rocard was keen to build on the consensual style which Mitterrand had adopted during *cohabitation* when the president had spoken of *ouverture*.[28] To this end, he made room in his cabinet for UDF ministers who had previously served under Chirac and Barre, men such as Jean-Pierre Soisson, Jacques Pelletier, Lionel Stoléru and Michel Durafour. He also attempted to give his government a non-sectarian appearance by calling on the services of prominent individuals outside the party cadres, notably Bernard Kouchner, the driving force behind Médecins sans Frontières, who became secretary of state for humanitarian action, and the sportsman and media pundit Roger Bambuck. In terms of policy, writes Cole, Rocard steered a path similar to that of Fabius: modest reform interlarded with prudent housekeeping, all aimed at a mixed economy which looked after the poor as well as creating the necessary preconditions for enterprise. To this end Cole continues, he reintroduced an amended wealth tax, abolished by Chirac in 1986; a minimum income was pledged for the very poor; education received substantial investments; the social security system was overhauled; further reforms aimed to cut through red tape in the public sector; and in New Caledonia, long afflicted by internal conflict, a settlement was promised which seemed to meet the demands of the autonomists.[29]

The results were encouraging. Unemployment, at long last, began to fall, inflation was held in check, productivity grew, the trade balance went into the black, and general confidence in the economy was high, something signalled by Mitterrand's willingness to support a single European currency at the Maastricht summit of 1991.

Confidence in Rocard was another matter. Mitterrand could never overcome his resentment of his long-time rival, and Rocard's widespread popularity clouded the president's judgement. In an act he almost certainly came to regret, and an episode which was not properly understood by the public, on 15 May 1991 he demanded Rocard's resignation. The replacement was Edith Cresson, France's first woman prime minister, a business school graduate who since 1981 had served in several economic ministries. In the light of Mitterrand's marital misdemeanours (it was revealed that he had both a mistress and illegitimate daughter) there was inevitable speculation over whether Cresson had been selected because she was a former lover of the president. Rather Mitterrand wanted a malleable premier, just as de Gaulle had wanted a more compliant deputy when he dismissed Pompidou in 1968.

Cresson's appointment marks the beginnings of the next phase of the second *septennat*. This was the nadir of Mitterrand's presidency, a time when ill health sapped his political judgement and left him out of touch with popular opinion, a time too when scandal threatened to engulf his government. Not that this was all Cresson's fault. Her sex invited much unwelcome press attention; she was no Socialist baron and lacked party support to offset presidential demands; she discovered that her choices of minister were made for her; the economy took an unfortunate turn for the worse in 1991; and her instinctive preference for an interventionist economic policy sat uneasily alongside the neo-liberal course mapped out by Rocard and Fabius. In her favour, she possessed boundless energy, but a lack of experience prompted her to make off-the-cuff remarks that played badly with public opinion not just in France. Angered at the Japanese for their protectionist trade policies, she compared their facial features to those of ants, the kind of crass comment that could be expected of the Duke of Edinburgh. She further speculated whether over 50 per cent of British males were homosexual simply because she was not ogled by men as she walked down the streets in London. Arrogant, abrasive and impetuous she was everything Rocard was not and, after a disastrous performance in the regional elections of March 1992, she was replaced.

At 11 months, Cresson's premiership was the shortest in the history of the Fifth Republic, but she was run close by her successor, Pierre Bérégovoy (March 1992–March 1993). As many commentators have observed, his career seemed to reflect the more general evolution of the French left. A former gas fitter who had taken various diplomas in management, in 1969 he had chosen politics as a career, working himself up through the apparatus of the Socialist Party, eventually serving as finance minister under Fabius and Rocard where he championed the *franc fort* (that is an attempt to keep the French currency at a parity with the *Deutschmark*), and a hard-line monetary policy which won him friends aplenty among European leaders but few among the party faithful. As prime minister, he ensured that fiscal conservatism was again the order of the day but this did little to cure recession and unemployment. In March 1993, the Socialists were trounced at the polls; along with their allies, they won a mere 67 seats as opposed to the 428 secured by the UDF/RPR coalition. Before Bérégovoy could witness the results of a second round of *cohabitation*, on 1 May 1993 he took his own life, depressed at recent poll results but traumatised by recent revelations that he had accepted an interest-free loan of 1,000,000 francs (£100,000) to buy a Paris appartment, a move eerily reminiscent of the loan that the British politician Peter Mandelson would later accept from a fellow politician. There was nothing illegal about the deal (as was true of the Mandelson affair), but for a man of upright probity Bérégovoy was deeply wounded by the inevitable speculation that raged in the press.

The details of the loan had come to light following an earlier investigation into the affairs of the businessman Roger-Patrice Pelat, a close friend of Mitterrand since resistance days, who was alleged to have been involved in insider dealing when Péchiney took over American Can. Further investigations revealed that he had often subsidised the Mitterrand family, and three of his associates, all with close links with the Socialist party, were eventually jailed for the Péchiney fraud. Further scandals were soon at hand, casting doubts on Mitterrand's choice of friends. The president's Vichy associates will be considered later. Mention here should be made of foreign minister, Roland Dumas who regularly drew on income which rightly belonged to the Quai d'Orsay. It was later uncovered that he had showered his mistress Christine Deviers-Joncour, an employee of Elf, with endless gifts, including a pair of shoes worth 11,000 *francs*, an arrangement blessed by Elf's director of *affaires générales*, Alfred Sirven, described as 'one of the few convicted armed robbers to have graduated to an executive position in a major multinational'.[30] Growing public despondency was compounded by the contaminated blood affair. In mid-1990s it was revealed that doctors at the national Centre for Blood Tranfusion, with the connivance of the Ministry of Health, had permitted the use of HIV-infected products in the treatment of haemophiliacs. Eventually three ministers deemed responsible – Fabius, Georgina Dufoix and Edmond Hervé – were committed to trial yet it was already clear that prosecutors had no real wish to probe the matter. Justice was at least pursued at a local level where several Socialist notables were found guilty of embezzlement – corruption seemed endemic in PS finances. And, on a national level, the impressario Bernard Tapie was convicted on charges of fraud and match-fixing on behalf of his football team, Marseille.

The fact that scandal continued after Mitterrand, and was far from being exclusively the preserve of the left, says Wolfreys, was a reflection of the changing nature of the French state: the decrease in presidential power, the slackening of government controls over the media, the spread of decentralisation and the growing independence of the judiciary. While this was of little consolation to Mitterrand, in the last two years of his second *septennat* he recovered a certain gravitas. This final phase was again a period of *cohabitation* in which he ruled alongside Edouard Balladur of the RPR as his prime minister, Chirac having earlier rejected the Matignon so that he could prepare his campaign for the presidency. A fussy and priggish individual, Balladur was a competent premier who had no wish to lock horns with a president who was displaying the outward signs of the cancer which would eventually take his life. This willingness to compromise had in the early 1970s earned him the nickname *Ballamou* ('soft not hard'); as prime minister, his easygoing manner won him a popularity akin to that enjoyed earlier by Rocard. Given his determination to stand as the right's candidate in the 1995 presidential elections, Chirac was suitably alarmed but, for reasons to be discussed later, outmanoeuvred his rivals to win the Elysée.

France Confronts its Past

As Mitterrand's presidency drew to a close, the historian Henry Rousso joined forces with the journalist Eric Conan to publish *Vichy. Un passé qui ne passe pas*, in essence a polemical work arguing that the obsession with the Second World War, which had recently overtaken France, was largely the creation of a cynical, manipulative and ever-hungry media, little concerned with historical fact.[31] In no sense apologists for the Holocaust, this obsession had been damaging in that it had focused too much attention on the fate of the Jews, a phenomenon they described as 'Judeo-Centrism', when other groups, for instance communists, freemasons, resisters and victims of the obligatory work service, suffered just as badly at the hands of the Nazis. If it had been hoped that this call would lead to less sensationalist accounts of the Occupation, the book failed in its purpose. The ghosts of the so-called 'dark years' lived on, fanned by shocking revelations about Mitterrand's past, the trial of the Vichy functionary and Fifth Republic stalwart Maurice Papon, and quarrels among

Resistance survivors. In the early 1990s, no-one's reputation was sacrosanct. Not only was the Lyon-based resister Raymond Aubrac charged with having been a Gestapo agent, claims that he vigorously denied, de Gaulle's lieutenant Jean Moulin, murdered by the Gestapo in 1943, was variously accused of having been a Soviet mole and an American agent.[32]

Why was there this belated desire to rake over the past? For many years after the Liberation, the French people had sought comfort in the Gaullist notion of 'a nation of resisters'. Through his war memoirs, published successively throughout the 1950s, the general peddled the idea that the Vichy regime had been an aberration imposed on the nation by the victorious Germans.[33] The Pétain government thus had no legitimacy. This was embodied instead in the figure of de Gaulle himself who had raised the standard of resistance through his 'call to honour' of 18 June 1940. This line of reasoning received unexpected approval from members of the historical profession. With French settlers in Algeria seemingly intent on defying the wishes of Paris, and with former Vichyites returning to public life, scholars belonging to the Comité d'Histoire de la Deuxième Guerre Mondiale (CHDGM), a semi-official body created in 1951 and led by the eminent academic and former resister Henri Michel, shared similar designs to de Gaulle in wishing to portray the Resistance as a valiant struggle which embodied the Republican legitimacy. As Gildea observes, while they admitted that the Resistance had been the work of a 'minority', it had still enjoyed the tacit support of the majority, and had embraced those values which could be traced back to the *Declaration of the Rights of Man and the Citizen* of 1789.[34]

Given the agonising choices posed by the Occupation and the bitter memories it engendered, it was inevitable that the Gaullist myth would struggle to maintain a consensus, even during the 1950s. Among resisters themselves, there were so-called 'dissenting memories'.[35] Some were angry that their wartime sacrifice should have been subsumed in the broader myth of a 'nation of resisters', whereas others were furious that the PCF – the party of the *75,000 fusillés*, an entirely misleading reference to the numbers of Communist resisters killed in the struggle against Nazism – had tried to appropriate the badge of resistance for itself. The experience of Algeria only exacerbated divisions within the Resistance camp. There were those such as Claude Bourdet who saw echoes of Gestapo-like tactics in the behaviour of French paratroopers; others, notably Georges Bidault, believed that granting independence to the Arabs was akin to sacrificing France to Hitler. Nor was it merely former resisters who took issue with the reassuring legends articulated by de Gaulle and others. Amnesty laws of 1951 and 1953 facilitated the re-entry into public life of former Vichyites, among them Jean-Louis Tixier-Vignancour and Georges Albertini, all of whom sought to portray the Resistance as blood-thirsty partisans who had arbitrarily murdered some 100,000 people at the Liberation. There was also the ADMP. Never numbering more than a few thousand supporters, it has nonetheless counted some 22 ministers in its ranks and has continued to campaign for the same things: a revindication of the values of the National Revolution, the transfer of their hero's body to its 'proper' resting place at Verdun and a judicial rehabilitation of the marshal himself.

For the most part, such arguments among former resisters and Vichyites could be contained within the body politic and generated little excitement among the wider public. In the 1970s, however, two factors conspired to bring the memory of the Occupation centre stage. The first was Marcel Ophuls' film, *Le Chagrin et la Pitié*. Released in 1971, this four hour documentary interspersed interviews with contemporary newsreels of life in wartime Clermont-Ferrand, a town whose experiences were held to be typical of the Occupation. Originally made for television it was deemed, in the words of the head of French state broadcasting, dangerous to the 'people's well-being and tranquillity', and for many years it could only be viewed in a small-art-house cinema in Paris.[36] As Richard Golson has observed, the film has been credited with almost 'single-handedly shattering the Gaullist myth of the resistance.'[37] As Golsan continues, de Gaulle himself was virtually absent from the footage which focused instead on the defeatism of French officials, the limits of resistance, the troubling pro-Nazi sentiments of the collaborators, the casual antisemitism of many ordinary people, and the callous racism of Vichy officials. Significantly it made a tremendous impact among the younger generation which was born after the Occupation and which, in the wake of the 1968 protests, was not afraid to embarrass its elders. As one '68 slogan had pronounced 'We are all Jews now'.

Revelations about the wartime treatment of Jews contributed to the second factor which made the Occupation central to public debate: the emerging self-consciousness of France's Jewish population. During the 1970s, some 750,000 Jews were resident in France; as Tyler Stoval reminds us, outside of the USSR, this was the largest concentration anywhere in Europe. Previously lacking self-confidence, he writes, this community came to acquire a collective identity thanks to a multitude of reasons: the victory of Israel in the Six-Day War; the influx of Algerian

Jews who were less afraid to speak their mind; the rise of the extreme right and racist crime which resulted in a terrorist attack on a Parisian synagogue in 1980; and the growth of 'negationism', that is a denial of the Holocaust. Embarrassingly, negationism originated in France. In 1974 the onetime resister, Paul Rassinier, contested the existence of the gas chambers, not having seen these himself when incarcerated at Buchenwald; he forgot to add that this was essentially a labour camp and thus did not possess machines of mass extermination. Similar claims were made by Robert Faurisson in *Le Monde*. Such denials could not be tolerated by an emboldened Jewish community. Especially outspoken was the lawyer Serge Klarsfeld who, together with his wife Beate, went to considerable lengths to show Vichy's complicity in the round-up of Jews, a theme also tackled in Claude Lanzmann's eight-hour film, *Shoah*, which was first broadcast on French television in 1985.[38]

The ebbing away of the old Gaullist myths of resistance, the advent of a new generation with fewer hang-ups about the Second World War and the growing assertiveness of France's Jewish population, ensured that by the late 1970s interest in the Occupation had become an 'obsession'. In the academic world, historians built on the brilliant study of Robert Paxton, *Vichy France. Old Guard and New Order*, published in 1972 and translated into French the following year. Drawing on German archival sources, this book conclusively demonstrated that Vichy was very much a 'home-grown' experiement. Within the artistic world, the fashion was for the so-called *mode rétro*, effectively a forties revival in which filmmakers, such as Louis Malle in *Lacombe Lucien* (1974), and novelists, such as Patrick Modiano in *La Place de l'Etoile* (1968), revisited the 'dark years', highlighting the desperate choices that had dominated daily life under occupation, thus denting yet further patriotic images of 'a nation of resisters'. And in politics the press was extremely sensitive to any echoes of the past. There was outrage in 1971 when Pompidou pardoned the former Milice leader in the Rhône, Paul Touvier. He had hoped the incident would pass off unnoticed. Coming in the wake of the furore over *Le Chagrin et la Pitié*, the president's actions caused a scandal, as did the ramblings of the former head of Vichy's Commissariat for Jewish Affairs, Louis Darquier de Pellepoix, who, in a notorious interview for *L'Express* of 1978, claimed that only lice had been gassed at Auschwitz.

Vichy was, therefore, already ever-present in French politics by the time of Mitterrand's presidency, yet a series of factors ensured that it would receive even greater prominence. The first was the figure of the president himself. At the time of his election, he had won the support of former resisters, notably Colonel Passy, because he himself had been a resister. His earlier ambivalent role under Vichy could not, however, be hidden forever. Much of this history was already well publicised. More came to light: his involvement in the right-wing Croix de Feu; his participation in a 1935 demonstration against immigration; his support for marshal Pétain; his membership of the Légion Française des Combattants; and his work for Vichy's prisoners of war service, for which he received the *francisque*.[39] What was striking was that, in the early 1990s, Mitterrand spoke openly of his past: in a series of interviews with the historian Olivier Wieviorka and the journalist Pierre Péan.[40] These revealed that, since 1987, he had made a habit of honouring the Armistice by placing a wreath at the tomb of Pétain's grave; he further asserted that Vichy's *Statuts des juifs* had only targeted foreign Jews, something simply not true; and he confessed to a life-long friendship with René Bousquet, Vichy's chief of police.

While such actions help explain why he was reluctant to accept that the French state was in any sense responsible for the deportations of Jews an others – 'Vichy was an accidental regime', he declared in 1993 – why did he so readily confess his past?[41] It has been speculated that it was an act of catharsis by an old man laid low by prostate cancer. Others have suggested that he had become so corrupted by power that he could no longer differentiate between himself and his position as president which placed him above the law.[42] Curiously the mildest criticism came from members of the right. Although they did not look to Mitterrand as one of their heroes, they were all too aware of the ambivalent choices posed by the Occupation period. It was an awareness of these decisions that most readily explains the president's confessions. As Jackson writes, 'Now that the Gaullist myth was shattered, Mitterrand was suggesting that the alternative was not to assert that the French had all been traitors, but that they had had struggled for solutions in a difficult period.'[43] As Mitterrand himself declared, whereas de Gaulle might have represented France, in his various wartime roles as soldier, prisoner, escapee, citizen, Vichy administrator and resister, he had represented the French.[44] This was all very well, but it did nothing to excuse the president's claims that the French state had not been involved in the targeting of Jews and that only foreign refugees had suffered under the Germans. In an oft-quoted review of Péan's *Une jeunesse française* in the *New York Review of Books*, Tony Judt made the telling point that Mitterrand could never denounce the past altogether, as he would inevitably have to denounce himself.[45]

The very public trials of former Vichy officials conducted in the 1980s and 90s were another reason why the Occupation overshadowed Mitterrand's presidency. Many of these figures had already been in the dock at the Liberation, only to receive token sentences. Their retrial was made possible by a law of 1964 which stated that 'crimes against humanity' were not subject to a statute of limitations and by the indefatigable efforts of the Klarsfeld family who were determined to see justice finally done. The first to be indicted, in March 1979, was Jean Lequay, Bousquet's right-hand man, who was responsible for the deportations of thousands of Jews, closely followed by Papon, initially charged in 1983; Touvier hauled before magistrates in 1989; and Bousquet, arrested in 1991. Thanks to lengthy legal delays, some engineered by Mitterrand himself, it was some time before these men actually appeared before a judge. Leguay died in July 1989 before his case could be heard while Bousquet was killed by an assassin's bullet in 1993. So it was that the first man to experience the belated wrath of French justice was Klaus Barbie, head of the Gestapo in Lyon, who had murdered Jean Moulin and who had escaped justice by taking refuge in Bolivia where he was eventually tracked down in 1971. Tried in Lyon in May–July 1987, Barbie was accused of the particular charge of having deported 44 Jewish children from a Red Cross colony to Auschwitz, together with overseeing the final convoy from Lyon in August 1944. He was defended by the skilful and highly controversial left-wing barrister Jacques Vergès, who in 2004 stepped forward to defend Saddam Hussein. It was the claim of Vergès that the Resistance had been riddled by informers who were just as guilty for the death of Moulin as was Barbie. Part-Vietnamese, this provocative lawyer also had a political axe to grind by likening Barbie's actions in Lyon to French behaviour in Indo-China. None of this saved Barbie from life imprisonment.

Less straightforward was the case of Touvier, head of the Milice in the Rhône. In this capacity, he had notoriously overseen the murder of Victor Basch, the octogenarian president of the League of Rights of Man. After the war, he had taken refuge among religious houses run by integralist Catholics and received a pardon in 1971. Rearrested at a priory in Nice in 1989, and charged with the murder of seven Jews at Rillieux-la-Pape, it initially seemed as though the legal apparatus did not possess the will to convict as it was decreed that the offence he had committed did not technically fall under the heading of 'crimes against humanity'. In the court's eyes, for such a charge to stick he had to be working for 'a state practising a policy of ideological hegemony', something which, it was said, Vichy was not; it was argued instead that Vichy was extremely confused in its ideological trajectories. Only after extensive protests was Touvier at last tried and given a life tariff in 1994, the first Frenchman to be convicted of 'crimes against humanity'.

His trial hardly acted as a moment of catharsis as some had hoped. The spectacle of an old man in the dock, unable to understand half of what was going on around him, did not satiate a desire for justice and there was irritation that the prosecution had been forced to change its line of attack. Thanks to the earlier legal definition of Vichy, he was charged with working for the Gestapo not on behalf of the Pétain regime. Touvier was, in any case, a minor figure. The same could not be said about Papon, a senior wartime administrator at Bordeaux, who went on to serve as the prefects of Corsica and Constantine, before taking charge of the Parisian police force in 1961, in which capacity he had overseen the murder of Algerian demonstrators in the demonstration of 17 October that year, something not properly confronted at his 1998 trial. In 1978, he had served as a budget minister in the Barre cabinet and it was said he even held presidential ambitions. Having already seen off his accusers in 1983, he eventually stood trial in 1997, accused of complicity in the deportation of some 1,500 Jews from the Gironde. His defence argued that he had merely been an administrator: by staying at his post, he had prevented the Germans taking over the deportation machine and he had secretly saved several Jewish lives by failing to carry out orders. This did not save him from a life sentence in April 1998, but his failing heath prompted his release from prison and, in the appeal courts, his lawyers were successful in challenging his conviction, asserting that he had indeed been a mere bureaucrat.

The trials of public functionaries, together with the revelations about Mitterrand's Vichy past, deeply unsettled public opinion, and herein might lie another reason why the French have pawed over their collective past. As Paxton has suggested, with the abandonment of the Gaullist myth of a 'nation of resisters', it was no longer possible to argue that France had been a victor in the Second World War.[46] This was an unwelcome conclusion coming at a time in the 1980s when the nation, confronted by yet further European integration, was suffering 'acute anxiety' about its national identity. It was only natural, therefore, that it should revisit its past, notably the 'dark years' when so much of the country's traditions were on parade. There are others, however, who argue that this fixation is a means of avoiding any true confrontation with history. In their eyes, it has been all too easy to land the sins of the nation on the likes of Touvier, Papon and Leguay. There may well be something in this argument as the concentration on Vichy has also enabled the French to avoid another painful legacy, that of the Algerian war. Maybe, just maybe, with the Papon trial over, and with no other silver-haired defendants likely to enter the dock, France might now discover the will to move away from Vichy and come to terms with the goings-on in North Africa.

Race and the Far Right

Understanding why the issue of race came to dominate the Mitterrand years requires another exploration of the French past. As the birthplace of the *Declaration of the Rights of Man and the Citizen*, France was also the birthplace of modern nationalism. This document declared that the sovereignty of the nation resided in its people who were no longer subjects, subservient to the will of the crown, but citizens. Thus to become French it was necessary to become a citizen which meant accepting the revolutionary ideals of liberty, equality and fraternity. Theoretically the mantle of citizenship was open to anyone regardless of their social status, racial background and geographical origin, although significantly the revolutionaries were not keen to include women. It was on this basis that the Revolution convinced itself that, when it embarked on its wars of conquest in 1792 turning faraway parts of Europe into bits of France, it was spreading enlightenment. Paradoxically, French military successes in the German lands, in particular, provided a fillip for a different type of national identity, revolving round mystical notions of blood and the soil. Such German notions of identity never truly made much headway in the France of the nineteenth century, nor did the revolutionary concepts of citizenship. It was not difficult for foreigners to become 'French' and to enjoy the same rights as everyone else.

Matters changed under the Third Republic. Inspired by positivist notions of progress, this regime endeavoured to create a modern nation, technologically advanced, proud of its achievements, forward looking and willing to defend itself from foreign encroachment, a fear particularly acute after defeat at the hands of the Prussians in 1870. Accordingly great play was once again made of producing citizens, a process Eugen Weber described as turning 'peasants into Frenchmen'. In this environment the school, workplace and the army all became vehicles for the inculcation of French values, and to accept those values was to attain nationhood. Assimilation was the watchword, something at the heart of the first French Code of Nationality in 1889, and it was expected that communities from the outside, for instance Russian Jews escaping the Tsarist pogroms by taking refuge in Paris, would abide by French traditions and practice their religious and ethnic traditions in private. In this way, immigrants could eventually become French and escape some of the punitive legislative measures, largely relating to tax and residence, which had been introduced to favour French nationals over foreigners.

In this context, France acquired a deserved reputation for being a welcoming country for all manner of immigrants. In the 1920s, it received White Russians escaping Bolshevik excesses, together with a huge influx of southern European and North Africans who, it was hoped, would make good the labour shortfall created by demographic decline and losses in the First World War; and before 1939, thousands of Spanish Republicans, on the run from Franco, made their way across the Pyrenees. As Vicki Caron has shown, this is not to say that France was free of xenophobia.[47] This was especially fierce in the Depression years when Algerians, Portuguese, Spaniards and Italians were accused of stealing French jobs, and the Vichy episode depressingly revealed how a biological racism, closely resembling that of the Nazis, had gained a foothold among elements of the far right. After the war, France accepted another influx of immigration, again largely from southern Europe. Overseen by the newly created Office National d'Immigration (ONI), these economic migrants made a telling contribution to the *trente glorieuses*. When the golden years came to an end, sometime in the early 1970s, French workers were again fearful for their jobs. Giscard responded by enforcing severe restrictions on immigration from non-EEC countries, even preventing the reuniting of families. Repatriation packages were quickly devised offering money to those who returned to their country of birth.

Notwithstanding this legislation, a steady flow of immigration, both legal and illegal, continued, primarily from the former colonies of the Maghreb: Tunisia, Morocco and Algeria. France also accepted large number of political refugees fleeing from war-torn African states, together with Vietnamese Boat people, and at last permitted the relatives of earlier immigrants to rejoin their families in France. So the number of immigrants in France more or less doubled between 1946 and 1990. Quoting the statistics of the Haut Conseil à l'Intégration, Cathie Lloyd recounts that there were 1.74 million immigrants in France at the start of the Fourth Republic and 4.16 million by 1990, although the proportion to the overall population had hardly changed since 1931, standing between six and eight per cent.[48] Of these ethnic groups, the largest were the Portuguese (649,000), closely followed by the Algerians (614,000) and Moroccans (572,000) whose numbers were swelled by second and third generations, children and grandchildren born to the first generation of North African arrivals. Lastly, recounts Lloyd, we should not forget the 340,000 from the DOM-TOMS now living on metropolitan soil, although these are not technically counted as immigrants because they possess French citizenship.

Inevitably the presence of large numbers of immigrants, especially Africans, gave rise to popular anxieties, especially during the recession years of the 1980s when several large towns witnessed rioting between white and non-white youths. The familiar refrain was that such newcomers were stealing French jobs, even though they were always the first to be sacked when the going got tough and suffered much higher levels of unemployment than other groups. More fundamentally Africans, especially from the Maghreb, were feared because of their racial distinctiveness. The colour of their skin, their 'strange' habits, and their language marked them out as outsiders. The fact that many of them congregated in specific geographical areas, often in crumbling HLMs on the outskirts of major cities, further underlined their distinctiveness. The violence of their lives on such estates was vividly captured in Jean-François Richet's film, *Ma 6T va crack-er*, which caused an uproar when released.[49] Even the one million or so second-generation immigrants, so-called *beurs* and *beurettes*, raised in state schools and largely accepting of French culture, were suspect, especially during the first Gulf War of 1991 when it was feared they might constitute a fifth column. It is telling that such men and women have often held on to vestiges of their traditional cultures, notably their Islamic faith, as a means of combating racial prejudice.

Without doubt Islam, that traditional bugbear of Christian Europe, has been the other reason why African immigrants have been so resented. Islam is now the second religion within France, counting 5 million devotees, the overwhelming majority being Sunni Muslims. Questioned about their faith in 1994, 42 per cent claimed to be vigilant in their practice, 36 per cent said they were believers, and 16 per cent, a proportion higher among the young, admitted they had no faith. Maybe it has been the ability of Islam to hold on to its flock, in contrast to Catholicism which has witnessed a steady slippage of believers since the 1960s, that has given rise to resentment, yet other reasons have been at play. The legacy of the Algerian war, and the presence of *pieds noirs* in areas such as Marseille and Toulon, has made acceptance of Muslims difficult; it was not forgotten that in colonial Algeria abandonment of Islam was one sure means of assimilating French culture. Nor has the rise of Islamic fundamentalism helped matters. The Iranian revolution of 1979, the founding of the FIS in Algeria ten years later, the Gulf War in 1991 and the spate of terrorist outrages in Paris during the 1980s and 90s (for instance the attempt to hijack a plane at Marseille airport in 1994 and crash it into the Eiffel tower, a chilling portent of 9/11) convinced many that the Muslim faith was a value system entirely at odds with French culture.

Despite these fears, Mitterrand spoke of 'le droit à la différence', an acceptance of multicultural pluralism, and an acknowledgement that his government sought integration rather than assimilation. To this end, the Socialists passed a series of bills granting freedoms to immigrants, for instance the ability to establish clubs and charities on an ethnic basis and the right for immigrants to teach their indigenous language within their own schools.[50] Yet government-led initiatives since the early 1980s have displayed little consistency. Both left and right have feared being seen as soft in the face of immigration, both have been perturbed by the rise in immigrants, and both have been frightened by the rise of the extremist Front National. It was partially to offset the rise of extreme right that, on coming to power in 1986, Chirac revived Giscard's policy of offering financial inducements to immigrants to return to their homeland. Certainly France was a less welcoming place under the new administration. Chirac's interior minister Charles Pasqua, himself of Corsican origin, quickly tightened entry restrictions on foreigners, and further envisaged stripping children born of immigrant parents of entitlement to French citizenship. This latter proposal foundered thanks to the opposition of centre-left deputies, the demonstrations organised by the protest group SOS Racisme and the obstruction of Mitterrand himself.

On regaining power in 1988, Mitterrand and the Socialists had to consider the recommendations of the government-sponsored Long Commission, established two years earlier, which proposed a toughening of the rules by which immigrants became French. The anger of Pasqua and his followers at the failure of the Socialists to act on these recommendations was soon overshadowed by the so-called headscarves affair of 1989 when a headteacher in Creil, Paris, invoked the secular laws prohibiting the ostentatious display of religious symbols in public buildings, to ban a trio of Muslim girls from wearing the *foulard*, or headscarf.[51]

When other establishments copied this example, Jospin called for tolerance, and the girls were readmitted, although the education minister
added that he saw little reason why the French model should be openly
flouted. Such sentiments were echoed elsewhere among the left, which
also believed the headscarf was demeaning to women, underscoring
their inferior status to men. It was the right, hitherto a fierce critic of the
secular bases of French education, that reopened the matter, thus raising suspicions that the implementation of laic legislation was racially
driven. Soon after the right's return to power in 1993, some 80 girls
were expelled for their wearing of the *foulard*. This prompted a ruling
from the Conseil d'Etat which stated that it was up to headteachers to
prove the scarf was being worn provocatively as a religious symbol. This
might have calmed matters matters, but did not prevent further expulsions: in November 1994, 24 girls from secondary schools in Maintes-
la-Joile and Lille were expelled; early the following year, further
expulsions centred round the Collège Xavier-Bichat in Natua. Eventually
in July 1995 another statement from the Conseil d'Etat ruled that the
wearing of the headscarf itself was not in itself 'ostentatious'. Students
could only be sent down if they combined the headscarf with provocative behaviour. This did not put an end to the matter. In 2004, the right-
wing Raffarin government, in the wake of the 9/11 outrage and the
second Iraq war, revisited and further tightened the legislation. This was
despite the fact that most girls have, so to speak, kept their heads down,
abandoning the *foulard* in the classroom.

   The headscarves affair was quickly followed by further crackdowns on
immigrants, legal or otherwise: the implementation of the Long proposals, the initiation of random police checks to uncover illegal aliens, and
the rescinding of the asylum rights. As the police combed the immigrant
districts of Paris, in August 1996 over 300 Africans congregated in the
Church of St Bernard at the heart of the capital. Fearing deportation
unless their papers were regularised, they undertook a hunger strike
and won the sympathy of many, including the archbishop of Paris. The
government's response was to order the police into the church, truncheons to hand, conjuring up unfortunate memories of the Occupation
when the police had colluded in the round-up of Jews. The subsequent
inability to prove cases against these asylum-seekers made the affair look
even grubbier, and there was hope that the Socialists, reelected in 1997,
would rescind the Pasqua legislation. In the event, the new government
failed to act decisively. Despite granting an amnesty to 150,000 illegal
immigrants, and despite revoking the infamous Debré law of 1997 which

stipulated that anyone housing foreigners should alert the authorities, the government was wary of public opinion. It thus kept open the squalid internment camp at Calais, Sangatte, housing asylum seekers, largely from eastern Europe, hoping that Britain would eventually accept the majority of these unwelcome visitors.

The inconsistency of government policy has undermined the assimilation process. While perfume manufacturers such as Clarins might have used black models to promote their product,[52] the reality is that in the workplace immigrants are clearly discriminated against. Statistics, quoted by John Ardagh, reveal that, in the late 1990s, the national unemployment rate was 12 per cent, yet it was 30 per cent among Maghrebis. Among young black Africans, unemployment was running as high as 50 per cent.[53] And within the world of work immigrants have usually had to accept menial occupations. Although the majority are admittedly poorly qualified, they remain woefully under-represented among the intellectual professions (law, medicine, and the civil service). Women immigrants, in particular, have found the job market an unwelcoming place. Discrimination is further apparent in the housing sector where North Africans, lacking a steady job, have discovered it difficult to find places even in HLMs. When spaces have been found, these HLMs, such as that of Les Bousquets, east of Paris, have become ghettos shunned by white inhabitants. To gain a sense of the fear these ghettos generate among white middle-class Parisians, it is only necessary to read Michel Houelbecque's novel *Plateforme* in which a high-profile tourism company, paradoxically arranging expensive holidays in the Far East and Africa, operates out of the suburbs, paying for its employees to go home in taxis rather than dare the RER where muggers congregate.[54] Perhaps the one success in racial integration has been the recent success of the French national football team which in 1998 won the World Cup, followed by Euro 2000. The team was overwhelmingly represented by players originating from former colonies, notably Zinedine Zidane (nicknamed 'Zizou'), the son of an Algerian immigrant who had settled in the La Castellane district of Marseille, a maze of tower blocks which had earned a reputation as a *quartier difficile*.[55]

The corollary to the rise of immigration has been the emergence of the far right. De Gaulle had been largely succeeded in neutering the extremists; with de Gaulle gone, in 1972 the former parachutist and Poujadist Jean-Marie Le Pen established the FN. Largely an irrelevance during the 1970s – Le Pen scored a pitiful 0.7 per cent in first ballot of the 1974 presidential elections – the Front's moment came in 1981 with the victory of the Socialists. Although he did badly in the presidential ballot that year, a growing fear of the left, coupled with the economic downturn of 1983, enabled his party to secure a small number of victories in the municipal elections that year, as well as winning a local by-election at Dreux, a town with a large immigrant population. Success was in the offing. In 1984, the Front managed 11 per cent of the vote in the European elections and returned ten members to Brussels; in the 1986 parliamentary elections, it secured 9.7 per cent of the votes which, thanks to Mitterrand's introduction of proportional representation, translated into 35 seats; in 1988, public opinion was shocked when in 1988 Le Pen attained 14.4 per cent of the poll in the first presidential ballot, coming only fractionally behind Raymond Barre and easily outstripping the Communist André Lajoinie, although in the legislative elections that same year his party managed one seat, primarily because the system of proportional representation, brought in by Mitterrand, was abandoned.

It was obvious, however, that, unlike previous right-wing phenomena (Boulangism, the extra-parliamentary leagues of the 1930s, Pétainism and Poujadism) the Front was here to stay. It won 14 per cent of the vote in the 1989 European elections, 12 per cent in the 1993 parliamentary ballot, and 15 per cent of voters rallied to Le Pen in the first round of the 1995 presidential elections. In 1999 the Front split, divided over electoral tactics. Alienated by Le Pen's autocratic behaviour and unwillingness to forge alliances with the mainstream right, supporters of Bruno Mégret broke off to form the Mouvement National Républicain (MNR).[56] Le Pen was nonplussed. As we shall see, in the 2002 presidential elections, he came second in the first round, outscoring the Socialist Jospin, and ensuring that he was in the run-off with Chirac. Although there was no possibility of him securing the most glittering of prizes, Le Pen's success caused a furore and indicated that not all was well in political life.

While the Front's vote might have fluctuated over the years, political commentators have identified a number of constants in its support.[57] First, they have noted a Caen-Montpellier dividing line. West of this divide the Front has struggled; to the east, it has done well, notably in Alsace and Provence, and those towns with high levels of immigrants, for instance Marseille, Toulon, Avignon and Nice. In terms of its voters, the Front does much better among men than it does among women. Support is spread across all age groups yet has been noticeably stronger among those in the 18–35 year old bracket, although less so in the 2002 elections. Most social groups may be identified in its constituency, which has broadened since the early days when it recruited chiefly among *pieds noirs*, onetime Poujadists, nationalist Catholics, former Pétainists and extreme radicals. Nonetheless, the core of its voters have stemmed from the petty *bourgeoisie* (shopkeepers, artisans, clerical workers, and farmers, traditionally groups most susceptible to parties offering instant panaceas to complex problems). Since 1999 it has attracted industrial workers who have feared for their livelihoods, although some of that backing tailed off in the 2002 presidential elections. More consistently, there has been a smattering of middle-class support, especially among integralist Catholics who would once have supported Action Française; yet generally Catholics have shied away from the Front, put off by its crude sermonising on race, as have many professionals. Teachers, trade unionists, ENA graduates, political commentators emphasise, are not its natural supporters.

The way in which the Front has unashamedly played to the gallery is one of the reasons behind its growth. It has answers to everything, particularly the problems thrown up by post-industrial society – unemployment, alienation, drugs, AIDS – and it has been all too easy to pin these ills on the immigrant population. Certain safety nets which had previously protected France from the far right have also crumbled, among them a decline of religion. There is a paradox here. Le Pen has regularly bemoaned the waning of Catholic values, sidestepping the fact that the Church has a proud assimilationist tradition, helping outsiders to adapt. The far left was another traditional restraint on the far right, but with the decline of Communism many natural militants have gravitated to the Front rather than to the PCF. More crucially, disenchantment with the main parties has benefited Le Pen. The parliamentary right has been seen as too soft on 'foreigners and crime', while the Socialists have been criticised for being out of touch with their traditional constituency of white, industrial workers whose lives have been blighted by immigration. Both left and right have been condemned for moving France closer to Europe, another reason for the Front's rise. At a time when France is becoming less French, Le Pen has trumpeted those national values purportedly threatened by the faceless bureaucrats in Brussels and Strasbourg. And there is finally Le Pen himself. He is undeniably a charismatic figure whose rabble-rousing speeches project an authority even if the solutions he proffers are both frightening and naïve. He has won particular support for speaking out on issues which mainstream politicians have shied away, most obviously immigration.

This brazen behaviour has also enabled him to overcome a series of scandals, some financial, some social (his former wife appeared naked in *Playboy*) and some political. His remark that the Holocaust was merely a 'detail' in the history of the Second World War was especially offensive. Even more disappointing has been the response of the mainstream parties to such statements. All too often they have allowed him to legitimate areas of debate, and they have then not found the language to match his ready-made answers.

More generally, historians have struggled to make sense of the Front's political characteristics. As H. G. Simmons pointed out, it has championed so many causes that it is not easy to label,[58] although that has not stopped some political scientists from suggesting that it really is a 'single-issue movement', obsessed with the question of race.[59] Because it has embraced so many causes, and provides a home for such an array of the discontented, it is also possible to view the FN as a 'protest party', ready to give the establishment a much-needed kick at any moment. In this sense, it seems to have supplanted the PCF, the most venerable of protest parties, whose vote now seems in free-fall, some of it going over to Le Pen.

In all of these debates there has been a reluctance, at least among scholars in France, to call the Front fascist. This is largely because historians and political scientists have cast doubts on whether a French fascism has ever existed. They have generally accepted the notion, first articulated by René Rémond, that the history of the French right has been a continuum made up of three constituent parts: Legitimism, Orleanism and Bonapartism.[60] Viewed from this perspective, the Front has been interpreted as a further manifestation of the Bonapartist tradition: a noisy, intensely nationalistic movement, organised on an authoritarian base. A variant of this argument, suggested by Pierre Milza, has been to define the Front as a form of 'national populism', a phenomenon which emerged after the Boulanger affair of the 1880s. In essence, 'national populism' may be defined as a form of mass right-wing politics, contemptuous of the establishment and eager to deploy new forms of political discourse, such as mass rallies, sloganeering and propaganda.[61]

All too often debates about fascism in France have degenerated into semantics, yet among Anglophone historians there is a consensus that, within France, a distinct fascism began to emerge in the 1930s. For some, this is a tradition the Front has continued. As Jim Wolfreys has argued, the Front has all the characteristics of a new form of French fascism.[62] In its origins, he writes, the party's founder deliberately aped

Doriot's Parti Populaire Français (PPF) of the 1930s, setting out to create a radical movement which allowed members, both officially and unofficially, to infiltrate important sectors of society such as town halls, trade unions and chambers of commerce. The aim has been to achieve durability, something largely accomplished (although how the FN will fare after the death of Le Pen remains uncertain) and mass support, less forthcoming (in 1993, it possibly had 60,000 members). Moreover, in its ideology the Front has all the hallmarks of fascism, continues Wolfreys. Despite standing in elections, it favours an authoritarian republic; it is fundamentally 'anti-egalitarian', preferring instead an oligarchical society comprising elites which the party itself would monopolise; it is rabidly xenophobic, its championing of *la préférence national* a rebuttal of all those elements (notably immigrants and Jews) who have worked to undermine French identity; and, in its economic policy, it is fundamentally anti-liberal, advocating instead a type of popular capitalism over which the state would rule supreme. To all extents and purposes, he concludes, the Front represents a type of neo-fascism.

Not everyone is convinced. Fascism was the product of a particular set of historical circumstances of the 1930s; the origins of the Front lie elsewhere, for instance in Poujadism; it still includes too many disparate elements to be given any one label; it plays the parliamentary game and seems content to operate within the system however much it despises that system. The one comforting factor is that, despite the recent success of Le Pen in the 2002 elections, the Front has never managed to harness, and hold on to, much more than 12–14 per cent of the popular vote. It has even been speculated that the Front does not truly want power, lending support to the view that it really sees itself as a protest party. Whatever the case, it has not come close to power in the manner of other extremist groups in Europe such as Jörg Haider's Freedom Party in Austria and Pym Fortune's List in the Netherlands. And it may be that as France becomes ever more a part of Europe, the Front will become ever more marginalised. It is to be hoped.

France and Europe

Six years into Mitterrand's first *septennat*, the influential historian of France Stanley Hoffmann famously suggested that, in his foreign policy, the president was little more than a reincarnation of de Gaulle.[63] There were undoubtedly similarities. The pursuit of French *grandeur*, the advocacy of the nation state, the retention of a *force de frappe*, the maintenance of good relations with former African colonies – these were all features of the Mitterrand years. Yet not everything was the same. It is possible to see several subtle differences, especially in France's relationship with the USA and Europe.

At least in France's relationship with the Third World it is possible to spot continuity with the past, even if the rhetoric was initially different. On election in 1981 Mitterrand appointed Jean-Pierre Cot, the son of Pierre Cot, one of the stalwarts of the Popular Front, Minister of Co-operation (in essence, says Lacouture, Minister for Africa). It was a brave move. A close associate of Rocard, a communist sympathiser, a supporter of Amnesty International and highly principled, he was minded to end the shabby neo-colonialism practised by Mitterrand's predecessors. To this end, he criticised human rights abuses, ensured that money invested in overseas aid programmes was not diverted into the coffers of African dictators, and cut Third World debt. It could not last. In 1982, a row erupted over the visit of Guinea's dictator Sekou Touré to Paris, and Cot resigned. In truth, this episode was merely a pretext for resignation. An argument had earlier brewed over Cot's plans to extend the fiefdom of his ministry so as to concentrate less on Africa and more on the Third World generally, in particular Latin America.[64] It must be added that the African leaders themselves did not like the new regime. Outwardly Cot's successor Christian Nucci embraced the cause of the Third World, establishing a Carrefour de Développement, to highlight the many hardships faced by emerging African nations. However, on taking over the Cooperation portfolio in 1986, Michel Aurillac discovered numerous accounting 'anomalies'. Money destined for Africa had instead gone to the Isère, where it had been used to buy Nucci a large house and pay for political favours, a scam which would eventually see him court, only to be pardoned by an amnesty law of 1989. Unruffled Mitterrand and his associates continued to speak of regenerating Africa, yet in reality practised a neo-colonialism little different to before. Support continued for some particularly brutish regimes, notably Omar Bongo in the Gabon and Mobuto Sese Seko, dictator of Zaire. Described by one minister as 'a walking bank balance with a leopard-skin cap', the corrupt Mobutu managed to hold on to power until 1997, largely thanks to French aid.[65] Even more squalid was the support lent to the pro-French Hutu regime of Juvénal Habyarimana in the former Belgian colony of Rwanda. When, in 1990, guerillas from the rival Tutsi tribe, congregated in the Rwanda Patriotic Front (RPF) and invaded from neighbouring Uganda, France was not slow to lend military support to Habyarimana, although it was claimed that this support was merely humanitarian in nature. There was subsequently much embarrassment in Paris when, in 1994, the Rwandan leader was assassinated, most likely by a French missile fired by a Tutsi soldier. This intensified the bloodbath in which Hutu militia groups, armed with machetes and French weaponry, and instructed by the national radio station, massacred Tutsis, murdering up to 800,000 and earning the chilling name *génocidaires* in the process, although it should be remembered that Tutsis also slaughtered Hutus. French troops on the ground (and for that matter the pitifully small numbers of UN peacekeepers, a mere 250 at one point) did little to stop the rapes, killings and floods of refugees who made for Tanzania. Ultimately, French backing for the Hutu regime could not stop an RPF victory. It is perhaps fortunate for the reputation of France that there are fewer unpleasant dictators left in Africa to support and that those who remain look increasingly to the USA.

Under Mitterrand France, too, looked increasingly across the Atlantic, a real shift in the focus of French foreign policy. As Gildea summarises, four factors brought about a shift in Franco-American relations, enabling the left to overcome at least some of its traditional worries about American imperialism.[66] First, he writes, the presence of Communists in government made Mitterrand determined to demonstrate France's 'commitment to NATO' so as to reassure the US and make life 'unbearable' for the PCF itself. Second, the Soviets were undergoing another of their periodic phases of unpopularity among left-wing intellectuals who were appalled at recent Russian initiatives: the 1979 invasion of Afghanistan and the crushing of the pro-democracy movement Solidarity in Poland. By contrast, among French youth, all things American were the rage. As a personal memoir, the author recalls meeting in 1985 with a large number of French students who were dismissive of Margaret Thatcher yet enamoured of Ronald Reagan. Third, the intensification of the arms race, posed some hard choices about nuclear weapons which many Socialists had previously opposed. Once in power, Mitterrand saw how the deployment of further US nuclear missiles on European soil – not French, that was asking too much – would facilitate the transfer of scientific know-how and discourage the West Germans from any policy of neutralism. As mentioned earlier in chapter three, the refusal to station such weapons on French soil ensured that France never saw a peace movement evolve in the way it did in West Germany and Britain. There would be no Greenham Common in France; instead anti-nuclear protestors had to travel half way round the world to protest against French nuclear testing in Polynesia, hence the *Rainbow Warrior* affair. When in 1987 the USSR and USA agreed to disassemble much of their nuclear arsenal in Europe, Mitterrand was alarmed fearing that French rockets would be decommissioned on the negotiating table. Finally, writes Gildea, the escalating crisis in the Gulf brought France increasingly into the American orbit. Although traditionally pro-Arab, in 1991 Mitterrand considered that he had little option but to provide French troops for the US-led coalition which had assembled to overturn the recent Iraqi invasion of Kuwait, even though this policy provoked the resignation of defence minister, Chevènement. Indeed, there were always limits to how far France was prepared to toe the American line but, with the ending of the Cold War, Paris increasingly understood that it could no longer attempt to assert an independence of the two superpowers, and that it had little option but to back the USA. This has not stopped France from attempting to beef up the defence possibilities of the European Union (EU), notably through the West European Union (WEU) which would at least offer some measure of independence from NATO and Washington. This, however, has not proved an easy ride.

It was in the relationship with Brussels that Mitterrand brought about a real shift with the result that he, more than any other French president, helped shape the destiny of Europe, although little of this could have been foreseen at his election in 1981. Then his priority was the pursuit of the *110 Propositions*, and many of his supporters argued that his primary concern should be domestic reform. Moreover, Mitterrand was not known for his burning interest in Europe, even though he reputedly said to Roland Dumas, his new minister for European Affairs, that 'together we are going to dig Europe out of the mud.'[67] These remarks were indeed strange. In his earlier incarnation as a Fourth Republic politician, Mitterrand had been preoccupied with empire, believing that France's destiny lay in providing leadership in the southern Mediterranean by which, notes Cole, he also meant North Africa.[68] When in the 1960s and 70s decolonisation forced him to think closer to home, there was little to distinguish his notion of European integration from that of de Gaulle, Pompidou and Giscard. Like them, he opposed opening the doors of the Community to all and sundry, especially Portugal and Spain whose inclusion he eventually countenanced only to placate West Germany. A small Europe was, in his mind, a manageable Europe. He further considered that the mantle of European leadership fell naturally on Paris and Bonn; Margaret Thatcher's behaviour merely confirmed him in his belief that Britain would weaken institutional structures. Not that he was a federalist. He championed the rights of national governments and was innately suspicious of European bodies even when they were headed by a fellow Frenchman, such as when Jacques Delors became president of the Commission in 1985.

It was Delors who, two years earlier, had focused Mitterrand's attention on Europe. The deflationary policies undertaken by his finance minister had made plain that France could no longer pursue economic policies independent of its international partners. If France had to take wider notice of what was happening in the world, then it was only right that it should fulfil its natural role as a leader in international affairs. It was this in mind that Mitterrand abandoned earlier limited projects, designed to realise such elusive projects as a 'social European space', and reprofiled himself as the forward-thinking, good European. This 'conversion' was aided by several other developments in 1984: France's six-month tenure of the European Council, the sloughing off of Communist support in the Assembly, and a dislike of Britain's constant carping over the CAP. With the faithful Dumas at his side as Minister for European Affairs, with Delors at the Commission, and with Helmut Kohl a valued partner, Mitterrand argued for a more tightly-knit Europe founded on federal ideals. With the victory of Chirac in the polls in 1986, and the onset of *cohabitation*, the president had in any case little choice but to focus on international matters. One additional factor concentrated the president's mind on Europe: the coming together of the two Germanys following the collapse of East European Communism in 1989. Born in the middle of the First World War, and a former resister, Mitterrand knew all too well the dangers of German expansionism, and he did not embrace reunification with any enthusiasm, although he did acknowledge the right of nations to self-determination. In the president's mind, the race was on to tie the new Germany ever more firmly to the European ideal lest it became a monster state, dwarfing France in terms of its demographic, economic and military power.

Although the reunification of Germany lay in the future, Mitterrand's interest in Europe resulted in French backing for the Single European Act (SEA) of 1987. Aware that European leaders were at sixes and sevens on such issues as a common defence policy and single currency, Delors sought to establish the ideal of a single market by promoting 'les quatre libertés', that is the free movement of goods, services, capital and people. To ensure that these developments were not thwarted by economic weaklings within the Community, the SEA also reformed the decision-making processes of European institutions. Most famously, within the European Council – the chief law-making body within the Community, comprising ministers from each of the member states – it abandoned unanimous voting to embrace Qualified Majority Voting (QMV). In the public presentation of the SEA, however, this political dimension was deliberately downplayed lest it exacerbated fears about national sovereignty, just as it did in the UK where, as John Campbell writes, Margaret Thatcher reconciled herself to the SEA primarily because it promoted deregulation and free enterprise.[69] This may also explain why Chirac, whose government had to steer the SEA through parliament, supported the Delors initiative, although dyed-in-the-wool Gaullists fretted that France had permitted 'a breach in the national veto'.[70] For the Socialists, however, arguments about liberal economics and national sovereignty were not all dominant. For them the SEA, and the Single European Market (SEM) it created, was a recognition that French businesses could no longer be protected by a *dirigiste* economic policy which provided state subsidies, cheap loans and guaranteed contracts. Economic development, in an age of increased global competition, was best achieved through the promotion of this huge internal market which would facilitate shared European endeavours and the overhauling of French concerns.

The next step in the relaunching of the European ideal was, of course, the Treaty on European Union (TEU), better known as the Maastricht Treaty. This comprised three 'pillars'. The first sought to consolidate the single market and strengthen infrastructural concerns (for instance, the CAP) by the gradual abandonment of fixed exchange rates – the Exchange Rate Mechanism (ERM) – which would be replaced by a single currency, eventually known as the euro, overseen by the European and Montery Union (EMU), essentially a central European bank.[71] As Anne Sa'Sadah reminds us, in these 'communitised areas', policy would be initiated by the European Commission; decisions would then be made by the European Council and European Parliament, QMV being the rule throughout. The second pillar looked towards the founding of a Common Foreign and Security Policy (CFSP) building on the WEU, something now thought possible with the ending of the Cold War although, as already remarked, agreement over foreign policy has proved as difficult as ever. And, finally, the third pillar recognised that the easier movement of people and goods and the abandonment of border controls required some supervisory body which was provided in the shape of the intergovernmental Justice and Home Affairs (JHA).[72]

The Treaty was, in turn, put to the French electorate in a referendum of 20 September 1992. As Alain Guyomarch and others write, outwardly the vote was designed to persuade the people of the merits of greater integration and incorporation of TEU within the constitution. Mitterrand's real intention was to highlight the divisions over Europe among his opponents and deflect attention from the unpopular aspects of his reign, notably the corruption scandals, high unemployment, the general lack of trust in the political elites and the failure to curb Serbian excesses in Yugoslavia.[73] Reminiscent of Munich in 1938, Maastricht cut through traditional party divides. While the Communists and the FN were naturally opposed, the Socialists, Greens, UDF and Gaullists were internally divided, albeit to different degrees, troubled by the apparent threats to national sovereignty. Thus voters had few steers from party leaders, and tended to follow their instincts, ensuring the overall vote was a close run thing: 51 per cent in favour, 49 opposed. As a survey for *Le Monde* of 25 September 1992 illustrated (neatly summarised by Guyomarch and others), several variables were identifiable in the decision making.[74] Regionally, they write, there was a clear town-countryside divide. 'No' votes were heavily cast in rural areas – for instance Picardy, where farmers had deep reservations about reforms to the CAP. Conservatives, gathered together in the Chasse, Pêche, Nature, Tradition ('Hunting, Fishing, Nature and Tradition') (CPNT) movement, were also opposed, angered that Brussels had curbed some of their bloodsports. In the towns, well-qualified professionals were more likely to support Maastricht, aware of how their own careers and living standards could be advanced by greater integration, although small shopkeepers and businessmen were extremely apprehensive, fearing the loss of state subsidies. Politically, the centre generally supported TEU while the extremes (both the Communists and the Le Pennistes) were opposed. Significantly Chirac, after much soul-searching, was pro-Maastricht, perhaps a vital factor in the victory of the 'yes' vote. Although it meant breaking a cherished Gaullist tenet of retaining state control over the national currency, he believed this was the best way to further his presidential ambitions in 1995 and of curbing German pretensions; in the event, Europe was hardly an issue in the campaign. Ideologically, there also appears to have been a division between liberals and authoritarians. The latter, inclined to support the death penalty and the secular laws on the headscarf, were generally 'no' voters. And, finally, there was a religious divide. Thanks to the lingering influence of MRP, a majority of Catholics favoured the integrationist path. It is significant that traditionally strong Catholic areas such as Brittany voted for the TEU (59.85 per cent 'yes', 40.14 per cent 'no').

Maastricht would not be easily forgotten. Europe had been presented to the public; it would not go away; and since there has been a hardening of positions. In the 1994 European elections, there was a five per cent increase in the numbers of French who visited the polls, while in the remainder of the European community participation was down. A prominent feature of these was the success of de Villiers, an independent-minded centre right deputy, who ran on an anti-European ticket, scoring 12.3 per cent of the vote. Yet, among society's elites, there has since been a wide-scale acceptance of the European ideal. On displacing the Socialists in 1993, Balladur pursued similar objectives, undertaking preparations for EMU and signing up to the General Agreement on Trade and Tariffs (GATT). We shall see in chapter seven how Chirac subsequently built on these initiatives overseeing the adoption of the euro, although like Mitterrand, this attention to international issues was in part prompted by *cohabitation*.

Conclusion: The Mitterrand Legacy

Evaluating the Mitterrand years is no easy task. After the excitement of 1981, and the far- reaching reforms executed during his first two years in office, his presidency came to be marked by a series of disappointments, beginning with the sharp U-turn in economic policy in 1984. Some of this disappointment came to be symbolised in the figure of Mitterrand himself. Increasingly dogged by ill-health, the one-time saviour of the French left had been unmasked as corrupt, a Vichy sympathiser and a friend of some unseemly people. It might well have been better for his reputation if he had not stood for a second term in office, although he agreed with Saint Just, the Jacobin revolutionary, that one could never rule 'innocently'.[75] Less able to initiate policy himself, especially after the *cohabitation* period of 1986–88, other issues came to dominate the political scene notably immigration, the legacy of the past and corruption in high places. In this swirl of discontents, it was no surprise that the FN should have flourished. Nonetheless, Mitterrand's contribution was, on balance, a positive rather than a negative one. The presence of a Socialist in the Elysée was another step in the maturation of the Fifth Republic as was the experience of the *cohabitation* something which many had dreaded. Through his leadership in Europe, Mitterrand was also a powerful figure in the transformation of France itself. As several commentators have pointed out, France is still distinct in several regards, yet it cannot be denied that it is less different than before. The division of left and right is less strong than previously and, despite the rise of the Front, the extremes are largely marginalised, witness the condition of the Communist party. No longer is the French state so centralist and, in its economic policy, it more or less resembles any other Western industrialised democracy. It could be argued that such changes would have happened anyway, thanks to the phenomenon of globalisation. Yet Mitterrand appreciated the limits in which he operated and was a master in the art of the possible.

Chapter 7: Le Chagrin: *Chirac's Presidency, 1995–2002*

Notwithstanding the fact that this chapter was written only a short time after the events had happened, it seems unlikely that historians and political scientists will look back on Chirac's first presidency (1995–2002) as an especially distinguished period in the history of the Fifth Republic. This is not to say that it was without its share of excitement. It was once more a period of *cohabitation*, yet this was entirely unnecessary. For reasons still not fully understood, but most likely in an attempt to catch his opponents on the backfoot, in 1997 Chirac took the unusual step of prematurely dissolving the National Assembly even though the government enjoyed a majority. Much to his astonishment, the voters duly returned a left-dominated Assembly forcing him to accept the Socialist Lionel Jospin as his prime minister. As commentators have argued, this blatant use of elections for short-term political gain smacked of the kind of partisanship that historic Gaullism had stood against. Was France in danger of reverting to the bad old days of the Fourth Republic? In another echo of an unhappy past, under Chirac the office of president seemed enfeebled. Having coveted the Elysée for so long, soon after assuming power he seemed incapable of controlling events. Not only had he lost the government's majority, he was also deserted by several of his close lieutenants who were deeply divided over Europe. To make matters worse he himself was mired in scandal, and came perilously close to prosecution. He was rescued by the 2002 presidential elections in which the racist Le Pen managed to outpoll Jospin so as to enter the second round of voting.

Inevitably, in 2002, there was much talk of crisis and even the possibility of a Sixth Republic. As in the past, such talk was misleading. Cooler heads understood that, in the presidential run-off, Le Pen had no chance of beating Chirac, and so it proved.[1] The legislative elections, conducted shortly afterwards, dealt Chirac a much kinder hand than in 1997, producing a handsome victory for his newly created Union pour la Majorité Présidentielle (UMP) which, it is agreed, was merely the RPR by another name. Chirac and his right-wing partners could thus look ahead to a period of unbroken rule. And, once again, politicians could boast of the durability of the Fifth Republic.

Except that few have chosen to do so. Rather there is a shared feeling that there is something amiss in the body politic, a feeling most visibly demonstrated by the high level of voter abstentions in all of the 2002 electoral contests. Corruption in the very highest places, the spread of globalisation, the continuing resentment against American culture (so-called McDomination, especially fierce after the second Iraq war), the further enlargement of the European community, the growth of terrorism, the fear of immigrants and continued economic uncertainties have led to a profound sense of 'insecurity', the very word on which Le Pen based his presidential campaign.[2] Given that there is no major crisis on the horizon, there is at present little possibility of a Sixth Republic, yet unless something is done by mainstream politicians to overcome these challenges, there is a danger that France will continue to be haunted by self-doubt, continually poring over its history and complaining about the present rather than looking ahead and building for the future.

Chirac elected

In early 1995 political talk inevitably revolved around the forthcoming presidential elections that year, the smart money being on prime minister Balladur to secure the Elysée. In the short period of *cohabitation*, he had proved himself a skilful and effective premier. As John Ardagh observes, his economic policy, which had witnessed a revival of the privatisation programme initiated by Chirac in 1986, had gradually eased France out of the bad times; he had lived up to his reputation as *Ballamou* by seeking the peaceful reconciliation of labour disputes; he had deliberately avoided goading the trade unions; at the 1993 GATT talks, held in Uruguay, he had successfully offset American criticism of European protectionism by securing a favourable deal for French farmers who were to receive state subsidies in return for a softening of the CAP; and, concludes Ardagh, he had enjoyed a good relationship with Mitterrand, respecting the president's decisions and observing sanctity of the *domaine réservé*.[3] In the minds of many political commentators, Balladur was the obvious man to take France into the twenty-first century.[4]

His prospects seemed even brighter given the disarray of the left. This time the Socialists had no Mitterrand to lead them into battle. Fourteen years as president, he had seemed immovable. Now he was an old man, engulfed in scandal and beset by illness. And there was no obvious heir apparent. Reduced to a mere 67 seats in the March 1993 legislative elections, the PS looked first to Michel Rocard. He promised a 'big bang', that is a radical overhaul of the party system to produce a dynamic socialist movement which would cater for 'the reformism of the ecologists, the loyalty to a social tradition of *centrisme*, and the authentic renovatory impulse of communism.'[5] The enmity of Mitterrand, personal rivalries within the Socialist camp and the precariousness of Rocard's own position ensured that this vision would not become a reality. A further setback came in the 1994 European elections, when the party failed to score more than 14 per cent of the vote, much of its energies siphoned off by Bernard Tapie's unofficial Energie Radicale list which received the backing of several of Mitterrand's cronies.

With Rocard no longer in the running, Socialists looked to Jacques Delors. His post at the European Commission was conveniently coming to an end, he was known to the voters and he possessed a reputation for decency and good sense. To the left's tangible disappointment, he announced that he would not stand as president. Outwardly, he declared that the political landscape was such that he would not be able to introduce the reforms he thought necessary. It remains questionable, however, whether Delors was prepared to throw himself into the hurly-burly of the hustings. He was an intelligent and sensitive man, in the words of Arnaud Teyssier, more a 'high functionary' than a political fighter.[6] He was thus reluctant to reduce complex matters to simple slogans and subject himself to intense media scrutiny. Socialist hopes thus turned to Henri Emmanuelli, onetime party treasurer who, in 1992, had been indicted for financial irregularities, and eventually to Lionel Jospin, formerly Rocard's education minister, who emerged the winner. While he performed much better in the presidential elections than anyone had predicted, as Mitterrand joked, he wanted to be president 'without being being a candidate'.[7]

Balladur's principal challengers were always going to emanate from the right. Le Pen could be relied upon to stand, and he duly did coming fourth with 15.2 per cent of the vote, instructing his supporters to hunt snails rather than go the electoral booths in the second round, which might account for the high level of abstentions (20 per cent), although at the time many others felt alienated by the elections. Another contender was Philippe de Villiers, onetime member of the UDF, whose anti-Maastricht instincts and authoritarian leanings had led him to found the Mouvement pour la France (MPF) which, in the 1994 European elections, secured 12.3 per cent of the vote. The real heavyweights of the right, however, chose not to come forward: Barre and Giscard. Balladur's principal challenger, then, was always going to be Chirac, who quickly caught up in the opinion polls and who, in the first round of the presidential vote in April 1995 scored 20.4 per cent of the votes as opposed to 18.5 per cent for Balladur, so as to enter the run-off against Jospin (23.2 per cent).

This reversal of fortunes is not difficult to explain.[8] Under the intense media spotlight, Balladur came across as a solid politician, but one lacking a popular touch, unable to talk to teenagers in the street and visibly embarrassed when, on the campaign trail in the countryside, a lamb urinated on his jacket, much to the amusement of the surrounding farmers and the watching television crew. Nor was he entirely free from the stench of corruption that seemed endemic in French political life. *Le Canard* revealed that he had benefited from selling shares in a computer company in which he had once worked, raising questions about insider trading, although no hard evidence was subsequently unearthed. The same newspaper also revealed that Chirac had received generous government grants for the upkeep of his house at Bity in the Corrèze and had offset spending on his château against income tax.[9] It was, though, Balladur's image that was most tarnished by this investigative journalism, something his lacklustre media performances could not rectify. Naturally, Chirac waged an energetic campaign, regularly appearing at mass rallies and on the television where his populist instincts were fully displayed, often resulting in him sending out contradictory messages. This inconsistency was, in part, a sign of nervousness. This was his third tilt at the presidency; another failure might mean oblivion. He was not prepared to allow this to happen and he thus pulled out all the stops to reach as wide an audience as possible. Aware that the electorate was frightened of economic insecurity, he spoke of *ouverture*, the need for government to heal the social divide, to eliminate unemployment and to create opportunity. It was the kind of language that would have come more naturally from Jospin, yet the Socialist contender seemed hesitant, just as he would in the 2002 presidential elections, thus allowing the unashamedly populist and racist Le Pen to slip into the run-off with Chirac.[10]

Most crucially, in his 1995 fight against Balladur, Chirac had the support of a majority on the French right. Apart from the backing of the RPR party machine and membership, political big-hitters rallied to his campaign: Alain Madelin, minister for business, Alain Juppé, foreign secretary, Philippe Séguin, president of the National Assembly, and even Giscard himself, who was keen to clear the way for a possible bid to become the first president of the European Union. Analysis of first round voting shows that Chirac even won over some UDF supporters. By contrast, Balladur was, as Andrew Knapp observes, largely dependent on 'the non-Gaullist moderate right'.[11]

Although seriously challenged by Jospin in the run off of May 1995, Chirac's popular touch, his promises to redress social inequalities, his increasingly presidential style which contrasted sharply with the timidity of his Socialist rival, and the willingness of Balladur's supporters to rally to the RPR man in the second ballot (some 85 per cent behaved thus) was enough to secure him the ultimate prize. 52.6 per of voters went for Chirac; 47.4 per cent for Jospin. For a man who had long yearned for the presidential prize, this should have been a moment of rejoicing; within months, he found himself the most unpopular president in the history of the Fifth Republic.

The Chirac Presidency: From Juppé to Jospin

It would be wrong to believe, as is sometimes alleged, that Chirac's campaign was nothing more than a shallow attempt to beat Balladur and Jospin. Elitist he might have been, but there was no doubting Chirac's wish to promote his own brand of inclusive Gaullism. Talk of healing *la rupture sociale* was genuine. This he hoped to achieve through a presidential style less aloof than that of his predecessors, a cutting back of government administration, the infusion of public monies into curing unemployment and the eradication of the public deficit, then running at 67 billion francs – in other words, four per cent of GDP and a figure much higher than previously realised. Of these targets, budgetary discipline was crucial as France was committed to putting into place the necessary financial criteria required for the introduction of a European single currency, as foreseen at Maastricht. Now was not the moment to back down although, outside of Europe, Chirac's foreign policy displayed all the traits to be expected of a Gaullist, the postponement in the abandoning of border controls for example. How though to rein in the budget? Given that Balladur's privatisation plans had not been as profitable as anticipated, the answer was to be found in an austerity package: the reduction of government healthcare spending, the biggest cause of the deficit; an extension in the years public employees needed to work to recoup their pensions; a hike in VAT; and, most controversially, a reform of the social security system so as to exclude trade union representatives. How this squared with Chirac's plans to cut unemployment through increases in state expenditure was never properly answered.

It was unfortunate that Chirac should have entrusted what was a delicate and difficult task to an indelicate and insensitive prime minister: Alain Juppé. He was a product of both the ENA and the ENS, making a name for himself first in the Inspection des Finances, then on Chirac's mayoral staff, and eventually as a minister under both Chirac (government spokesperson, 1986–8) and Balladur (foreign minister, 1993–5). 'Super Enarque' or 'Amstrad', as he was variously known, was every part the technocrat, ruthless in government, able to move from one post to another, and the holder of a multitude of offices (mayor of Bordeaux, a member of the European parliament, and deputy for a Paris constituency). Although there were already suspicions about his probity, which would eventually lead in 2004 to his prosecution for financial irregularities, in 1995 it was his off-handed and self-satisfied manner which alienated public opinion and exacerbated the inevitable protests which met the publication of the government's austerity package.

Throughout November and December France was wracked by a three-week general strike. Beginning in the universities, this soon spread to other public sectors, notably the civil service and railways, the principal targets of the so-called *Plan Juppé*, and culminated in a series of nation-wide demonstrations of 12 December when some two million people protested, many mobilised by the Fédération des Syndicats Unitaires et Démocratiques (FSUD) which had split from the CFDT. These were the largest demonstrations since 1968 and marked a clear reversal in the attitude of government towards the unions. It will be remembered that one of the consequences of 1968 was a fear of unnecessarily unleashing union and worker power, although this had not prevented strike breaking and other violent clashes with organised labour. Inspired by free-market economics, as practised in the USA and UK, and aware that trade union representation was, in 1995, the lowest in its history, Juppé was free of the ghosts of the 1960s, and understood that December 1995 was not May 1968.[12] Most strikers, even among the student body, were little concerned with ideology, but with securing their own sectional interests. Calls for a radical overhauling of political and economic institutional structures were few and far between.

Unruffled by the invective directed at his government, Juppé was able to see through most of his reforms, particularly those designed to curb overspending on health. (Significantly, they would be continued by the Socialists under Jospin, albeit with far more tact.) Some of this unpopularity inevitably rubbed off on Chirac, whose approval ratings slumped to under 50 per cent, yet he was wily enough to keep a distance from his prime minister, notably at the worst moments of industrial unrest, and he did not hesitate to project himself as the symbol of France overseas. He also took a particular interest in defence policies, finally ending France's long-standing commitment to military conscription, and cementing closer ties with NATO. Aware that the reduction of US troops in Germany offered Paris a wonderful opportunity to assert its leadership of Western Europe, Chirac took France back into the NATO military command structure as well as into the Mediterranean fleet.

Juppé might have been unpopular, but this does not explain why, on 21 April 1997, Chirac decided to dissolve the National Assembly. This unusual behaviour was reminiscent of 1976 when he had been the first prime minister in the Republic's history to have resigned although, admittedly, at the time he was waiting to be pushed. As Anne Sa'Sadah comments he was now the first president to have called a midterm 'tactical' election, when his government already held a majority, simply to secure a short-term political advantage rather than having been pushed into this decision by a political crisis.[13] When in 1962 de Gaulle dissolved the National Assembly, it was to cement his particular vision of the presidency which seemed threatened by his political opponents. When, on 30 May 1968, de Gaulle called fresh elections, it was to put the left-wing demonstrations of that month behind him so that France could rediscover a sense of stability.

In view of the 1997 results, Chirac's behaviour seems even stranger. In a stroke, he wiped out the majority which the RPR (258 seats) and the UDF (206) commanded in parliament. Reduced to 67 seats in 1993, PS representation grew to 253. Together with its left-wing allies, Greens

(7 seats), the Communists (38) and assorted left-wingers (21), the Socialists now possessed a majority (319) over the combined forces of the right which returned 257 deputies (134 RPR, 108 UDF/allies, 15 various right-wingers, always discounting the one FN representative). In retrospect, Chirac would have done better to have gone to the country in 1995 straight after his election just as Mitterrand did in 1981 and in 1988, and just as Balladur had intended. Yet, during his campaign, Chirac had promised not to pursue Balladur's proposed tactics which, he argued in a fine Gaullist flourish, made the government of France dependent on the manipulation of elections. Now, of course, Chirac appeared to be doing exactly that: using a tactical ploy to steal a march on his opponents.

That was not how Chirac explained his actions. His interest, he solemnly declared, was the 'cohesion of Europe'. Backed by a refreshed mandate, he would have the authority to see through France's entry into a single currency, the most contentions and important issue of the day, and a move which would have to be accompanied by yet further government cutbacks if EMU criteria for convergence were to be met. France was paying the price, he declared on 21 April 1997, for 14 years of *Mitterrandisme* in which vital reforms, especially in the public sector, had been neglected. That Europe weighed on his mind is unquestionable. He did not want anti-Europeanism to gather any more momentum and was aware that few of his ministers, notably Juppé and Charles Pasqua, were enamoured of the euro. *Dans le fond*, Chirac hoped to catch his opponents on the hop, and may have been swayed by opinion polls indicating a rise in his own popularity, albeit not that of his prime minister. Might not this support harden if the president made clear to his people the overwhelming need for what he called a *nouvel élan*. In any case, he figured, elections would have to be held in 1998 and was there not a danger in holding out that long? As Philip Thody writes, in the past, when elections had been held at the normal point in the cycle, the president's party had lost or had nearly lost, witness the UNR in 1967 (reduced to a tiny majority) and more recently the PS, defeated in both 1986 and 1993.[14]

Whatever his motives, Chirac grossly miscalculated. He and his advisers had not taken on board the ways in which the Socialist defeat of 1993 and the presidential setback of 1995 had inadvertently strengthened Jospin's hold over his party, enabling him to develop a pragmatic strategy of *une gauche plurielle*, ready to undertake electoral alliances with the Greens, the principal ecology party, which itself had overcome its scruples of doing deals at election time, and the Communists who, under the new leadership of Robert Hue, were likewise prepared to enter into alliances, recognising that such cooperation was vital if the party was to stave off its seemingly unstoppable decline. As Jospin articulated his campaign, the principal themes emerged as job creation, a halt to further privatisations and a reduction of the working week to 35 hours. Although this latter proposal was truly radical, there was little else to grip the imagination of the electorate, not that this imagination was dormant. Already wanting to give Juppé a kick up the backside for the insensitive way in which he had pursued the politics of austerity, fears grew that his government must have some terrible new economic cut-backs up its sleeve. Why else had elections been called so early?

It was, above all, a resentment at being forced into the voting booths, when there was no compelling need, that most counted against the government. In 1995, Chirac had promised not to go the polls; he had broken that pledge. Unlike his predecessors at the Elysée, even Mitterrand at the very end of his term of office, Chirac had come across as 'unpresidential', a man no longer in control of events, overly reliant on his prime minister, ready to do quick fixes – in sum, a calculating politician looking for short-term political gain. It would do the president good, reflected many, if he now had to share power with the left, just as he had shared power with Mitterrand.

So began another phase of *cohabitation*. Developing the themes of *la gauche plurielle*, in his first cabinet Jospin appointed Dominique Voynet, the Green Party leader, to the Ministry of the Environment, made room for three Communists, and placed the indefatigable left-winger Jean-Pierre Chevènement, who presided over his own party the Mouvement des Citoyens (MdC), at the Interior, although naturally it was the Socialists who commanded the lion's share of ministerial portfolios, 19 out of 27. When, in 2000, Jospin reshuffled his cabinet, ministers were again selected from the disparate strands of the left, care being taken even to include internal Socialist critics of government policy. As David Hanley observes, thereafter it was only die-hard left-wing radicals who were excluded from 'the magic circle'.[15]

As will be seen, holding together such a coalition of interests did not prove easy yet, as Alistair Cole writes, Jospin was 'an astute coalition manager',[16] and initially the fortunes of new government looked good. The election of Tony Blair's New Labour in Britain, some four weeks after Jospin's triumph, seemed to augur a new European-wide future for social democracy; the triumph in the World Cup of the French national football team, captained by the extraordinarily talented Zinedine Zidane, gave the nation a sense of well being and seemed to bode well for a tolerant France in which immigrants were truly valued; and the upturn in the US economy stimulated the growth of French industries, producing a fall in unemployment and a reduction of the deficit. Popular, pragmatic and non-ideological measures followed, and significantly the constitution was reformed so that the presidential term of office was cut from seven to five years, something which both Giscard and Mitterrand had toyed with but never found the inclination to deliver. Elections for the presidency and the National Assembly would now be conducted within a period of two months, the contest for the Elysée coming first, so as to reduce the possibility of *cohabitation*. This is something de Gaulle had opposed believing the presidential mandate would be tarnished, reducing the supreme office holder into little more than a politician.[17] Indeed, there may well have been something calculating in Jospin's move. As Jonathan Fenby wryly observes, this new procedure improved his chances of winning the Elysée, as he and his government continued to enjoy high public opinion approval ratings.[18]

In truth, many of Jospin's policies were not that dissimilar from those of the ill-fated Juppé. Privatisation continued, notably that of the motorways, and EMU criteria meant that the government had little choice but to extend anti-deficit measures, resulting in further tax rises and reductions in government spending. The difference was that Jospin had a better way with words and a better public style than had Juppé.[19] The one truly radical measure was the 35 hour week, although it soon proved necessary to introduce this in stages rather than in one fell swoop.

Not everything went well for Jospin. Apart from unwelcome press reports about his Trotskyist past, in November 1999 the talented Dominique Strauss-Kahn, minister of Finance and Industry, decided to quit amid a welter of fraud allegations, later unproven, centring round the work he had previously performed while acting as an attorney to a student welfare scheme. The problems in holding together *la gauche plurielle* also proved trying for Jospin, despite his abilities. Tensions with the Greens were never far from the surface, whereas the Communists were often troublesome. In the event, differences over policy – notably the euro, Kosovo, the disposal of nuclear waste, and hunting – were contained, but it was difficult to keep these out of the public's eye.[20] Most serious was Chevènement's resignation over plans to grant Corsica some limited measure of autonomy, a move which the MdC leader saw as a threat to national sovereignty. While Chevènement did not overdramatise the affair, he and his supporters were disappointed that the MdC was thereafter excluded from cabinet. Commentators have since suggested that Jospin's failure to win the 190,000 extra votes needed to ease him into the second round of the 2002 presidential elections may be put down to disgruntled MdC sympathisers, who put their crosses elsewhere on the ballot papers.[21] Certainly Jospin was overly complacent. Despite the many successes of *la gauche plurielle*, and the continued divisions on the right, it was telling that in both the 1998 regional council elections and the 2001 municipal elections, the centre right vote was firm, despite the fact that the left won all the headlines by taking control of the mayoralties of Paris and Lyon. What eventually went wrong for Jospin will be considered in the next section.

What of Chirac? After the fiasco of the 1997 dissolution of the National Assembly, was he destined to play the part of a Fourth Republic president, little more than a power-broker, cast out to the margins.[22] The pain and disbelief at the 1997 results were clearly caught by the television cameras and seemed etched into his face. Thereafter it was said by *Le Canard* that he had sunk into depression, retreating into the Elysée, where he sat in front of the televison, watching his favourite sport (Japanese sumo wrestling), perhaps himself trying to put on those extra pounds by eating a lot of charcuterie and drinking a lot of beer. Not only did he enjoy poor relations with his new prime minister, his right-wing allies were deserting him, their many divisions exposed and hardened by the moves towards European integration.[23]

Naturally, Giscard remained sweet on Europe but was increasingly sour towards Chirac, a man he had never liked or trusted. Giscard's party, the UDF now under the direction of François Bayrou, made it very plain it wanted to have little to do with the Elysée. Meanwhile, the president's onetime allies Alain Madelin, a Thatcherite liberal economist, and Charles Millon, former Minister of Defence, worried at the gathering pace of European integration, formed a new centre right grouping which called itself La Droite. This promised to rally all like-minded rightists, even supporters of Le Pen's FN, with whom Millon had already done electoral deals at a local level. Worse still, splits appeared among the president's own party when Chirac's close electoral adviser Philippe Séguin and loyal lieutenant Charles Pasqua joined forces with the hardline Eurosceptic Philippe de Villiers to found a Rassemblement pour la France et l'Indépendance de l'Europe (RPFIE) which, of course, shared a similar acronym to de Gaulle's Rassemblement du Peuple Français. As Serge Berstein has observed, these splits effectively marked the end of

Gaullism as *the* dominant force on the right; its demotion into the strands that make up French conservatism was confirmed.[24]

To confound it all, Chirac had to fend off charges of electoral fraud and corruption dating back to his time as mayor of Paris. Enquiries by the judge Eric Halphen revealed that the city of Paris housing department had been subsidising the RPR for many years, a process which had continued under Chirac's successor as mayor, Jean Tibéri.[25] As the judicial net closed in, and subsequent associated frauds were uncovered (illegal property deals, false expense claims, vote rigging, jobs for the boys and girls) Juppé and Tibéri both faced prosecution. Much to the president's embarrassment, recall Howarth and Varouxakis, his former chauffeur published a book in which he revealed that Chirac had conducted several affairs, earning the nickname 'trois minutes, douche compris' ('three minute man, shower included'), which made a change from his previous nickname, 'bulldozer', which had been earned for his formidable political stamina. In 2001, Chirac seemed destined to go on trial, but was saved by the Constitutional Council which ruled that the trial of a sitting president could only proceed on charges of treason. This, say Howarth and Varouxakis did not stop the satirical television programme *Les Guignols de l'Info*, similar to *Spitting Image*, dubbing *Chirac Super-menteur*.[26]

In an astonishing reversal of fortunes, Chirac was rescued, both from the criminal justice system and political oblivion, by his victory in the 2002 presidential elections. More remarkable than the fact that he had won, was the failure of Jospin to reach the second round. Rather than have to confront his prime minister, as everyone had predicted, Chirac discovered himself in the run-off face to face with the extreme rightist Le Pen.

Chirac's Salvation: The 2002 Elections

'Etat de choc', 'Le cauchemar Le Pen', 'La blessure', 'Séisme', 'Démolition'.[27] Such were the headlines of the leading political journals in the wake of the first round of presidential voting on 21 April 2002. The votes were as follows: Chirac came first with 19.71 per cent of the vote, then amazingly Le Pen with 16.95 per cent, and third Jospin with 16.2 per cent, whose political career was effectively ruined, something indicated by his immediate resignation as leader of the PS. Other candidates were far behind, among them: Bayrou (UDF) 6.8 per cent; Arlette Laguillier (Trotskyite Lutte Ouvrière) 5.7 per cent; Jean-Pierre Chevènement (MdC)

5.2 per cent; Olivier Besancenot (Ligue Communiste Révolutionnaire) 4.25 per cent; Robert Hue (PCF) 3,37 per cent; Bruno Mégret (MNR) 2.35 per cent; Christine Boutin (Forum des Républicains Sociaux) 1.19 per cent; and Daniel Gluckstein (Parti des Travailleurs) 0.47 per cent.

In truth, the vote for Le Pen was not so dissimilar to his past showing: in 1995 he had managed 15.2 per cent, coming fourth after Jospin, Chirac and Balladur. It was also understood, at least among political commentators, that he had little chance of success in the second round of presidential voting on 5 May 2002 when he won 5,525, 907 votes (17.79 per cent) as opposed to 25,540,874 votes for Chirac (82.21 per cent). As anticipated, many voters obeyed the instructions of the defeated candidates, rallying to the incumbent president as a means of defeating Le Pen, even though thousands of protestors marched under the banner 'Votez escroc, pas fascho' ('Vote for a crook, not a fascist').[28] Undaunted, Chirac put together a new political party, the UMP, which in the ensuing legislative elections of June that year emerged triumphant with 369 seats, as opposed to 178 for the combined forces of *la gauche plurielle*. No seats went to the FN which managed 11.3 per cent of the first round voting. As his new prime minister, Chirac turned to the uncompromising Jean-Pierre Raffarin who inaugurated his premiership with a series of tough social measures, aimed at cracking down on illegal immigrants, prostitutes and criminals.

If Chirac's victory in the second round of the presidential elections could have been foreseen, what had earlier gone wrong for Jospin and what had gone right for Le Pen? As has been pointed out, Jospin had an admirable record: 'No prime minister had ever achieved such a durable presence since Pompidou between 1962 and 1968. No left-wing government had ever achieved – remotely – such coherence and stability.'[29] In the event, not enough was made of this record. He was further damaged by a fracturing of the left-wing vote.[30] The damage done to Jospin's cause by Chevènement's followers has already been commented on, but it did not help that there were so many left-wing candidates, even though several were on the fringes. Analysis of the voting patterns has further uncovered that many people used their initial vote to register a protest, often siding with Le Pen even though they had no real desire for him to win. As we have noted, in recent years the FN has succeeded in becoming *the* party of protest, displacing both the Communists and Greens. Abstentions were also high which undeniably favoured Le Pen (27.83 per cent as opposed to 20.3 per cent in 1995 and 15.9 per cent in 1988, 14.1 per cent in 1981 and 12.7 per cent in 1974).[31]

Above all, Jospin had miscalculated his political strategy. He had naturally assumed that he would be in the second round run-off and had
grossly underestimated the challenge of the far right, relying on opinion
polls which ultimately proved misleading. As a result, he waged an inef-
fectual campaign when measured against that of Le Pen. As the present
author, together with Frank Tallett, has observed:

> Whereas Le Pen spoke the language of the *métallo*, Josin hesitated to
> speak of *les travailleurs*; whereas Le Pen embraced the working
> classes, Jospin appeared to be surrounded by elitist intellectuals;
> whereas Le Pen appropriated *La Marseillaise*, Jospin vaunted the
> merits of the European union; whereas Le Pen denounced weekly
> car burnings by 'yobs' from immigrant ghettos, Jospin alluded to
> 'incivilities' caused by 'youths'; whereas Le Pen happily revealed his
> antisemitism, Jospin believed to address such matters was to descend
> to the level of gutter politics; whereas Le Pen's electioneering was its
> usual crude sloganeering, Jospin failed to use the media to its full
> potential; whereas Le Pen's campaign was clear from the outset,
> Jospin's was anything but (he himself ordered various last-minute
> alterations to the manifesto); whereas Le Pen blasted the record of
> the government, Jospin failed to play up the very real achievements
> of his premiership.[32]

It was an unequal campaign, but should not have been. Jospin should
have passed the first round, thus enabling him to launch a serious challenge to Chirac who, up to that point, had appeared mechanical and
uninspirational. As the anti-Le Pen vote rallied round the incumbent
president, Chirac was guaranteed a second term, regardless of what he
said or did. The only question was how many votes he would garner.

That Chirac's UMP went on to win the June legislative elections may
be attributed to several factors: the willingness of an electorate to end
the uncertainty of national politics by rallying to the president's party;
the failure of the FN to build on its early success; the fragmentation of
right-wing parties outside of the UMP; the ability of the UMP to focus
the campaign on traditional right-wing issues, notably tax cuts and crime
reduction; the continued demoralisation of the left, which was further
disadvantaged by Jospin's resignation; and a general dissatisfaction with
politics resulting in record abstention rates (35.58 per cent in the first
ballot). Even so, the scale of Chirac's victory had not been predicted.
Gaullism might no longer be the force it once was among the French

right but, as has been observed, this was the first occasion since the 1970s that the right can expect 'to govern on its own' for a full term of office.[33]

The Fifth: Past, Present and Future

Any prediction about what might happen within French politics over the next ten years – will the presidency recover something of its power and dignity, will the right repeat the dominance it commanded in the period 1958–81, will the Socialists emulate the renaissance they initiated at Epinay in 1971 – takes us out of the realm of history into that of futurology. At the time of writing in 2004, the UMP had taken a terrible pounding in the regional elections, suggesting that voters are already fed up with Raffarin's austerity package.

It is easier to speak of the past, and to reflect on the remarkable durability of the Fifth Republic. Like the Third Republic, it has stood up to repeated challenges and, on each occasion, has emerged unscathed: the crisis of decolonisation; the 1968 protests; the death of its creator in the shape of de Gaulle; the election of a non-Gaullist presidents (Giscard and Mitterrand); the advent of *cohabitation*; and the rise of the extreme right. Admittedly many of these crises were non-crises, talked up at the time in characteristic Gallic fashion, and it is fortunate that the regime has not had to confront military defeat either on metropolitan or colonial soil. Nevertheless, the Fifth has repeatedly confounded the prophets of doom. One textbook in 1968 stated that in the minds of many French men and women the Fifth seemed 'provisional', although it did acknowledge that the regime seemed to be more than a mere 'interlude'.[34] As Richard Vinen has recently observed, if there is to be major constitutional change then this is more likely to 'come from Brussels or Strasbourg' rather than from Paris.[35]

Unlocking the key to the durability of the Fifth Republic is no easy matter, but allows us a penetrating insight into the successes and failings of the regime. The traditional Gaullist explanation for the longevity of the Fifth would, of course, be to stress the primacy of the constitution which, it is argued, rescued the country from its natural propensity for division. Whether these divisions were ever truly contained must remain debatable. Under the Fifth, politics have retained the power to astonish, witness the spontaneity of the 1968 demonstrations, the size of Mitterrand's victory in 1981 and Le Pen's surprise showing in 2002.

Political parties have also continued to behave like political parties – even the Gaullists, especially the Gaullists – and in recent years politics have come to display the kind of gamesmanship we would normally associate with the Fourth Republic.

There is no doubting that, in the 1960s, the constitution provided much-needed backbone, yet its sanctity has come to matter less. This is partially because globalisation has meant that the national governments can no longer take decisions in isolation, but most importantly because politicians have never been overly wedded to its content, permitting an organic flexibility which has assisted in the promotion of stability. For instance, the tension that existed, from the very start, in the relationship between president and prime minister has been contained, most obviously during periods of *cohabitation* which have often proved popular among the electorate. The Fifth is also fortunate in that it has not had to confront the dilemma of the Fourth which saw two formidable political players, in the shape of the Gaullists and Communists, arraigned against the system. Even the FN seems content to work within the system, despite its criticisms of liberal democracy.

The stability of the Fifth Republic has been further underpinned by a dulling of the old ideological fissures which had repeatedly flared up in the past, for instance the sterile anticlerical and clerical debate which dogged politics in the 1950s. Ironically, this has happened at a time when a two-party system has gradually taken a hold, always remembering that French party discipline still remains relatively loose. It would, however, be a mistake to believe that ideological differences have completely disappeared. The recent debates over the Occupation have shown a reluctance on the part of politicians from all parties to come to terms with the past, and the legacy of Algeria has yet to be truly confronted, partially because of the formidable presence of Muslims within French society. Catholicism might no longer arouse passions, but Islam certainly does.

The success of the Fifth's longevity further lies in the ability of its politicians to respond to a society in mutation. This had been a key failing of the Fourth whose political structures had been designed to reflect a society dominated by small holders, peasants and *notables*, a world that was rapidly disappearing. For all his talk of modernisation and preparing for the future, De Gaulle's Republic was also in danger of being out of kilter with those transformations initiated by the *trente gloriueses*. The state was all too keen to tell people what was good for them, limiting their opportunities and freedoms of expression. The

1968 demonstrations were a protest against these very restrictions. Since, then, political life has been more attuned to underlying social and economic changes – the growth in consumerism, urbanisation, the communications revolution and the onset of globalisation.

This has not been, in any sense, an easy process, and has meant a redrawing of the powers of the state which, since the onset of planning, has been at the forefront of economic and social organisation. Inevitably, with the onset of privatisation, some of these powers have been rolled back, and there remain those frustrated by the suffocating power of centralisation, for instance Disney executive Pierre-Yves Gerbeau brought in to rescue the Dome project in the UK. Nonetheless, as James McMillan writes, on balance the influence of the French state has not been entirely negative, and has contributed to wider political stability.[36] The state, he continues, is still the largest provider of jobs, a willing regulator of the market place, and an instrument of change. This intervention, for all its drawbacks, has enabled France to make the leap from a rural society to a sophisticated and dynamic economy which can compete in the global markets. The price, concludes McMillan, has been persistently high levels of unemployment which have bemused successive governments, even Jospin's, the one administration in recent times to have increased significantly the numbers in work.

The other factors that have contributed to the durability of the Fifth lie in its relationship with the wider world. To shake off the Algerian conundrum in the early years of the Republic was a great boon, although the broader history of French decolonisation has not been especially honourable. Still believing itself to be imbued with certain fundamental truths, France has attempted to retain its links with its former empire. This might have led to the promotion of *Francophonie*, but it has also led to a policy of neo-colonialism, maintained by both left and right, which has often seen Paris and French companies propping up some particularly nasty regimes, as well as feeding the arms trade. Elf was directly implicated in the Rwanda masscres of 1994 and, in 1998 at Brazzaville in the Congo, French arms and aircraft assisted dictator Sasso Ngnesso in the murder of some 25,000 of his citizens and the forced flight of many more.[37]

In a bipolar world, involvement in the Third World was seen as vital to maintain an impression of French *grandeur*. The extent to which Paris has been truly able to influence international affairs is extremely debatable. Successive presidents since de Gaulle have maintained the fiction that France, through its *force de frappe*, its partnership with Germany, its close ties with Europe, its links with former colonies, and its courting of the Soviet Union/Russia, has constituted a independent presence in international affairs, able to restrain the USA. Yet as Mitterrand discovered in the 1980s, France had little option but to follow the American lead. Since the ending of the Cold War that freedom has been even more severely curbed. Not that the French public have necessarily recognised this. Traditionally ambivalent towards the USA, since the fall of Communism an anti-Americanism has hardened. When, in the 1990s, NATO chose to intervene in Kosovo, where the Serbian leader Slobodan Milosevic was pursuing policies of ethnic cleansing, fears were expressed that France was merely facilitating American hegemony in the post-Cold War world, even though the French had initially been keener on intervention.[38] Anxieties about the USA also flared up in the wake of the 9/11 terrorist attack on the twin towers. Both politicians and intellectuals were troubled that sympathy for the Americans, especially within the anglo-saxon world, might encourage US pretensions. There were even anxieties lest the Germans became part of a renewed anglo-saxon partnership, thus weakening France's leadership of the Continent.[39] Against this backdrop, French criticism of the Iraq war in 2003 was highly predictable.

It is within Europe that France has been able to exert the greatest influence, and the benefits of closer integration have clearly aided stability at home. Most obviously, integration contained the Franco-German rivalry which, since 1870, had led to three wars, two of which had produced regime change in Paris. Yet, the process of integration has not been a smooth one. Closer involvement with its neighbours might have brought economic benefits to France, but has also led to a dilution of French culture, symbolised in the gradual disappearance of the black tobacco Gitanes and Gauloises cigarettes, sold in soft-packets, which have recently fallen foul of European health legislation although, to be fair, successive French government have been attempting to cure the nation's addiction to smoking. Inevitably, European integration has also raised questions about national sovereignty. Already troubled by the onset of globalisation in which decisions which formerly belonged to governments and national officials are now taken by multi-corporations, France is decidedly apprehensive in the face of the enlargement of the Community. Will Paris, together with Berlin, still be able to control the pace of integration so as to preserve national identity? Some fear that France will be swamped by economic migrants from Eastern Europe who will dilute French identity already threatened in their eyes by the presence of large numbers of non-white immigrants from North Africa.

In this environment of self-doubt, in which there is frequently talk of a *malaise*, it is the responsibility of mainstream politicians to win back the trust of the public, so as to restore a faith in the political system. Almost certainly this will entail a radical rethink of the Fifth Republic's structures. Corruption, for so long a cancer in the French body politic, requires major surgery; the power of the state, admittedly on the wane, still needs further pruning; the integration of minorities must be speeded up; and somehow France has to come to terms with its reduced status in the world, overcoming the paranoia which has often clouded its judgement of other nations. Even without this major surgery, the Fifth will undoubtedly continue, yet faith in its procedures and institutions will steadily diminish. Voter abstentions will grow and Le Pen, and his politics of hate, will thrive. The start of this section promised that it would not indulge in futurology, yet it seems that the present populist policies of the Raffarin government – cost cutting, linked to various high profile campaigns against crime, which is all too often presented as the work of Magrehbi immigrants – lack the necessary imagination.

In the past, France has frequently prided itself on its ability to enlighten the rest of humankind. Given that these aforementioned problems are common to the post-modern western world, France may again have the opportunity to lead the way. It has since been suggested that should France be able to repeat such a role, the Fifth Republic would be heralded as the most successful and illustrious of French regimes.

Notes

Introduction

1. Among the many French studies, see J.-J. Becker, *Histoire politique de la France depuis 1945* (Paris, Armand Colin, 1996 ed), J. Chapsal, *La Vie politique sous la Vème République* (Paris, Presses Universitaires de France, 1987) 2 vols, J. M. Donegani & M. Sadoun, *La Ve République* (Paris, Calmann Lévy, 1998), G. Elgey & J. M. Colombani, *La Cinquième ou la République des phratries* (Paris, Fayard, 1998), H. Portelli, *La Politique en France sous la Vème République* (Paris, Grasset, 1987), S. Sur, *La Vie politique en France sous la Vème République* (Paris, Montchrestien, 1982), P. Viannson-Ponté, *Histoire de la République gaullienne* (Paris, Fayard, 1970) 2 vols, and A. Teyssier, *La Vème République, 1958–1995. De de Gaulle à Chirac* (Paris, Pygmalion, 1995).
2. R. N. Gildea, *France since 1945* (Oxford, Oxford University Press, 2002 2nd ed). See too T. Stovall, *France since the Second World War* (London, Longman, 2002).
3. See notably J. McMillan, *Twentieth-Century France* (London, Arnold, 1991), M. Larkin, *France since the Popular Front* (Oxford, Clarendon Press, 1997 2nd ed) and R. Vinen, *France, 1934–70* (Basingstoke, Macmillan, 1996).
4. See especially A. Cole, *French Politics and Society* (London, Longman, 1998), P. Morris, *French Politics Today* (Manchester, Manchester University Press, 1994), A. Stevens, *The Government and Politics of France* (Basingstoke, Macmillan, 1996 2nd ed), and V. Wright, *The Government and Politics of France* (London, Routledge, 1989 3rd ed).
5. See J. Fenby, *France on the Brink. The Trouble with France* (London, Abacus, 2002 ed), J. Ardagh, *France in the New Century. Portrait of a*

Changing Society (London, Penguin, 1999), J. Forbes & N. Hewlett, *Contemporary France. Essays and Texts on Politics, Economics and Society* (London, Longman, 1994) and S. Perry (ed.) *Aspects of Contemporary France* (London, Routledge, 1997).

6. O. Duhamel, *Le Pouvoir politique en France* (Paris, Seuil, 2003 5th ed), p. 31.

7. See P. Thody, *The Fifth Republic. Presidents, Politics and Personalities* (London, Routledge, 1997).

8. Elgey & Colombani, *La Cinquième*, pp. 13–15.

9. 'The Fifth Republic as Parenthesis? Politics since 1945', in J. McMillan (ed.), *Modern France. Short Oxford History of France* (Oxford, Oxford University Press, 2003), pp. 74–102.

10. P. Gordon & S. Meunier, *The French Challenge. Adapting to Globalisation* (Washington, Brookings, 2001).

11. See B. Boccara, *L'Insurrection démocratique. Manifeste pour la Sixième République* (Paris, Démocratie, 1993). See, too, G. Raynaud, 'Preparing the Sixth Republic', in M. Allison & O. Heathcote (eds), *Forty Years of the French Fifth Republic. Action, Dialogue and Discourse* (Bern, Lang, 2002), pp. 373–82.

12. W. G. Andrews & S. Hoffmann (eds), *The Fifth Republic at Twenty* (Albany, University of New York Press, 1981), p. xi.

13. See the essay by the author, in collaboration with Frank Tallett, in their edited collection, *The Right in France from Revolution to Le Pen* (London, I. B. Tauris, 2003 2nd ed), pp. 293–304. A more nuanced and informed essay is that by P. Buffotot & D. Hanley, 'The Normalisation of French Politics? The Elections of 2002', *Modern and Contemporary France*, (11), 2, 2003, pp. 131–46.

14. Teyssier, *La Ve République*, p. 13.

15. *L'Express*, 2–8 May 2002.

16. J. Horne, 'The Transformation of Society', in McMillan, *Modern France*, p. 149.

17. Vinen, *France 1934–1970*, pp. 196–8, and for the general observations about French society.

18. Cole, *French Politics and Society*, p. 253, see too pp. 236–52.

Chapter 1: *La Coagulation*: The Fourth Republic, 1944–1958

1. J. M. Donegani & M. Sadoun, *La Ve République. Naissance et mort* (Paris, Calmann Lévy, 1998), p. 25.

2. D. Hanley, *Party, Society, Government. Republican Democracy in France* (Oxford, Berg, 2002), p. 122.
3. This argument may be followed in P. Williams, *Crisis and Compromise. The Politics of the Fourth Republic* (London, Longman, 1964), G. Elgey, *Histoire de la Quatrième République* (Paris, Fayard, 1965–92), 3 vols, P. Courtier, *La Quatrième République* (Paris, Presses Universitaires de France, 1994), J.-P. Rioux, *La France de la Quatrième République* (Paris, Seuil, 1980–83), 2 vols, and J. Gacon, *Quatrième République* (Paris, Messidor, 1987).
4. For the most recent analysis of 1940, see J. Jackson, *The Fall of France. The Nazi Invasion of 1940* (Oxford, Oxford University Press, 2003).
5. H. R. Kedward, *In Search of the Maquis. Resistance in Rural France* (Oxford, Oxford University Press, 1993).
6. See G. Madjarian, *Conflits, pouvoirs et société à la Libération* (Paris, Union Générale, 1980).
7. A. Peyrefitte, *C'était de Gaulle* (Paris, Fayard, 1997), vol. 2, p. 85.
8. On this particular issue, see F. Virgili, *La France virile. Des Femmes tondues à la Libération* (Paris, Payot, 2000). On the purges more generally, astonishingly the venerable P. Novick, *The Resistance versus Vichy. The Purge of Collaborators in Liberated France* (London, Chatto and Windus, 1966) is still the most comprehensive oversight, although it should be read alongside H. Rousso, 'L'Epuration en France. Une histoire inachevée', *Vingtième Siècle*, 33, 1992, pp. 106–17.
9. A readily accessible discussion of the constitution, from which much material here has been taken, is M. Larkin, *France since the Popular Front* (Oxford, Clarendon Press, 1997 2nd ed), pp. 137–50.
10. Quoted in F. Giles, *The Locust Years. The Story of the Fourth Republic* (London, Secker & Warburg, 1991), p. 38.
11. This possibility is discussed and dismissed in A. Shennan, *De Gaulle* (London, Longman, 1993), p. 47.
12. See notably P. Viannay, *Du bon usage de la France* (Paris, Ramsay, 1988).
13. Quoted in Giles, *Locust Years*, p. 27.
14. *Ibid.*
15. V. Auriol, *Journal du Septennat* (Paris, Armand Colin, 1949), vol. 3, p. 49.
16. D. S. Bell, 'The French Communist Party: From Revolution to Reform', in J. Evans (ed.), *The French Party System* (Manchester, Manchester University Press, 2003), p. 32.

17. Hanley, *Party, Society, Government*, p. 129.
18. R. Vinen, *France, 1934–1970* (Basingstoke, Macmillan, 1996), pp. 82–101, and his *Bourgeois Politics in France, 1945–51* (Cambridge, Cambridge University Press, 1995).
19. On the MRP, R. Bosworth, *Catholicism and Crisis in Modern France. French Catholic Groups at the Threshold of the Fifth Republic* (Princeton, Princeton University Press, 1962), is still good.
20. Quoted in Giles, *Locust Years*, p. 104. See F. de Tarr, *Henri Queuille en son temps, 1884–1970. Biographie* (Paris, La Table Ronde, 1995).
21. J. Monnet, *Memoirs* (London, Collins, 1978), p. 231.
22. République Française, *Ecole Nationale d'Administration* (Paris, ENA, 1975), p. ix.
23. D. Johnson, 'Pierre Poujade', *The Guardian*, 28 August 2003. See too S. Hoffmann, *Le Mouvement Poujade* (Paris, FNSP, 1956) and D. Borne, *Petits bourgeois en révolte? Le Mouvement Poujade* (Paris, Flammarion, 1977). See too P. Poujade, *J'ai choisi le combat* (St Céré, Société Générale d'Editions et des Publications, 1956).
24. A. Collovald, 'Les Poujadistes ou l'échec en politiques', *Revue d'Histoire Moderne et Contemporaine* 36 (1), 2000, pp. 111–33, and J. G. Shields, 'The Poujadist Movement. A Faux Fascism?', *Modern and Contemporary France*, 8 (1), 2000, pp. 19–34.
25. Quoted in A. Horne, *A Savage War of Peace. Algeria, 1954–1962* (London, Pan, 2002 ed), p. 29.
26. R. N. Gildea, *France since 1945* (Oxford, Oxford University Press, 2002 2nd ed), p. 7.
27. A. Guyomarch, H. Machin & E. Ritchie, *France in the European Union* (Basingstoke: Macmillan, 1998), p. 19.
28. For more or less a definitive list, see X. Yacono, *Les Etapes de la décolonisation française* (Paris, Presses Universitaires de France, 1982 3rd ed), p. 6.
29. De Gaulle quoted in Peyrefitte, *C'était de Gaulle*, vol. 1, p. 233.
30. A. Clayton, *The French Wars of Decolonisation* (London, Longman, 1994), p. 8.
31. R. N. Gildea, *France since 1945*, p. 21.
32. Quoted in M. S. Alexander, 'Duty, Discipline and Authority: The French Officer Elites Between Professionalism and Politics, 1900–1962', in N. Atkin & F. Tallet (eds), *The Right in France from Revolution to Le Pen* (London, I. B. Tauris, 2003 2nd ed), p. 143.
33. Clayton, *French Wars*, pp. 6–7.
34. Quoted in Horne, *A Savage War of Peace*, p. 176.

35. See M. Evans, *The Memory of Resistance. French Opposition to the Algerian War, 1954–62*, pp. 24–8 (Oxford, Berg, 1997). See too J. E. Talbott, *The War Without a Name. France in Algeria, 1954–1962* (New York, Knopf, 1980), R. Betts, *France and Decolonisation, 1900–1960* (Basingstoke, Macmillan, 1991), and C. R. Ageron, *Modern Algeria. A History from 1830 to the Present* (London, Hurst, 1991).

36. Clayton, *French Wars*, p. 109.

37. Horne, *A Savage War of Peace*, p. 242.

38. Vinen, *France, 1934–70*, pp. 159–60.

39. Quoted in Horne, *A Savage War of Peace*, p. 175.

40. Quoted in K. Ross, *Fast Cars, Clean Bodies. Decolonisation and the Reordering of French Culture* (Cambridge Mass., MIT Press, 1995), p. 124.

41. Figures from D. L. Hanley, P. Kerr & N. Waites, *Contemporary France. Politics and Society since 1945* (London, Routledge, 1979), p. 13.

42. See D. Porch, *The March to the Marne. The French Army, 1871–1914* (Cambridge, Cambridge University Press, 1981).

43. Quoted in Peyrefitte, *C'était de Gaulle*, vol. 1, p. 67.

44. *Ibid.*, vol. 2, p. 207.

45. S. Berstein, *Histoire du gaullisme* (Paris, Perrin, 2001).

46. A. Teyssier, *La Ve République, 1958–1995. De de Gaulle à Chirac* (Paris, Pygmalion, 1995), p. 36.

47. Peyrefitte, *C'était de Gaulle*, vol. 1, p. 435.

48. Shennan, *De Gaulle*, p. 37.

49. M. S. Alexander & J. Keiger (eds) *France and the Algerian War, 1954–1962. Strategy, Operations and Diplomacy* (London, Frank Cass, 2002), p. 7.

50. This point is made by Teyssier, *La Ve République*, p. 32.

51. Williams, *Crisis and Compromise*, p. 449.

52. Hanley, *Party, Society, Government*, p. 139.

Chapter 2: *La Crise*: The Founding of the Fifth, 1958–62

1. C. de Gaulle, *Mémoires d'espoir* (Paris, Plon, 1970), vol. 1, pp. 22–3.

2. A. Shennan, *De Gaulle* (London, Longman, 1994), pp. 74–5.

3. A. Malraux, *Les Chênes qu'on abat* (Paris, Gallimard, 1971), p. 43.

4. R. Rémond, *Les Droites en France* (Paris, Aubier-Montagne, 1982).

5. R. Turner, 'The Presidency', in S. Perry (ed.), *Aspects of Contemporary France* (London, Routledge, 1997), p. 26.

6. Quoted in full in C. S. Maier & D. S. White (eds), *The Thirteenth of May. The Advent of de Gaulle's Republic* (New York, Oxford University Press, 1968), p. 43.

7. *Ibid.*

8. A. Peyrefitte, *C'était de Gaulle* (Paris, Fayard, 1994), vol. 1, p. 437. See R. Aron, *Chroniques de guerre. La France Libre, 1940–1945* (Paris, Gallimard, 1990).

9. *Ibid.*, p. 190.

10. D. Schoennbrun, *The Three Lives of Charles de Gaulle. A Biography* (London, Hamish Hamilton, 1966), p. 193.

11. S. Berstein, *The Republic of de Gaulle, 1958–1969* (Cambridge, Cambridge University Press, 1993), p. 11.

12. P. Morris, *French Politics Today* (Manchester, Manchester University Press, 1994), p. 22.

13. M. Larkin, *France since the Popular Front* (Oxford, Clarendon Press, 1986), p. 284. The alternate was listed on the ballot paper at the time of the initial election.

14. *Ibid*, p. 282. See too J. Frears, 'Parliament' in W. G. Andrews & S. Hoffmann (eds), *The Fifth Republic at Twenty* (Albany, University of New York Press, 1981), pp. 57–78.

15. See J. Hayward, *De Gaulle to Mitterrand. Presidential Power in France* (London, Hurst, 1993).

16. D. S. Bell, *Presidential Power in Fifth Republic France* (Oxford, Berg, 2000).

17. D. Howarth & G. Varouxakis, *Contemporary France. An Introduction to French Politics and Society* (London, Arnold, 2003), pp. 41–2.

18. See J. Frears & P. Morris, 'La Britannicité de la Ve République', in *Espoir*, 1992, no. 85. See, too, A. Teyssier, *La Ve République, 1958–1995. De de Gaulle à Chirac* (Paris, Pygmalion, 1995), p. 38.

19. J. Jackson, *De Gaulle* (London, Cardinal, 1990) p. 54.

20. M. Winock, 'De Gaulle and the Algerian Crisis, 1958–1962', in H. Gough & J. Horne (eds), *De Gaulle and Twentieth-Century France* (London, Edward Arnold, 1992), p. 72.

21. The words belong to Albert Camus cited in the collection, *Resistance, Rebellion and Death* (London, Hamish Hamilton, 1961), p. 98.

22. A. Horne, *A Savage War of Peace. Algeria, 1954–1962* (London, Pan, 2002 ed) p. 232.

23. See F. Bédarida & E. Fouilloux (eds), *La Guerre d'Algérie et les chrétiens*, Cahiers de l'Institut du Temps Présent, 9, October 1988.

24. For a commentary on de Beauvoir's novel, see K. Ross, *Fast Cars, Clean Bodies. Decolonisation and the Reordering of French Culture*

(Cambridge Mass., MIT Press, 1995), pp. 57–9, 61–5, 108, 133–7, 142–50. See too M. Atack, *May 68 in French Fiction and Film. Rethinking Society, Rethinking Representation* (Oxford, Oxford University Press, 1999), pp. 9–25.

25. See J. Soustelle, *Vingt-huit ans de gaullisme* (Paris, La Table Ronde, 1968).

26. Quoted in Winock, 'De Gaulle and the Algerian Crisis, 1958–1962', p. 72.

27. Quoted in Horne, *Savage War of Peace*, p. 302.

28. *Ibid.*, p. 377.

29. Quoted in Berstein, *The Republic of de Gaulle*, p. 29.

30. Peyrefitte, *C'était de Gaulle*, vol. 1, p. 73.

31. R. N. Gildea, *France Since 1945* (Oxford, Oxford University Press, 2002 2nd ed), pp. 29–30.

32. Peyrefitte, *C'était de Gaulle*, vol. 1, p. 73.

33. See G. Halimi & S. de Beauvoir, *Djamila Boupacha* (Paris, Gallimard, 1961).

34. See M. Evans, *The Memory of Resistance. French Opposition to the Algerian War, 1954–1962* (Oxford, Berg, 1997).

35. See J. House & N. MacMaster, 'Une journé portée disparue. The Paris massacre of 1961 and memory', in K. Mouré & M. S. Alexander (eds), *Crisis and Renewal in France* (New York, Berghahn, 2001), pp. 267–90, J.-P. Brunet, *Police contre FLN. Le drame d'octobre 1961* (Paris, Flammarion, 1999) and J. Luc Einaudi, *La Bataille de Paris, 17 octobre 1961* (Paris, Seuil, 1991).

36. D. Blair, *Simone de Beauvoir* (London, Vintage, 1990), p. 483.

37. Jean-Jacques Servan-Schreiber, *L'Express*, 13 July 1956, reprinted in *L'Express*, 15–21 May 2003, p. 15.

38. R. Vinen, *France, 1934–1960* (Basingstoke, Macmillan, 1996), p. 170.

39. M. S. Alexander & J. Keiger (eds), *France and the Algerian War, 1954–62. Strategy, Operations and Diplomacy* (London, Frank Cass, 2002), p. 14.

40. See Horne, *Savage War of Peace*, p. 538.

41. See A. Roche, 'Pieds noirs. Le retour', *Modern and Contemporary France*, (2), 2, 1994, pp. 151–64.

42. Vinen, *France*, p. 174.

43. R. N. Gildea, *France since 1945*, (Oxford, Oxford University Press, 1996) p. 28.

44. See B. Droz, 'Le cas très singulier de la guerre d'Algérie', in *Vingtième siècle*, no. 5, January–March 1985, and P. Dine, 'A la

recherche du soldat perdu. Myth, Metaphor and memory in the French Cinema of the Algerian War', in V. Holman & D. Kelly (eds), *France at War in the Twentieth Century. Propaganda, Myth and Metaphor* (Oxford, Berghahn Books, 2000), p. 143.

45. See P. Dine, *Images of the Algerian War. French Fiction and Film, 1954–1992* (Oxford, Clarendon Press, 1994).

46. See G. M. Benamou (ed.), *Un Mensonge Français. Enquête sur la guerre d'Algérie* (Paris, Robert Laffont, 2003), P. Nora, *Les Lieux de mémoire* (Paris, Seuil, 1990, 3 vols), B. W. Sigg, *Le silence et la honte. Névroses de la guerre d'Algérie* (Paris, Messidor, 1989), B. Stora, *La Gangène et l'oubli. La Mémoire de la guerre d'Algérie* (Paris, La Découverte, 1992), and his 'La Guerre d'Algérie quarante ans après. Connaissances et reconnaissance', *Modern and Contemporary France*, (2), 2, 1994, pp. 131–9.

47. See J.-P. Rioux, (ed.), *La Guerre d'Algérie et les français* (Paris, Fayard, 1990).

48. Evans, *Memory of Resistance*, p. 21.

49. See especially *Le Monde*, 23 November and 24 November 2000.

50. See P. Aussaresses, *Services Spéciaux. Algérie, 1955–1957* (Paris, Perrin, 2001).

51. S. Hazaressingh, 'Guard Dogs of Good Deeds. Remembering badly and forgetting well: history and memory in modern France', in *Times Literary Supplement*, 21 March 2003, pp. 12–3.

52. C. De Gaulle, *Lettres, Notes et carnets, 1961–3* (Paris, Plon, 1980–88), p. 27.

53. Shennan, *De Gaulle*, p. 109.

54. Peyrefitte, *C'était de Gaulle*, vol. 1, p. 179.

55. Berstein, *Republic of de Gaulle*, p. 67 from where this summary of political positions has been taken.

56. Peyrefitte, *C'était de Gaulle*, vol. 1, p. 70.

57. Berstein, *Republic of de Gaulle*, p. 77.

Chapter 3: *La Consolidation*: De Gaulle's Republic, 1963–1967

1. G. Perec, *Les Choses* (Paris, René Julliard, 1965).

2. T. Stovall, *France since the Second World War* (London, Longman, 2002), p. 124.

3. D. Borne, *Histoire de la société française depuis 1945* (Paris, Armand Colin, 2000 3rd ed), p. 40.

4. H. Mendras, *La Seconde Révolution française, 1965–1984* (Paris, Gallimard, 1988), p. 9.

5. A. Shennan, *De Gaulle* (London, Longman, 1994), p. 132.

6. A. Peyrefitte, *C'était de Gaulle* (Paris, Perrin, 1997), vol. 2, p. 178, p. 385.

7. *Ibid.*, vol. 1, p. 101.

8. V. Wright, *The Government and Politics of France* (London, Routledge, 1989 3rd ed), pp. 16–20.

9. Peyrefitte, *C'était de Gaulle*, vol. 1, p. 506.

10. S. Perry, 'Television', in S. Perry (ed.), *Aspects of Contemporary France* (London, Routledge, 1997), p. 117.

11. Quoted in J. Jackson, *De Gaulle* (London, Cardinal, 1990), p. 85.

12. Peyrefitte, *C'était de Gaulle*, vol. 1, p. 500.

13. A. Peyrefitte, *Le Mal français* (Paris, Plon, 1976).

14. Jackson, *De Gaulle*, p. 85.

15. R. Cayol, *La nouvelle communication politique* (Paris, Larousse, 1986), p. 36.

16. S. Berstein, *The Republic of de Gaulle, 1958–1969* (Cambridge, Cambridge University Press, 1993), p. 87.

17. J. Foccart, *Journal de l'Elysée* (Paris, Fayard, 2001), 3 vols.

18. *Le Canard Enchainé*, 26 November 1958 reproduced in J. Watson, 'The Internal Dynamics of Gaullism', unpublished University of Oxford D. Phil, 2001.

19. Watson, 'The Internal Dynamics of Gaullism'.

20. Berstein, *Republic of de Gaulle*, p. 90.

21. Wright, *The Government and Politics of France*, p. 164.

22. P. Morris, *French Politics Today* (Manchester, Manchester University Press, 1994), pp. 117–8.

23. See especially A. Knapp & V. Wright, *The Government and Politics of France* (London, Routledge, 2000), chapter 9, J. Charlot, *The Gaullist Phenomenon* (London, Allen & Unwin, 1971), and P. Martin, *Comprendre les évolutions électorales* (Paris, Presses de Sciences Po, 2000).

24. Berstein, *De Gaulle's Republic*, pp. 87–100, and for much of the subsequent discussion.

25. Peyrefitte, *C'était de Gaulle*, vol. 3, p. 74.

26. F. Mitterrand, *The Wheat and the Chaff. The Personal Diaries of the President of France, 1971–1978* (London, Weidenfeld & Nicolson, 1982), p. 12.

27. R. N. Gildea, *France since 1945* (Oxford, Oxford University Press, 2002 2nd ed), p. 58.

28. A. Teyssier, *La Ve République, 1958–1995. De de Gaulle à Chirac* (Paris, Pygmalion, 1995), p. 109.
29. T. H. White, *The Making of the President 1960* (New York, Atheneum, 1961), p. 378.
30. D. Hanley, *Party, Society, Government. Republican Democracy in France* (Oxford, Berghahn Books, 2003), pp. 163–6.
31. A. Cole, *French Politics and Society* (London, Longman, 1999), p. 146.
32. *Ibid.*
33. Borne, *Histoire de la société française*, p. 40.
34. J. Fourastié, *Les trente glorieuses ou la Révolution invisible* (Paris, Fayard, 1979).
35. R. Vinen, *France 1934–1970* (Basingstoke, Macmillan, 1996), p. 112.
36. E. Weber, *The Hollow Years. France in the 1930s* (New York, Norton, 1994), p. 37.
37. K. Mouré, 'The French Economy since 1930', in M. S. Alexander (ed.), *French History since Napoleon* (London, Arnold, 1999), p. 372.
38. Mendras, *La Seconde Révolution*, p. 30.
39. G. Dupeux, *French Society, 1789–1970* (London, Methuen, 1976), p. 244.
40. R. N. Gildea, *France since 1945*, pp. 102–3.
41. *Ibid.*, pp. 100–1.
42. See A.-D. Schor, *La Politique économique et sociale de la Ve République* (Paris, Presses Universitaires de France, 1993), pp. 112–4.
43. Berstein, *De Gaulle's Republic*, p. 114.
44. A. Bleton, *Les Hommes qui viennent* (Paris, Editions Ouvrières, 1956), p. 200.
45. D. Holter, *The Battle for Coal. Miners and the Politics of Nationalisation in France, 1940–1950* (DeKalb, Northern Illinois University Press, 1992), p. 193.
46. R. Kuisel, *Seducing the French. The Dilemma of Americanisation* (Berkeley, University of California Press, 1993).
47. Peyrefitte, *C'était de Gaulle*, vol. 3, pp. 81–3.
48. A. Sigaux, *A History of Tourism* (London, Leisure Arts, 1966), p. 71.
49. E. Furlough, 'The Business of Pleasure. Creating Club Méditerranée', in K. Steven Vincent & A. Klairmont-Lingo, *The Human Tradition in Modern France* (Wilmington, SR Books, 2000), p. 187. See too A. Faujas, *Trigano. L'aventure du Club Med* (Paris, Flammarion, 1994), P. Blednick, *Another Day in Paradise? The Real Club Méd Story* (London, Macmillan, 1988) and A. Rauch, *Vacances en France de 1830 à nos jours* (Paris, Hachette, 1996).

50. See D. Lacorne (ed.), *The Rise and Fall of Anti-Americanism. A Century of French Perceptions* (Basingstoke, Macmillan, 1990).

51. Kuisel, *Seducing the French*, pp. 52–69.

52. G. Le Bras, *Etudes de sociologie religieuse* (Paris, Presses Universitaires de France, 1955–56), 2 vols, and F. Boulard, *An Introduction to Religious Sociology* (London, Darton, Longman and Todd, 1960).

53. G. Lambert, *Dieu change en Bretagne* (Paris, Cerf, 1985).

54. See C. Duchen, *Feminism in France from May '68 to Mitterrand* (London, Routledge, 1986) and C. Laubier (ed.) *The Condition of Women in France, 1945 to the Present* (London, Routledge, 1990).

55. Laubier, *The Condition of Women in France. 1945 to the Present*, p. 71.

56. Duchen, *Feminism in France from May 68 to Mitterrand*.

57. J. Ardagh, *France in the New Century* (London, Penguin, 1999), p. 598.

58. *Ibid.*, for much of the material here, p. 199 et seq.

59. L. R. Roos, 'Tales of the City. Representing the HLM in Contemporary French Culture', in M. Allison & O. Heathcote (eds), *Forty Years of the Fifth French Republic. Action, Dialogue and Discourse* (Bern, Lang, 2001), pp. 339–54.

60. P. Cerny, *The Politics of Grandeur. Ideological Aspects of de Gaulle's Foreign Policy* (Cambridge, Cambridge University Press, 1980) and M. Vaïsse, *La Grandeur. Politique étrangère du général de Gaulle* (Paris, Fayard, 1998).

61. D. Gvichianin, 'Les relations franco-soviétiques pendant la présidence du général de Gaulle', in Institut Charles de Gaulle, *De Gaulle en son siècle* (Paris, Institut Charles de Gaulle, 1992) vol. 3, p. 382.

62. J. Dalloz, *La France et le monde depuis 1945* (Paris, Armand Colin, 1993), pp. 116–8.

63. See Foccart, *Journal de l'Elysée*, vol. 3.

64. N. Wahl, 'De Gaulle and the Americans' in R. O. Paxton & N. Wahl (eds), *De Gaulle and the US. A Centennial Reappraisal* (Oxford, Berg, 1994), p. xiv.

65. Peyrefitte, *C'était de Gaulle*, vol. 1, p. 282.

66. Quoted in A. Pierre, 'Conflicting Visions. Defence, Nuclear Weapons and Arms Control in the Franco-American Relationship during the de Gaulle Era' in Paxton & Wahl (eds), *De Gaulle and the US*, p. 299.

67. Jackson, *De Gaulle*, p. 68 and for much of the information here.

68. R. Kuisel, 'The American Economic Challenge. De Gaulle and the French', in Paxton & Wahl (eds), *De Gaulle and the US*, p. 195.

69. Peyrefitte, *C'était de Gaulle*, vol. 1, p. 374, vol. 2, p. 48.

70. *Ibid.*, vol. 2, p. 313.
71. R. O. Paxton, 'Introduction', in Paxton & Wahl (eds), *De Gaulle and the US*, p. 5.
72. A. Guyomarch, H. Machin & E. Ritchie, *France in the European Union* (Basingstoke, Macmillan, 1998), p. 21.
73. Peyrefitte, *C'était de Gaulle*, vol. 1, p. 356.
74. D. Johnson, 'De Gaulle's Foreign Policy', *International Affairs*, 1966.
75. Jackson, *De Gaulle*, pp. 77–8.

Chapter 4: *Le Contestation*: 1968

1. Quoted in M. Agulhon, A. Nouschi & R. Schor, *La France de 1940 à nos jours* (Paris, Nathan, 2001 3rd ed), p. 238.
2. Quoted in M. Atack, *May 68 in French Fiction and Film. Rethinking Society, Rethinking Representation* (Oxford, Oxford University Press, 1999), p. 12.
3. A. Marwick, *The Sixties. Cultural Revolution in Britain, France, Italy and the United States, c.1958–c.1974* (Oxford, Oxford University Press, 1998), p. 602.
4. P. Viansson-Ponté, *Histoire de la république gaullienne* (Paris, Robert Laffont, 1970–71), p. 250.
5. E. Balladur, *L'Arbre de mai* (Paris, Atelier Marcel Jullian, 1977), pp. 303–4.
6. See D. Caute, *Sixty-Eight. The Year of the Barricades* (London, Hamish Hamilton, 1988), p. 210 and J. Jackson, 'De Gaulle and May 1968', in H. Gough & J. Horne, *De Gaulle and Twentieth-Century France* (London, Edward Arnold, 1994), p. 126.
7. R. Frank, 'Introduction', in G. Dreyfus-Armand, R. Frank, M.-F. Lévy & M. Zacarini-Fournel (eds), *Les Années 68. Le temps de contestation* (Brussels, Editions Complexe, 2000), p. 14. For recent sociological commentaries, Teyssier recommends P. Yonnet, *Voyage au centre du malaise française* (Paris, Gallimard, 1993) and J. Capdevieille & R. Mouriaux, *Mai 68. L'entre-deux de la modernité. Histoire de trente ans* (Paris, FNSP, 1985). For an historical approach see L. Joffrin, *Mai 68. Histoire des événements* (Paris, Seuil, 1988) and O. Rudelle, *Mai 68. De Gaulle et la République* (Paris, Plon, 1988).
8. A. Touraine, *Le Communisme utopique. Le mouvement de Mai 68* (Paris, Seuil, 1968).

9. Cited in R. Vinen, *France 1934–1970* (Basingstoke, Macmillan, 1996), p. 184.
10. T. Ali, *Street Fighting Years. An Autobiography of the Sixties* (London, Fontana, 1987), p. 197.
11. Quoted in Caute, *Sixty Eight*, p. 192. See, too, Agulhon et al., *La France de 1940*, p. 241, and R. Johnson, *The French Communist Party versus the Students* (New Haven, Yale University Press, 1972).
12. Quoted in *ibid.*, p. 184.
13. R. Aron, *La Révolution introuvable* (Paris, Fayard, 1968), p. 257.
14. Quoted in Marwick, *The Sixties*, p. 611. See too the collection, O. Bernard, *The Finger Points at the Moon. Inscriptions from Paris, May 1968* (New York, Tuba Press, 1999).
15. See P. Bénéton & J. Touchard, 'The Interpretation of the Crisis on May/June 1968', in K. Reader, *The May Events in France. Reproductions and Reinterpretations* (New York, St Martin's Press, 1993), pp. 31–2.
16. Marwick, *The Sixties*, p. 611.
17. See J.-P. Le Goff, *Mai 68, l'héritage impossible* (Paris, Editions La Découverte, 1998).
18. Quoted in D. Sassoon, *One Hundred Years of Socialism. The West European Left in the Twentieth Century* (London, Fontana, 1997), p. 390.
19. S. Berstein, *The Republic of de Gaulle, 1958–1969* (Cambridge, Cambridge University Press, 1993), p. 211.
20. A. Peyrefitte, *C'était de Gaulle* (Paris, Perrin, 1997), vol. 2, p. 186.
21. J. Jennings. 'Introduction', in J. Jennings (ed.), *Intellectuals in Twentieth-Century France. Mandarins and Samurais* (Basingstoke, Macmillan, 1993), p. 13. See too D. Howarth & G. Varouxakis, *Contemporary France. An Introduction to French Politics and Society* (London, Arnold, 2003), pp. 123–40, and G. Varouxakis, *Victorian Political Thought on France and the French* (Basingstoke, Palgrave, 2002).
22. C. Charle, *Naissance des 'intellectuels', 1880–1900* (Paris, Minuit, 1990).
23. See L. Bodin, *Les Intellectuels* (Paris, Presses Universitaires de France, 1962), S. Hazareesingh, *Political Traditions in Modern France* (Oxford, Oxford University Press, 1994), J. Jennings, *Intellectuals in Twentieth-Century France* (Basingstoke, Macmillan, 1993), P. Ory & J.-F. Sirinelli, *Les Intellectuels en France de l'Affaire Dreyfus à nos jours* (Paris, Colin, 1986), and T. Judt, *Past Imperfect. French Intellectuals, 1944–1956* (Berkeley, University of California Press, 1992).

24. See J. Benda, *La Trahison des clercs* (Paris, Grasset, 1933) and P. Nizan, *Les Chiens de garde* (Paris, Grasset, 1932).

25. See S. Khilnani, *Arguing Revolution. The Intellectual Left in Postwar France* (New Haven, Yale University Press, 1993).

26. R. N. Gildea, *France since 1945* (Oxford, Oxford University Press, 2002 2nd ed), pp. 182–4, for much of the information here.

27. Caute, *Sixty Eight*, p. 200.

28. Quoted in Khilnani, *Arguing Revolution*, p. 108.

29. Judt, *Past Imperfect* pp. 3–4.

30. J. Jennings, 'Of Treason, Blindness and Silence. Dilemmas of the Intellectual in Modern France', in J. Jennings & T. Kemp-Welch (eds), *Intellectuals in Politics. From the Dreyfus Affair to Salman Rushdie* (London, Routledge, 2000), pp. 65–85.

31. Jackson, 'De Gaulle and May 1968', p. 129.

32. K. Ross, *May '68 and its Afterlives* (Chicago, University of Chicago Press, 2002), p. 26.

33. J.-P. Legois, A. Monchablon & R. Morder, 'Le Mouvement étudiant et l'Université: entre réforme et révolution, 1964–1976', in Dreyfus-Armand, Frank, Lévy & Zacarini-Fournel (eds), *Les Années 68. Le temps de contestation*, p. 285.

34. R. Turner, 'Higher Education', in S. Perry (ed.), *Aspects of Contemporary France* (London, Routledge, 1997), pp. 98–9.

35. Quoted in Atack, *May 68*, p. 29.

36. Quoted in M. Archer, 'Education', in J. Flower (ed.), *France Today* (London, Methuen, 1977 3rd ed), p. 72.

37. J. F. McMillan, *Twentieth-Century France. Politics and Society* (London, Arnold, 1991), p. 180.

38. Marwick, *The Sixties*, p. 603. See the correspondence in Peyrefitte, *C'était de Gaulle*, vol. 3, pp. 558–9.

39. K. Ross, *May '68*, p. 107.

40. Le Goff, *Mai 68*, p. 192.

41. *Ibid.*, pp. 95–7, and Marwick, *The Sixties*, p. 617.

42. See J. Bridgford, 'The Events of May. Consequences for Industrial Relations in France', in D. Hanley & P. Kerr (eds), *May '68. Coming of Age* (Basingstoke, Macmillan, 1989), pp. 100–16.

43. Berstein, *The Republic of de Gaulle*, p. 217.

44. H. Koning, *1968. A Personal Report* (London, Unwin Hyman, 1987), p. 75.

45. Quoted in Caute, *Sixty Eight*, p. 205.

46. Peyrefitte, *C'était de Gaulle*, vol. 3, p. 604. *L'Huma* is the popular title for the communist paper, *L'Humanité*.
47. *Ibid.*, vol. 1, 11 June 1963. See too Reader, *The May Events*, p. 3.
48. Quoted in A. Teyssier, *La Ve République, 1958–1995. De de Gaulle à Chirac* (Paris, Pygmalion, 1995), p. 142. See too p. 145.
49. Berstein, *The Republic of de Gaulle*, p. 219.
50. Bridgford, 'The Events of May', pp. 102–6.
51. See A. de Boissieu, *Pour servir le Général* (Paris, Plon, 1983), J. Massu, *Baden 68. Souvenirs d'une fidelité gaulliste* (Paris, Plon, 1979), F. Flohic, *Souvenirs d'outre-Gaulle* (Paris, Plon, 1979), G. Pompidou, *Pour rétablir une vérité* (Paris, Flammarion, 1982) and C. Fouchet, *Les Feux du crépuscule. Journal, 1968, 1969, 1970* (Paris, Plon, 1977).
52. Jackson, 'De Gaulle and May 1968'. See too J. Lacouture, *De Gaulle*, vol. 2, *The Leader* (London, Collins, 1991) and D. S. Bell, 'May 68: Explaining the Power Vacuum', in M. Allison & O. Heathcote, *Forty Years of the Fifth French Republic. Action, Dialogue and Discourse* (Bern, Lang, 2001), pp. 21–35.
53. See F. Broche, *De Gaulle Secret* (Paris, Pygmalion, 1993).
54. J. Charlot, 'The Aftermath of May 68 for Gaullism, the Right and the Centre', in Hanley & Kerr (eds), *May '68*, pp. 62–81.
55. Peyrefitte, *C'était de Gaulle*, vol. 3, p. 625.
56. J. Charlot, 'The Aftermath of May 68 for Gaullism, the Right and the Centre', in Hanley & Kerr (eds), *May '68*, pp. 62–81.
57. D. Hanley & P. Kerr, 'Introduction: Elusive May. The Paradox of a Moment in History', in Hanley & Kerr (eds), *May '68*, pp. 1–9. See too H. Weber, *Vingt ans après* (Paris, Seuil, 1988).
58. Teyssier, *La Ve République, 1958–1995*, p. 131.
59. *Le Monde*, 26/27 December 1999.
60. A. Prost, 'Ecoles, Collèges and Lycées in France since 1968', in Hanley & Kerr (eds), *May '68*, pp. 23–41.
61. Hanley & P. Kerr, 'Introduction: Elusive May. The Paradox of a Moment in History', in Hanley & Kerr (eds), *May '68*, p. 7.
62. N. Hewlett, *Modern French Politics. Analysing Conflict and Consensus since 1945* (London, Polity, 1998), p. 163.
63. See R. Inglehart, *Culture Shift in Advanced Industrial Society* (Princeton, Princeton University Press, 1990).
64. S. Wharton, 'Progress. What Progress? The Gay and Lesbian Liberation Movement in the Fifth Republic', in Allison & Heathcote (eds), *Forty Years of the Fifth Republic*, pp. 191–204.

65. Quoted in D. Blair, *Simone de Beauvoir* (London, Vintage, 1990), p. 535.
66. See C. Duchen, *Feminism in France from 68 to Mitterrand* (London, Routledge, 1986), p. 20 and C. Laubier, *The Condition of Women in France. 1945 to the Present. A Documentary Anthology* (London, Routledge, 1990), p. 71.

Chapter 5: *La Confiance*: Pompidou and Giscard, 1969–81

1. J.-J. Becker *Histoire politique de la France depuis 1945* (Paris, Armand Colin, 1996 ed), p. 126.
2. S. Berstein & J.-P. Rioux, *The Pompidou Years, 1970–1974* (Cambridge, Cambridge University Press, 2002), p. 9.
3. *Ibid.*, p. 16, see too A. Teyssier, *La Ve République, 1958–1995. De Gaulle à Chirac* (Paris, Pygmalion, 1995), p. 171.
4. P. Thody, *The Fifth Republic. Presidents, Politics and Personalities* (London, Routledge, 1998), p. 38.
5. See F. Abadie & J.-P. Corcette, *Georges Pompidou, 1911–1974. Le désir et le destin* (Paris, Balland, 1994) and E. Roussel, *Georges Pompidou* (Paris, P. Lattès, 1994).
6. Teyssier, *La Ve République*, p. 196.
7. A. Peyrefitte, *C'était de Gaulle* (Paris, Perrin, 1994), vol. 1, 8 December 1958.
8. See J. Foccart, *Journal de l'Elysée* (Paris, Fayard, 2001), vol. 5.
9. A. F. Knapp, *Gaullism after de Gaulle* (Aldershot, Dartsmouth, 1994), p. 33.
10. Berstein & Rioux, *The Pompidou Years, 1970–1974*, p. 55.
11. V. Wright, *The Government and Politics of France* (London, Routledge, 1989 3rd ed), p. 193.
12. See Knapp, *Gaullism after de Gaulle, passim.*
13. Wright, *The Government and Politics of France*, p. 193.
14. F. Mitterrand, *The Wheat and the Chaff* (London, Weidenfeld & Nicolson, 1982) p. 120.
15. Berstein & Rioux, *The Pompidou Years*, p. 25.
16. O. Todd, *La Marelle de Giscard, 1924–74* (Paris, Robert Laffont, 1977), p. 191.
17. V. Giscard d'Estaing, *Démocratie française* (Paris, Fayard, 1976). See too J. C. Petitfils, *La Démocratie giscardienne* (Paris, PUF, 1989).

18. See Hasard d'Estin, *Tout fout le camp* (Paris, Le Sagittaire, 1976).
19. J. R. Frears, *France in the Giscard Presidency* (London, George Allen & Unwin, 1981), pp. 128–97, and for much of the information in this paragraph.
20. *L'Express*, 26 February 1973, reprinted in *L'Express*, 15–21 May 2003.
21. P. Favier & M. Martin-Roland, *La Décennie Mitterrand* (Paris, Seuil, 1990), vol. 1, p. 214. As the authors relate, Badinter in 1974 had published a polemic against the guillotine, *L'Exécution* (Paris, Grasset).
22. Quoted in Frears, *France in the Giscard Presidency*, p. 150.
23. J. Fenby, *On the Brink, The Trouble with France* (London, Abacus, 1998), p. 328.
24. Mitterrand, *The Wheat and the Chaff*, p. 176. See too p. 126.
25. R. N. Gildea, *France since 1945* (Oxford, Oxford University Press, 2002 2nd ed), pp. 110–4, for much of the information here.
26. J. Forbes & N. Hewlett, *Contemporary France. Essays and Texts on Politics, Economics and Society* (London, Longman, 1994), p. 182.
27. J. Ardagh, *France in the New Century. Portrait of a Changing Society* (London, Penguin, 1999), pp. 109–12.
28. *Ibid.*, p. 67.
29. *Ibid.*, p. 700.
30. R. Barre, *Questions de confiance* (Paris, Flammarion, 1988) p. 54, quoted in Teyssier, *La Ve République, 1958–1995*, p. 261.
31. A. Cole, *French Politics and Society* (London, Longman, 1998), p. 33.
32. F.-X. Vershave, *Noir silence. Qui arrêtera la Françafrique* (Paris, Lesarènes, 2000).
33. R. N. Gildea, *France since 1945*, p. 267–8 Fenby, *On the Brink*, pp. 165–7 for much information here.
34. A. Cole, *Franco-German Relations* (London, Longman, 2001), p. 15.
35. A. Guyomarch, H. Machin & E. Ritchie, *France in the European Union* (Basingstoke, Macmillan, 1998), p. 27.
36. J. Campbell, *Margaret Thatcher*, vol. 2, *The Iron Lady* (London, Jonathan Cape, 2003), p. 62.
37. Fenby, *On the Brink*, p. 330.
38. Cole, *French Politics and Society*, p. 34.
39. See O. Duhamel and J. Jaffré, *SOFRES. L'état de l'opinion* (Paris, Seuil, 1997).
40. J. Jennings, 'Introduction' in J. Jennings (ed.), *Intellectuals in Twentieth-Century France. Mandarins and Samurais* (Basingstoke, Macmillan, 1993), p. 3.

41. See S. Hazareesingh, *Intellectuals and the French Communist Party. Disillusion and Decline* (Oxford, Oxford University Press, 1991).

42. D. S. Bell & B. Criddle, *The French Communist Party in the Fifth Republic* (Oxford, Clarendon Press, 1994), pp. 87–8. Also see M. Adereth, *The French Communist Party. A Critical History, 1920–1984* (Manchester, Manchester University Press, 1984).

43. Wright, *Government and Politics of France*, pp. 222–3.

44. Among the many new studies of Mitterrand, see J. Lacouture, *Mitterrand. Une histoire de français* (Paris, Seuil, 1998) 2 vols.

45. A. Cole, *François Mitterrand. A Study in Political Leadership* (London, Routledge, 1994), p. 6.

46. See D. S. Bell & B. Criddle, *The French Socialist Party. The Emergence of a Party of Government* (Oxford, Clarendon Press, 1988 2nd ed).

47. Mitterrand, *The Wheat and the Chaff*, p. 35.

48. D. S. Bell, 'The French Communist Party. From Revolution to Reform', in J. Evans (ed.), *The French Party System* (Manchester, Manchester University Press, 2003), p. 34 and R. N. Gildea, *France since 1945*, p. 213.

49. L. Stoléru, *Les Français à deux vitesses* (Paris, Flammarion, 1982).

50. *Le Monde. Dossiers et Documents. L'Election présidentielle*, May 1988.

51. Lacouture, *Mitterrand*, vol. 2, p. 12.

Chapter 6: *Le Caméléon*: The Mitterrand Presidencies, 1981–1995

1. Quoted in T. Stovall, *France since the Second World War* (London, Longman, 2002), p. 133.

2. A. Cole, *François Mitterrand. A Study in Political Leadership* (London, Routledge, 1997 2nd ed), pp. 32–52.

3. Quoted in W. Northcutt, *Mitterrand. A Political Biography* (New York, Holmes & Meier, 1992), p. 83.

4. J. Favier & M. Martin-Roland, *La Décennie Mitterrand* (Paris, Seuil, 1990), vol. 1, p. 96, p. 122.

5. Northcutt, *Mitterrand*, p. 83.

6. D. Lochak, *La Haute Administration à l'épreuve de l'alternance* (Paris, Presses Universitaires de France, 1985). See, too, Favier & Martin-Roland, *La Décennie Mitterrand*, vol. 1, p. 622.

7. Favier & Martin-Roland, *La Décennie Mitterrand*, vol. 1, p. 66, pp. 68–9.

8. C. Nay, *Les sept Mitterrand, ou les metamorphoses d'un septennat* (Paris, Grasset, 1988).

9. *Le Monde*, 12 May 1981, cited in Favier & Martin-Roland, *La Décennie Mitterrand*, vol. 1, p. 119.

10. Cole, *Mitterrand*, p. 33, p. 35.

11. This point is made in T. R. Christofferson, *The French Socialists in Power, 1981–1986. From Autogestion to Cohabitation* (Delaware, University of Delaware Press, 1991).

12. M. Agulhon, A. Nouschi & R. Schor, *La France de 1940 à nos jours* (Paris, Nathan, 2001 ed), p. 289.

13. Quoted in J. Lacouture, *Mitterrand. Une histoire de français* (Paris, Seuil, 1998), vol. 2, p. 32.

14. Favier & Martin-Roland, *La Décennie Mitterrand*, vol. 1, p. 230. For Lang more generally, see D. L. Looseley, *The Politics of Fun. Cultural Policy and Debate in Contemporary France* (Oxford, Berg, 1995).

15. Lacouture, *Mitterrand*, vol. 2, p. 54.

16. See M. Larkin, 'The Catholic Church and Politics in Twentieth-Century France', in M. S. Alexander (ed.), *French History Since Napoleon* (London, Arnold, 1999), pp. 147–171, and N. Beattie, 'Yeast in the Dough? Catholic Schooling in France, 1981–95', in K. Chadwick (ed.), *Catholicism, Politics and Society in Twentieth-Century France* (Liverpool, Liverpool University Press, 2000), pp. 197–218.

17. P. Holmes, 'Broken Dreams. Economic Policy in Mitterrand's France', in S. Mazey & M. Newman (eds), *Mitterrand's France* (London, Croom Helm, 1987), pp. 33–55. For an in-depth study, A. Founteneau & P.-A. Muet, *La Gauche face à la crise* (Paris, FNSP, 1985).

18. See Favier & Martin-Roland, *La Décennie Mitterrand*, vol. 1, p. 510.

19. See M. McLean, *Economic Management and French Business from de Gaulle to Chirac* (Basingstoke, Palgrave, 2002).

20. P. Clarke, *A Question of Leadership. Gladstone to Thatcher* (London, Hamish Hamilton, 1991), p. 316.

21. *L'Express*, 27 July 1984.

22. Quoted in Favier & Martin-Roland, *La Décennie Mitterrand*, vol. 2, p. 199.

23. *L'Express*, 16 August 1985, and 20 September 1985.

24. Favier & Martin-Roland, *La Décennie Mitterrand*, vol. 2, p. 434.

25. *Ibid.*, vol. 2, p. 380.

26. V. Wright, *The Government and Politics of France* (London, Routledge, 1989 3rd ed), pp. 71.

27. A full list to be found in A.-D. Schor, *La politique économique et sociale de la Ve République* (Paris, Presses Universitaires de France, 1993).

28. Favier & Martin-Roland, *La Décennie Mitterrand*, vol. 3, pp. 16–7.

29. Cole, *Mitterrand*, p. 44 and R. N. Gildea, *France since 1945* (Oxford, Oxford University Press, 2002 2nd ed), p. 221.

30. J. Wolfreys, 'Shoes, Lies and Videotape. Corruption and the French State', *Modern and Contemporary France*, 2001, 9 (4), p. 440.

31. E. Conan & H. Rousso, *Vichy, un passé qui ne passe pas* (Paris, Fayard, 1994).

32. See R. Aubrac, *Où la mémoire s'attarde* (Paris, Odile Jacob, 1996). See too D. Cordier, *Jean Moulin. L'inconnu du Panthéon* (Paris, Lattès, 1989–93), 3 vols and A. Clinton, *Jean Moulin, 1899–1943. The French Resistance and the Republic* (Basingstoke, Palgrave, 2002).

33. H. Rousso, *The Vichy Syndrome. History and Memory in France since 1944* (Cambridge MA, Harvard University Press, 1989), pp. 243–5.

34. R. N. Gildea, *France since 1945* (Oxford, Oxford University Press, 2002 2nd ed), p. 75.

35. J. Jackson, *France. The Dark Years, 1940–1944* (Oxford, Oxford University Press, 2001), pp. 605–8.

36. *Ibid.*, p. 613.

37. R. Golson, *Vichy's Afterlife. History and Counterhistory in Postwar France* (Lincoln, University of Nebraska Press, 2000), p. 73.

38. See S. Klarsfeld, *Vichy-Auschwitz* (Paris, Fayard, 1982–5), 2 vols. Also see T. Stovall, *France since the Second World War* (London, Longman, 2002), p. 90 for much information related here.

39. See C. Nay, *Le Noir et le rouge* (Paris, Grasset, 1984).

40. P. Péan, *Une Jeunesse française. François Mitterrand, 1934–1947* (Paris, Fayard, 1994) and O. Wieviorka, *Nous entrerons dans la carrière, De la Résistance à l'exercice du pouvoir* (Paris, Seuil, 1994).

41. Quoted in Favier & Martin-Roland, *La décennie Mitterrand*, vol. 4, pp. 561–2.

42. Golson, *Vichy's Afterlife*, pp. 104–5, and P. Thibaud, 'L'Homme au-dessus des lois', *Le Débat*, September–November, 1994.

43. Jackson, *France. Dark Years, 1940–1944*, p. 621.

44. Quoted in J. Lacouture, *Mitterrand*, vol. 2, p. 110.

45. *New York Review of Books*, 23 November 1994 quoted in Jackson, *The Dark Years*, p. 622.

46. R. O. Paxton, *Vichy France. Old Guard and New Order, 1940–1944* (New York, Columbia University Press, 2001 ed).

47. V. Caron, *Uneasy Asylum. France and the Jewish Refugee Crisis, 1933–42* (Stanford, Stanford University Press, 1999).

48. C. Lloyd, 'Race and Ethnicity', in M. Cook & G. Davie (eds), *Modern France. Society in Transition* (London, Routledge, 1999), p. 40.

49. L. R. Koos, 'Tales of the City. Representing the HLM in Contemporary French Culture', in M. Allisson & O. Heathcote (eds), *Forty Years of the Fifth Republic. Action, Dialogue and Discourse* (Bern, Lang, 2001), pp. 339–54.

50. See P. R. Ireland, 'Race, Immigration and hate', in A. Daley (ed.), *The Mitterrand Era. Policy Aternatives and Politics in France* (Basingstoke, Macmillan, 1996).

51. For a chronology of this issue see G. Davie, 'Religion and Laïcité', in M. Cook & G. Davie (eds), *Modern France. Society in Transition* (London, Routledge, 1999), pp. 207–8.

52. See G. Mermet, *Francoscopie. 2003* (Paris, Larousse, 2003), p. 231.

53. J. Ardagh, *France in the New Century. Portrait of a Changing Society* (London, Penguin, 1999), p. 223.

54. M. Houellebecq, *Plateforme* (Paris, Flammarion, 1999).

55. See A. Hussey, 'ZZ Top', *The Observer Sport Monthly*, April 2004, pp. 15–23.

56. G. Ivaldi, 'The FN Split. Party System Change and Electoral Prospects' in J. Evans (ed.), *The French Party System* (Manchester, Manchester University Press, 2003), pp. 137–51.

57. See J.-Y. Camus, *Le Front National. Histoire et analyses* (Paris, Livre de Poche, 1998), N. Mayer, *Ces français qui votent FN* (Paris, Flammarion, 1999), and R. Dély, *Histoire secrète du Front National* (Paris, Grasset, 1999).

58. See H. G. Simmons, *The French National Front. The Extremist Challenge to Democracy* (Oxford, Westview, 1996).

59. S. Mira, 'The National Front in France. A Single Issue Movement?', *West European Politics*, (11), 2, 1988.

60. See R. Rémond, *Les Droites en France* (Paris, Aubier, 1982).

61. See, for example, P. Milza, *Fascisme français* (Paris, Flammarion, 1987).

62. J. Wolfreys, 'Neither Right nor Left? Towards an Integrated Analysis of the Front National', in N. Atkin & F. Tallett (eds), *The Right in France from Revolution to Le Pen* (London, I. B. Tauris, 2003 2nd ed), pp. 261–76. See too M. Dobry, *Le Mythe de l'allergie française au fascisme* (Paris, Albin Michel, 2003).

63. S. Hoffmann, 'Gaullism by any other name', in G. S. Ross, S. Hoffmann & S. Malzacher (eds), *The Mitterrand Experiment* (Oxford, Polity Press, 1987).

64. Lacouture, *Mitterrand*, vol. 2, pp. 514–8. See too R. N. Gildea, *France since 1945*, p. 269 for much information here.

65. Quoted in J. Fenby, *On the Brink. The Trouble with France* (London, Abacus, 2002 ed), p. 37.
66. See R. N. Gildea, *France since 1945*, pp. 251–7.
67. Favier & Martin-Roland, *La Décennie Mitterrand*, vol. 2, p. 244.
68. Cole, *Mitterrand*, pp. 116–7.
69. Campbell, *Margaret Thatcher*, vol. 2, p. 308.
70. A. Knapp, 'From the Gaullist Movement to the President's Party', in Evans (ed.), *The French Party System*, p. 125.
71. Provisions of the TEU taken from A. Guyomarch, H. Machin & E. Ritchie, *France in the European Union* (Basingstoke, Macmillan, 1998), p. 34.
72. A. Sa'Adah, *Contemporary France. A Democratic Education* (Lanham, Roman & Littlefield, 2003), p. 268.
73. Guyomarch, Machin & Ritchie, *France in the European Union*, pp. 97–102.
74. *Le Monde*, 25 September 1992 reproduced in *ibid.*, p. 99.
75. Quoted in Lacouture, *Mitterrand*, vol. 1, p. 13.

Chapter 7: *Le Chagrin*: Chirac's Presidency, 1995–2002

1. *L'Express*, 2–8 May 2003.
2. On Americanisation, see *The Sunday Times*, 22 February 2004.
3. J. Ardagh, *France in the New Century. Portrait of a Changing Society* (London, Penguin, 1999), p. 25.
4. See, for example, *L'Evénement du jeudi*, 2 February 1992.
5. Quoted in B. Clift, 'PS Intra-Party Politics and Party System Change' in J. Evans (ed.), *The French Party System* (Manchester, Manchester University Press, 2003), p. 50.
6. A. Teyssier, *La Ve République, 1958–1995. De de Gaulle à Chirac* (Paris, Pygmalion, 1995), p. 524.
7. Quoted in J. Fenby, *On the Brink. The Trouble with France* (London, Abacus, 2002), p. 396.
8. See P. Perrineau & C. Ysmal, *Le Vote de crise. L'élection présidentielle de 1995* (Paris, FNSP, 1995).
9. *Le Canard Enchaîné*, 2 March 1995.
10. This point is made in A. Sa'Adah, *Contemporary France. A Democratic Education* (Lanham, Rowman & Littlefiled, 2003), p. 149, who is good on Chirac's 1995 campaign.
11. A. Knapp, 'From the Gaullist movement to the President's Party', in Evans, *The French Party System*, p. 125.

12. See the discussion in D. Howarth & G. Varouxakis, *Contemporary France. An Introduction to French Politics and Society* (London, Arnold, 2003), pp. 94–5 and C. Groux, *Vers un renouveau du conflit social* (Paris, Bayard, 1998).

13. Sa'Adah, *Contemporary France*, p. 150.

14. P. Thody, *The Fifth French Republic. Presidents, Politics and Personalities* (London, Routledge, 1998), p. 125.

15. See D. Hanley, 'Managing the Plural Left. Implications for the Party System', in Evans, *The French Party System*, pp. 81–6.

16. A. Cole, 'Understanding Jospin', *Modern and Contemporary France*, (1), 3, 2002, p. 295.

17. A. Peyrefitte, *Cétait de Gaulle* (Paris, Perrim, 1997), vol. 2, p. 143.

18. Fenby, *On the Brink*, p. 411.

19. See J. Gaffney, 'Protocol, Image and Discourse in Political Leadership Competition. The Case of Prime Minister Lionel Jospin, 1997–2002', *Modern and Contemporary France*, (10), 3, 2002, pp. 313–323.

20. See C. Amar & A. Chemin, *Jospin et Cie. Histoire de la gauche plurielle, 1993–2002* (Paris, Seuil, 2002).

21. P. Buffotot & D. Hanley, 'The Normalisation of French Politics? The Elections of 2002', *Modern and Contemporary France*, (11), 2, 2003, pp. 131–46.

22. See R. Elgie, 'La Cohabitation de longue durée. Studying the 1997–2002 experience', *Modern and Contemporary France*, (10), 3, 2002, pp. 297–311.

23. R. Vinen, 'The Fifth Republic as Parenthesis?', in J. F. McMillan (ed.), *Modern France. Short Oxford History of France* (Oxford, Oxford University Press, 2003), p. 97.

24. S. Berstein, *Histoire du gaullisme* (Paris, Perrin, 2001).

25. See E. Halpen, *Sept ans de solitude* (Paris, Denoël, 2002).

26. J.-C. Laumond, *Vingt-Cinq Ans ave Lui* (Paris, Ramsay, 2001) . See, too, Chirac's wife's rebuttal: B. Chirac, *Conversation, entretiens avec Patrick de Carolis* (Paris, Plon, 2001). See too Howarth & Varouxakis, *Contemporary France*, p. 88 for information here.

27. *Le Point*, 25 April 2002, *L'Express*, 2–8 May 2002, *Le Monde*, 23 April 2002, *Le Parisien*, 22 April 2002 and *Le Figaro*, 23 April 2002.

28. *The Observer*, 28 April 2002.

29. Gaffney, 'Protocol, Image, Discourse in Political Leadership Competition. The Case of Prime Minister Lionel Jospin, 1997–2002', p. 321.

30. *Libération*, 22 April 2002.

31. *Le Point*, 25 April 2002.
32. N. Atkin & F. Tallett, 'Towards a Sixth Republic? Jean-Marie Le Pen and the 2002 Elections', in N. Atkin & F. Tallett (eds), *The Right in France from Revolution to Le Pen* (London, I. B. Tauris, 2003), pp. 298–9.
33. Howarth & Varouxakis, *Contemporary France*, p. 87.
34. J. Blondel & E. Drexel Godfrey Jnr, *The Government of France* (London, Methuen, 1968 3rd ed), p. vii & p. 188.
35. Vinen, 'The Fifth Republic as parenthesis', p. 102.
36. J. F. McMillan, 'France in the Twenty-First Century', in McMillan, *Modern France*, pp. 228–9.
37. See F.-X. Vershave, *Noir silence. Qui arrêtera la Françafrique?* (Paris, Lesarènes, 2000).
38. *Le Monde*, 27 March 1999.
39. Howarth & Varouxakis, *Contemporary France*, p. 210.

Bibliography

Primary Sources

Ali, T., *Street Fighting Years. An Autobiography of the Sixties* (London, Fontana, 1987).

Aron, R., *La Révolution introuvable* (Paris, Fayard, 1968).

Aubrac, R., *Où la mémoire s'attarde* (Paris, Odile Jacob, 1996).

Auriol, V., *Journal du Septennat* (Paris, Armand Colin, 1970–80), 7 vols.

Aussaresses, P., *Services Spéciaux. Algérie, 1955–1957* (Paris, Perrin, 2001).

Balladur, E., *L'Arbre de mai* (Paris, Atelier Marcel Jullian, 1977).

Barre, R., *Questions de confiance* (Paris, Flammarion, 1988).

Benda, J., *La Trahison des clercs* (Paris, Grasset, 1933).

Bernard, O., *The Finger Points at the Moon. Inscriptions from Paris, May 1968* (New York, Tuba Press, 1999).

Bleton, A., *Les hommes qui viennent* (Paris, Editions Ouvrières, 1956).

Boccara, B., *L'Insurrection démocratique. Manifeste pour la Sixième République* (Paris, Démocratie, 1993).

Camus, A., *Resistance, Rebellion and Death* (London, Hamish Hamilton, 1961).

Chirac, B., *Conversation, entretiens avec Patrick de Carolis* (Paris, Plon, 2001).

De Beauvoir, S., *The Second Sex* (London, Jonathan Cape, 1953).

De Beauvoir, S., *Les Belles Images* (Paris, Gallimard, 1966).

de Boissieu, A., *Pour servir le Général* (Paris, Plon, 1983).

De Gaulle, C., *Mémoires de guerre* (Paris, Plon) 3 vols.

De Gaulle, C., *Mémoires d'espoir* (Paris, Plon, 1970) 3 vols.

De Gaulle, C. *Lettres, notes et carnets, 1961–3* (Paris, Plon, 1980–88) 12 vols.

Flohic, F., *Souvenirs d'outre-Gaulle* (Paris, Plon, 1979).

Foccart, J., *Journal de l'Elysée* (Paris, Fayard, 2001).

Fouchet, A., *Les Feux du crépuscule. Journal, 1968, 1969, 1970* (Paris, Plon, 1977).

Giscard d'Estaing, V., *Démocratie française* (Paris, Fayard, 1976).

Halimi, G. and de Beauvoir, S., *Djamila Boupacha* (Paris, Gallimard, 1961).

Halpen, E., *Sept ans de solitude* (Paris, Denoël, 2002).

Hasard, d' Estin, *Tout fout le camp* (Paris, Le Sagittaire, 1976).

Houellebecq, M., *Plateforme* (Paris, Flammarion, 1999).

Koning, H., *1968. A Personal Report* (London, Unwin Hyman, 1987).

Kriegel, A., *The French Communists. Profile of a People* (London, 1968).

Lambert, F., *Dieu change en Bretagne* (Paris, Cerf, 1985).

Laubier, C., *The Condition of Women in France. 1945 to the Present. A Documentary Anthology* (London, Routledge, 1990).

Laumond, J.-C., *Vingt-Cinq Ans ave Lui* (Paris, Ramsay, 2001).

Le Monde. Dossiers et Documents. L'Election présidentielle, May 1988.

Maier, C. & White, D. S. (eds), *The Thirteenth of May. The Advent of de Gaulle's Republic* (New York, Oxford University Press, 1968).

Malraux, A., *Les Chênes qu'on abat* (Paris, Gallimard, 1971).

Massu, J., *Baden 68. Souvenirs d'une fidelité gaulliste* (Paris, Plon, 1979).

Mitterrand, *The Wheat and the Chaff. The Personal Diaries of the President of France, 1971–1978* (London, Weidenfeld & Nicolson, 1982).

Nizan, P., *Les Chiens de garde* (Paris, Grasset, 1932).

Péan, P., *Une Jeunesse française. François Mitterrand, 1934–1947* (Paris, Fayard, 1994).

Perec, G., *Les Choses* (Paris, René Juillard, 1965).

Peyrefitte, A., *Le Mal français* (Paris, Plon, 1976).

Peyrefitte, A., *C'était de Gaulle* (Paris, Perrin, 1994–1997), 3 vols.

Pompidou, G., *Pour rétablir une vérité* (Paris, Flammarion, 1982).

Poujade, P., *J'ai choisi le combat* (Saint Céré, Société Générale d'Editions et Publications, 1956).

Soustelle, J., *Vingt-huit ans de Gaullisme* (Paris, La Table Ronde, 1968).

Touraine, A., *Le Communisme utopique. Le mouvement de Mai 68* (Paris, Seuil, 1968).

Viannay, P., *Du bon usage de la France* (Paris, Ramsay, 1988).

Viansson-Ponté, P., *Histoire de la république gaullienne* (Paris, Robert Laffont, 1970–71).

White, T. H., *The Making of the President 1960* (New York, Atheneum, 1961).

Wieviorka, O., *Nous entrerons dans la carrière, De la Résistance à l'exercice du pouvoir* (Paris, Seuil, 1994).

Secondary Sources

Abadie, F. & Corcette, J.-P., *Georges Pompidou, 1911–1974. Le désir et le destin* (Paris, Balland, 1994).

Adereth, M., *The French Communist Party. A Critical History, 1920–1984* (Manchester, Manchester University Press, 1984).

Ageron, C. R., *Modern Algeria. A History from 1830 to the Present* (London, Hurst, 1991).

Agulhon, M., Nouschi, A. & Schor, R., *La France de 1940 à nos jours* (Paris, Nathan, 2001 3rd ed).

Aldrich, R., *Greater France. A History of French Overseas Expansion* (Basingstoke, Macmillan, 1996).

Alexander, M. S. (ed.), *French History Since Napoleon* (London, Arnold, 1999).

Alexander, M. S., 'Duty, Discipline and Authority: The French Officer Elites Between Professionalism and Politics, 1900–1962', in Atkin, N. & Tallet, F. (eds), *The Right in France from Revolution to Le Pen* (London, IB Tauris, 2003 2nd ed).

Alexander, M. S. & Keiger, J. (eds), *France and the Algerian War, 1954–1962. Strategy, Operations and Diplomacy* (London, Frank Cass, 2002).

Allison, M. & Heathcote, O. (eds), *Forty Years of the Fifth French Republic. Action, Dialogue and Discourse* (Bern, Lang, 2001).

Amar, C. & Chemin, A., *Jospin et Cie. Histoire de la gauche plurielle, 1993–2002* (Paris, Seuil, 2002).

Andrews, W. G. & Hoffmann, S. (eds), *The Fifth Republic at Twenty* (Albany, University of New York Press, 1981).

Archer, M., 'Education', in J. Flower (ed.), *France Today* (London, Methuen, 1977 3rd ed).

Ardagh, J., *France in the New Century. Portrait of a Changing Society* (London, Penguin, 1999).

Atack, M., *May 68 in French Fiction and Film. Rethinking Society, Rethinking Representation* (Oxford, Oxford University Press, 1999).

Atkin, N. & Tallett, F., 'Towards a Sixth Republic? Jean-Marie Le Pen and the 2002 Elections', in Atkin, N. & Tallett, F. (eds), *The Right in France from Revolution to Le Pen* (London, Tauris, IB 2003).

Atkin, N. & Tallett, F. (eds), *The Right in France from Revolution to Le Pen* (London, IB Tauris, 2003).

Beattie, N., 'Yeast in the Dough? Catholic Schooling in France, 1981–95', in Chadwick, K. (ed.), *Catholicism, Politics and Society in Twentieth-Century France* (Liverpool, Liverpool University Press, 2000).

Becker, J.-J., *Histoire politique de la France depuis 1945* (Paris, Armand Colin, 1996 ed).

Becker, J.-J. & Ory, P., *Crises et alternances, 1974–1995* (Paris, Seuil, 1998).

Bédarida, F. & Fouilloux, E. (eds), *La Guerre d'Algérie et les chrétiens*, Cahiers de l'Institut du Temps Présent, 9, October 1988.

Bell, D. S., *Parties and Democracy in France* (Aldershot, Ashgate, 2000).

Bell, D. S., *Presidential Power in Fifth Republic France* (Oxford, Berg, 2000).

Bell, D. S., 'May 68: Explaining the Power Vacuum', in Allison, M. & Heathcote, O. (eds), *Forty Years of the Fifth French Republic. Action, Dialogue and Discourse* (Bern, Lang, 2001).

Bell, D. S., 'The French Communist Party: From Revolution to Reform', in Evans. J. (ed.), *The French Party System* (Manchester, Manchester University Press, 2003).

Bell, D. S. & Criddle, B., *The French Socialist Party. The Emergence of a Party of Government* (Oxford, Clarendon Press, 1988 2nd ed).

Bell, D. S. & Criddle, B., *The French Communist Party in the Fifth Republic* (Oxford, Clarendon Press, 1994).

Benamou, G. M. (ed.), *Un Mensonge Français. Enquête sur la guerre d'Algérie* (Paris, Robert Laffont, 2003).

Bénéton, P. & Touchard, J., 'The Interpretation of the Crisis of May/June 1968', in Reader, K., *The May Events in France. Reproductions and Reinterpretations* (New York, St Martin's Press, 1993).

Berstein, S., *The Republic of de Gaulle, 1958–1969* (Cambridge, Cambridge University Press, 1993).

Berstein, S., *Histoire du gaullisme* (Paris, Perrin, 2001).

Berstein, S. & Rioux, J.-P., *The Pompidou Years, 1970–1974* (Cambridge, Cambridge University Press, 2002).

Betts, R., *France and Decolonisation, 1900–1960* (Basingstoke, Macmillan, 1991).

Blair, D., *Simone de Beauvoir* (London, Vintage, 1990).

Blednick, P., *Another Day in Paradise? The Real Club Med Story* (London, Macmillan, 1988).

Blondel, J. & Drexel Godrey, E., *The Government of France* (London, Methuen, 1968 3rd ed).

Bodin, L., *Les Intellectuels* (Paris, Presses Universitaires de France, 1962).

Borne, D., *Petits bourgeois en révolte? Le Mouvement Poujade* (Paris, Flammarion, 1977).

Borne, D., *Histoire de la société française depuis 1945* (Paris, Armand Colin, 2000 3rd ed).

Boulard, F., *An Introduction to Religious Sociology* (London, Darton, Longman and Todd, 1960).

Bosworth, R., *Catholicism and Crisis in Modern France. French Catholic Groups at the Threshold of the Fifth Republic* (Princeton, Princeton University Press, 1962).

Bridgford, J., 'The Events of May. Consequences for Industrial Relations in France', in Hanley, D. & Kerr, P. (eds) (Basingstoke, Macmillan, 1989).

Broche, F., *De Gaulle Secret* (Paris, Pygmalion, 1993).

Brunet, J.-P., *Police contre FLN. Le drame d'octobre 1961* (Paris, Flammarion, 1999).

Buffotot, P. & Hanley, D., 'The Normalisation of French Politics? The Elections of 2002', *Modern and Contemporary France*, (11), 2, 2003, 131–46.

Campbell, J., *Margaret Thatcher*, vol. 2, *The Iron Lady* (London, Jonathan Cape, 2003).

Camus, J.-Y., *Le Front National. Histoire et analyses* (Paris, Livre de Poche, 1998).

Capdevieille, J. & Mouriaux, R., *Mai 68. L'catre-deux de la modernite' Histoire de trente ans* (Paris, FNSP, 1985).

Caron, V., *Uneasy Asylum. France and the Jewish Refugee Crisis, 1933–42* (Stanford, Stanford University Press, 1999).

Caute, D., *Sixty-Eight. The Year of the Barricades* (London, Hamish Hamilton, 1988).

Cayol, R., *La nouvelle communication politique* (Paris, Larousse, 1986).

Cerny, P., *The Politics of Grandeur. Ideological Aspects of De Gaulle's Foreign Policy* (Cambridge, Cambridge University Press, 1980).

Chadwick, K. (ed.), *Catholicism, Politics and Society in Twentieth-Century France* (Liverpool, Liverpool University Press, 2000).

Chapsal, J., *La Vie politique sous la Ve République* (Paris, PUF, 1987).

Charle, A., *Naissance des 'intellectuels', 1880–1900* (Paris, Minuit, 1990).

Charlot, J., *The Gaullist Phenomenon* (London, Allen & Unwin, 1971).

Charlot, J., *Le Gaullisme d'opposition, 1946–1958* (Paris, Fayard, 1983).

Charlot, J., 'The Aftermath of May 68 for Gaullism, the Right and the Centre', in Hanley, D. & Kerr (eds), *May '68* (London, Macmillan, 1989)

Christofferson, T. R., *The French Socialists in Power, 1981–1986. From Autogestion to Cohabitation* (Delaware, University of Delaware Press, 1991).

Clark, M. (ed.), *The Algerian War and the French Army, 1954–62. Experiences, Images, Testimonies* (Basingstoke, Palgrave, 2002).

Clarke, P., *A Question of Leadership. Gladstone to Thatcher* (London, Hamish Hamilton, 1991).

Clayton, A., *The French Wars of Decolonisation* (London, Longman, 1994).

Clift, B., 'PS Intra-Party Politics and Party System Change', in Evans, J. (ed.), *The French Party System* (Manchester, Manchester University Press, 2003).

Clinton, A., *Jean Moulin, 1899–1943. The French Resistance and the Republic* (Basingstoke, Palgrave, 2002).

Cole, A., *François Mitterrand. A Study in Political Leadership* (London, Routledge, 1997 2nd ed).

Cole, A., *French Politics and Society* (London, Longman, 1998).

Cole, A., *Franco-German Relations* (London, Longman, 2001).

Collovald, A., 'Les Poujadistes ou l'échec en politiques', *Revue d'Histoire Moderne et Contemporaine* 36 (1), pp. 111–33.

Collovald, A., *Jacques Chirac et le gaullisme. Biographie dun héritier à histoires* (Paris, Belin,1999).

Conan, E. & Rousso, H., *Vichy, un passé qui ne passe pas* (Paris, Fayard, 1994).

Cook, M. & Davie, G. (eds), *Modern France. Society in Transition* (London, Routledge, 1999).

Cordier, D., *Jean Moulin. L'inconnu du Panthéon* (Paris, Lattès, 1989–93) 3 vols.

Courtier, P., *La Quatrième République* (Paris, Presses Universitaires de France, 1994).

Daley, A. (ed.), *The Mitterrand Era. Policy Alternatives and Politics in France* (Basingstoke, Macmillan, 1996).

Dalloz, J., *La France et le monde* (Paris, Armand Colin, 1993).

Davie, G., 'Religion and Laïcité', in Cook, M. & Davie, G. (eds), *Modern France. Society in Transition* (London, Routledge, 1999), pp. 207–8.

Dély, R., *Histoire secrète du Front National* (Paris, Grasset, 1999).

Dine, P., 'A la recherche du soldat perdu. Myth, Metaphor and memory in the French Cinema of the Algerian War', in Holman, V. & Kelly, D. (eds), *France at War in the Twentieth Century. Propaganda, Myth and Metaphor* (Oxford, Berghahn Books, 2000).

Dine, P., *Images of the Algerian War. French Fiction and Film, 1954–1992* (Oxford, Clarendon Press, 1994)

Dobry, M., *Le Mythe de l'Allergie française au fascisme* (Paris, Albin Michel, 2003).

Donegani, J. M. & Sadoun, M., *La Ve République. Naissance et mort* (Paris, Calmann Lévy, 1998).

Drake, D., *Intellectuals and Politics in Post-War France* (Basingstoke, Palgrave, 2002).

Dreyfus-Armand, G., Frank, R., Lévy, M. F., & Zacarini-Fournel, M. (eds), *Les Années 68. Le temps de contestation* (Brussels, Editions Complexe, 2000).

Droz, B., 'Le cas très singulier de la guerre d'Algérie', in *Vingtième sècle*, no. 5, January–March 1985.

Duchen, C., *Feminism in France from 68 to Mitterrand* (London, Routledge, 1986).

Duhamel, O., *Le Pouvoir politique en France* (Paris, Seuil, 2003).

Duhamel, O. and Jaffré, J., *SOFRES. L'état de l'opinion* (Paris, Seuil, 1997).

Dupeux, G., *French Society, 1789–1970* (London, Methuen, 1976).

Elgey, G., *Histoire de la Quatrième République* (Paris, Fayard, 1965–92) 3 vols.

Elgey, G. & Colombani, J. M., *La Cinquième ou la République des phratries* (Paris, Fayard, 1998).

Elgie, R. (ed.), *The Changing French Political System* (London, Frank Cass, 1999).

Elgie, R., 'La Cohabitation de longue durée. Studying the 1997–2002 Experience', *Modern and Contemporary France*, (10), 3, 2002, pp. 297–311.

Evans, J. (ed.), *The French Party System* (Manchester, Manchester University Press, 2003).

Evans, M., *The Memory of Resistance. French Opposition to the Algerian War, 1954–62* (Oxford, Berg, 1997).

Faujas, A., *Trigano. L'aventure du Club Med* (Paris, Flammarion, 1994).

Favier, J. & Martin-Roland, M., *La Décennie Mitterrand* (Paris, Seuil, 1990–9) 4 vols.

Fenby, J., *On the Brink. The Trouble with France* (London, Abacus, 2002).

Flynn, G. (ed.), *Remaking the Hexagon. The New France in the New Europe* (Boulder, Westview Press, 1995)

Founteneau, A. and Muet, P.-A., *La Gauche face à la crise* (Paris, FNSP, 1985).

Fourastié, J., *Les trente glorieuses ou la Révolution invisible* (Paris, Fayard, 1979).

Forbes, J. & Hewlett, N. (eds), *Contemporary France. Essays and Texts on Politics, Economics and Society* (London, Longman, 1994).

Frank, R., 'Introduction', in Dreyfus-Armand, G., Frank, R., Lévy, M.-F., & Zacarini-Fournel, M. (eds), *Les Années 68. Le temps de contestation* (Brussels, Editions Complexe, 2000).

Frears, J. R., *France in the Giscard Presidency* (London, George Allen & Unwin, 1981).

Frears, J., 'Parliament', in Andrews, W. G. & Hoffmann, S. (eds), *The Fifth Republic at Twenty* (Albany, University of New York Press, 1981).

Frears, J. & Morris, P., 'La Britannicité de la Ve République', in *Espoir*, 1992, no. 85.

Furlough, E., 'The Business of Pleasure. Creating Club Méditerranée', in Steven Vincent, K. & Klairmont-Lingo, A. (eds), *The Human Tradition in Modern France* (Wilmington, SR Books, 2000).

Gacon, J., *Quatrième République* (Paris, Messidor, 1987).

Gaffney, J., 'Protocol, Image and Discouse in Political Leadership Competition. The Case of Prime Minister Lionel Jospin, 1997–2002', *Modern and Contemporary France*, (10), 3, 2002, pp. 313–23.

Gildea, R. N., *France since 1945* (Oxford, Oxford University Press, 2002 2nd ed).

Giles, J., *The Locust Years. The Story of the Fourth Republic* (London, Secker & Warburg, 1991).

Golson, R., *Vichy's Afterlife. History and Counterhistory in Postwar France* (Lincoln, University of Nebraska Press, 2000).

Gorce, P.-M. de la, *Charles de Gaulle* (Paris, Perrin, 1999).

Gordon, P. & Meunier, S., *The French Challenge. Adapting to Globalisation* (Washington, Brookings, 2001).

Gough, H. & Horne J. (eds), *De Gaulle and Twentieth-Century France* (London, Edward Arnold, 1994).

Groux, C., *Vers un renouveau du conflit social* (Paris, Bayard, 1998).

Guyomarch, A., Machin, H. & Ritchie, E., *France in the European Union* (Basingstoke, Macmillan, 1998).

Guichard, J.-P., *De Gaulle et les Mass Media. L'image du général* (Paris, France Empire, 1985).

Gvichiani, D., 'Les relations franco-soviétiques pendant la présidence du général de Gaulle', in Institut Charles de Gaulle, *De Gaulle en son siècle* (Paris, Institut Charles de Gaulle, 1992) vol. 3, p. 382.

Hanley, D., 'Managing the Plural Left. Implications for the Party System', in Evans, *The French Party System* (Manchester, Manchester University Press, 2003).

Hanley, D., *Party, Society, Government. Republican Democracy in France* (Oxford, Berg, 2002).

Hanley, D. & Kerr, P. (eds), *May '68. Coming of Age* (Basingstoke, Macmillan, 1989).

Hanley, D. & Kerr, P., 'Introduction: Elusive May. The Paradox of a Moment in History', in Hanley, D. & Kerr, P. (eds), *May '68. Coming of Age* (Basingstoke, Macmillan, 1989).

Hanley, D. L., Kerr, P. and Waites, N. *Contemporary France. Politics and Society since 1945* (London, Routledge, 1979).

Hayward, J., *Governing France. The One and Indivisible Republic* (London, Weidenfeld & Nicolson, 1983, 2nd ed).

Hayward, J., *De Gaulle to Mitterrand. Presidential Power in France* (London, Hurst, 1993).

Hazareesingh, S., *Intellectuals and the French Communist Party. Disillusion and Decline* (Oxford, Oxford University Press, 1991).

Hazareesingh, S., *Political Traditions in Modern France* (Oxford, Oxford University Press, 1994).

Hazaressingh, S., 'Guard Dogs of Good Deeds. Remembering badly and forgetting well: history and memory in modern France', in *Times Literary Supplement*, 21 March 2003, pp. 12–3.

Hoffmann, S., *Le Mouvement Poujade* (Paris, FNSP, 1956).

Hoffmann, S., *Decline or Renewal? France since the 1930s* (New York, Viking, 1974).

Hoffmann, S., 'Gaullism by any other name', in Ross, G. S., Hoffmann, S., & Mazacher, S. (eds), *The Mitterrand Experiment* (Oxford, Polity Press, 1987).

Holman, V. & Kelly, D. (eds), *France at War in the Twentieth Century. Propaganda, Myth and Metaphor* (Oxford, Berghahn Books, 2000).

Holmes, P., 'Broken Dreams. Economic Policy in Mitterrand's France', in Mazey, S. & Newman, M. (eds), *Mitterrand's France* (London, Croom Helm, 1987).

Holter, D., *The Battle for Coal. Miners and the Politics of Nationalisation in France, 1940–1950* (DeKalb, Northern Illinois University Press, 1992).

Horne, J., 'The Transformation of Society', in McMillan J. F. (ed.), *Modern France*, Short Oxford History of France (Oxford University Press, 2003).

Horne, A., *A Savage War of Peace. Algeria, 1954–1962* (London, Pan, 2002 ed).

Hewlett, N., *Modern French Politics. Analysing Conflict and Consensus since 1945* (London, Polity, 1998).

House, A. & MacMaster, N., 'Une journé portée disparue. The Paris massacre of 1961 and memory', in Mouré, K. & Alexander, M. S. (eds), *Crisis and Renewal in France* (New York, Berghahn, 2001).

Howarth, D. & Varouxakis, G., *Contemporary France. An Introduction to French Politics and Society* (London, Arnold, 2003).

Hussey, A., 'ZZ Top', *The Observer Sport Monthly*, April 2004, pp. 15–23.

Inglehart, R., *Culture Shift in Advanced Industrial Society* (Princeton, Princeton University Press, 1990).

Institut Charles de Gaulle, *De Gaulle en son siècle* (Paris, Institut Charles de Gaulle, 1992) 6 vols.

Ireland, P. R., 'Race, Immigration and Hate', in Daley, A. (ed.), *The Mitterrand Era. Policy Aternatives and Politics in France* (Basingstoke, Macmillan, 1996).

Ivaldi, G., 'The FN Split. Party System Change and Electoral Prospects' in Evans, J. (ed.), *The French Party System* (Manchester, Manchester University Press, 2003).

Jackson, J., *France. The Dark Years, 1940–1944* (Oxford, Oxford University Press, 2001).

Jackson, J., *The Fall of France. The Nazi Invasion of 1940* (Oxford, Oxford University Press, 2003).

Jackson, J., *De Gaulle* (London, Cardinal, 1990).

Jackson, J., 'De Gaulle and May 1968', in Gough, H. & Horne J. (eds), *De Gaulle and Twentieth-Century France* (London, Edward Arnold, 1994).

Jennings, J., *Intellectuals in Twentieth-Century France. Mandarins and Samurais* (Basingstoke, Macmillan, 1993).

Jennings, J., 'Of treason, blindness and silence. Dilemmas of the Intellectual in modern France', in Jennings, J. & Kemp-Welch, T. (eds), *Intellectuals in Politics. From the Dreyfus Affair to Salman Rushdie* (London, Routledge, 2000).

Jennings, J. & Kemp-Welch, T. (eds), *Intellectuals in Politics. From the Dreyfus Affair to Salman Rushdie* (London, Routledge, 2000).

Johnson, D., 'De Gaulle's Foreign Policy', *International Affairs*, 1966.

Johnson, D., 'Pierre Poujade', *The Guardian*, 28 August 2003.

Johnson, R., *The French Communist Party versus the Students. Revolutionary Politics in May–June 1968* (New haven, Yale University Press, 1972).

Judt, T., *Past Imperfect. French Intellectuals, 1944–1956* (Berkeley, University of California Press, 1992).

Kedward, H. R., *In Search of the Maquis. Resistance in Rural France* (Oxford, Oxford University Press, 1993).

Kieger, J. F. V., *France and the World since 1870* (London, Arnold, 2001).

Khilnani, S., *Arguing Revolution. The Intellectual Left in Postwar France* (New Haven, Yale University Press, 1993).

Klarsfeld, S., *Vichy-Auschwitz* (Paris, Fayard, 1982–5) 2 vols.

Knapp, A. F., *Gaullism after de Gaulle* (Aldershot, Dartsmouth, 1994).

Knapp, A., 'From the Gaullist Movement to the President's Party', in Evans, J. (ed.), *The French Party System* (Manchester, Manchester University Press, 2003).

Knapp, A. & Wright, V., *The Government and Politics of France* (London, Routledge, 2000).

Koos, L. R., 'Tales of the City. Representing the HLM in Contemporary French Culture', in Allisson, M. & Heathcote, O. (eds), *Forty Years of the Fifth Republic. Action, Dialogue and Discourse* (Bern, Lang, 2001).

Kuisel, R., 'The American Economic Challenge. De Gaulle and the French', in R. O. Paxton & N. Wahl (eds), *De Gaulle and the US. A Centennial Reappraisal* (Oxford, Berg, 1994).

Kuisel, R., *Seducing the French. The Dilemma of Americanisation* (Berkeley, University of California Press, 1993).

Kuisel, R., *Capitalism and the Stae in Modern France. Renovation and Economic Management in the Twentieth Century* (Cambridge, Cambridge University Press, 1981).

Lacorne, D. (ed.), *The Rise and Fall of Anti-Americanism. A Century of French Perceptions* (Basingstoke, Macmillan, 1990).

Lacouture, J., *De Gaulle*, vol. 2, *The Leader* (London, Collins, 1991).

Lacouture, J., *Mitterrand. Une Histoire de Français* (Paris, Seuil, 1998) 2 vols.

Larkin, M., *France since the Popular Front* (Oxford, Clarendon Press, 1986).

Larkin, M., 'The Catholic Church and Politics in Twentieth-Century France', in Alexander, M. S. (ed.), *France since Napoleon* (London, Arnold, 1999).

Le Bras, G., *Etudes de sociologie religieuse* (Paris, Presses Universitaires de France, 1955–56), 2 vols.

Le Goff, J.-P., *Mai 68, l'héritage impossible* (Paris, Editions La Découverte, 1998).

Legois, J.-P., Monchablon, A. & Morder, R. 'Le mouvement étudiant et l'Université: entre réforme et révolution, 1964–1976', in Dreyfus-Armand, G., Frank, R. Lévy, M. F. & Zacarini-Fournel, M. (eds), *Les Années 68. Le temps de contestation* (Brussels, Editions Complexe, 2000).

Lloyd, C., 'Race and Ethnicity', in Cook, M. & Davie, G., *Modern France. Society in Transition* (London, Routledge, 1999).

Lochak, D., *La Haute administration à l'épreuve de l'alternance* (Paris, Presses Universitaires de France, 1985).

Looseley, D., *The Politics of Fun. Cultural Policy and Debate in Contemporary France* (Oxford, Berg, 1995).

Luc Einaudi, J., *La Bataille de Paris, 17 octobre 1961* (Paris, Seuil, 1991).

Madjarian, G., *Conflits, pouvoirs et société à la Libération* (Paris, Union Générale, 1980).

Martin, P., *Comprendre les évolutions électorales* (Paris, Presses de Sciences Po, 2000)

Marwick, A., *The Sixties. Cultural Revolution in Britain, France, Italy and the United States, c.1958–c.1974* (Oxford, Oxford University Press, 1998).

Mayer, N., *Ces français qui votent FN* (Paris, Flammarion, 1999).

Mazey, S. & Newman, M. (eds), *Mitterrand's France* (London, Croom Helm, 1987).

McLean, M., *Economic Management and French Business from de Gaulle to Chirac* (Basingstoke, Palgrave, 2002).

McMillan, J. F. (ed.), *Modern France. Short Oxford History of France* (Oxford, Oxford University Press, 2003).

McMillan, J. F., 'France in the Twenty-First Century', in McMillan, J. F. (ed.), *Modern France. Short Oxford History of France* (Oxford, Oxford University Press, 2003).

McMillan, J. F., *Twentieth-Century France. Politics and Society* (London, Arnold, 1992).

Mendras, H., *La Seconde Révolution française, 1965–1984* (Paris, Gallimard, 1988).

Mermet, G., *Francoscopie. 2003* (Paris, Larousse, 2003).

Milza, P., *Fascisme français* (Paris, Flammarion, 1987).

Mira, S., 'The National Front in France. A Single Issue Movement?', *West European Politics*, (11), 2, 1988.

Morris, P., *French Politics Today* (Manchester, Manchester University Press, 1994).

Mouré, K., 'The French Economy since 1930', in Alexander M. S. (ed.), *French History since Napoleon* (London, Arnold, 1999).

Mouré, K. & Alexander, M. S. (eds), *Crisis and Renewal in France* (New York, Berghahn, 2001).

Nay, C., *Le Noir et le rouge* (Paris, Grasset, 1984).

Nay, C., *Les sept Mitterrand, ou les metamorphoses d'un septennat* (Paris, Grasset, 1988).

Nora, P., *Les Lieux de mémoire* (Paris, Seuil, 1990) 3 vols.

Northcutt, W., *Mitterrand. A Political Biography* (New York, Holmes & Meier, 1992).

Novick, P., *The Resistance vesus Vichy. The Purge of Collaborators in Liberated France* (London, Chatto & Windus, 1966).

Ory, P. and J.-F., *Sirinelli, Les Intellectuels en France de l'Affaire Dreyfus à nos jours* (Paris, Colin, 1986).

Paxton, R. O., *Vichy France. Old Guard and New Order, 1940–1944* (New York, Columbia University Press, 2001 ed).

Paxton, R. O., and Wahl, N. (eds), De Gaulle and the US. A Centennial Reappraisal (Oxford, Berg, 1994).

Perrineau, P., *Le Sympton Le Pen* (Paris, Fayard, 1997).

Perrineau, P. & Ysmal, C., *Le vote de crise. L'élection présidentielle de 1995* (Paris, FNSP, 1995).

Perry, S. (ed.), *Aspects of Contemporary France* (London, Routledge, 1997).

Perry, S., 'Television', in Perry, S. (ed.), *Aspects of Contemporary France* (London, Routledge, 1997).

Petitfils, J.-C., *La Démocratie giscardienne* (Paris, PUF, 1989).

Pierre, A., 'Conflicting Visions. Defence, Nuclear Weapons and Arms Control in the Franco-American Relationship during the de Gaulle era' in R. O. Paxton & N. Wahl (eds), *De Gaulle and the US. A Centennial Reappriasal* (Oxford, Berg, 1994).

Porch, D., *The March to the Marne. The French Army, 1871–1914* (Cambridge, Cambridge University Press, 1981).

Portelli, H., *La Politique en France sous la Vème République* (Paris, Grasset, 1987).

Prost, A., 'Ecoles, Collèges and Lycées in France since 1968', in Hanley, D. & Kerr, P. (eds), *May '68. Coming of Age* (Basingstoke, Macmillan, 1989).

Ruach, A., *Vacances en France de 1830 à nos jours* (Paris, Hachette, 1996).

Raynaud, G., 'Preparing the Sixth Republic', in Allison, M. & Heathcote, O. (eds), *Forty Years of the French Fifth Republic. Action, Dialogue and Discourse* (Bern, Lang, 2002).

Rémond, R., *Les Droites en France* (Paris, Aubier-Montagne, 1982).

Rioux, J.-P., *La France de la Quatrième République* (Paris, Seuil, 1980–83) 2 vols.

Rioux, J.-P. (ed.), *La Guerre d'Algérie et les français* (Paris, Fayard, 1990).

Roche, A., 'Pieds noirs. Le retour', *Modern and Contemporary France*, (2), 2, 1994, pp. 151–64.

Roos, L. R., 'Tales of the City. Representing the HLM in Contemporary French Culture', in Allison, M. & Heathcote, O. (eds), *Forty Years of the Fifth Republic. Action, Dialogue and Discourse* (Bern, Lang, 2001).

Ross, K., *May '68 and its Afterlives* (Chicago, University of Chicago Press, 2002).

Ross, K., *Fast Cars, Clean Bodies. Decolonisation and the Reordering of French Culture* (Cambridge Mass., MIT Press, 1995).

Ross, G. S., Hoffmann, S., & Mazacher, S. (eds), *The Mitterrand Experiment* (Oxford, Polity Press, 1987).

Roussel, E., *Georges Pompidou* (Paris, P. Lattès, 1994).

Roussel, E., *Charles de Gaulle* (Paris, Gallimard, 2002).

Rousso, H., *The Vichy Syndrome. History and Memory in France since 1944* (Cambridge, MA, Harvard University Press, 1989).

Rousso, H., 'L'Epuration en France. Une histoire inachevée', *Vingtième Siècle*, 33, 1992, pp. 106–17.

Sa'Adah, A., *Contemporary France. A Democratic Education* (Lanham, Rowman & Littlefield, 2003).

Sassoon, D., *One Hundred Years of Socialism. The West European Left in the Twentieth Century* (London, Fontana, 1997).

Schoennbrun, A., *The Three Lives of Charles de Gaulle. A Biography* (London, Hamish Hamilton, 1966).

Schor, A.-D., *La Politique économique et sociale de la Ve République* (Paris, Presses Universiatires de France, 1993).

Shennan, A., *De Gaulle* (London, Longman, 1994).

Shields, J. G., 'The Poujadist Movement. A Faux Fascism?', *Modern and Contemporary France*, 8 (1), 200, pp. 19–34.

Sigaux, A., *A History of Tourism* (London, Leisure Arts, 1966).

Sigg, A. W., *Le Silence et la honte. Névroses de la guerre d'Algérie* (Paris, Messidor, 1989).

Simmons, H. G., *The French National Front. The Extremist Challenge to Democracy* (Oxford, Westview, 1996).

Sirinelli, J.-F. (ed.), *Histoire des droites en France* (Paris, Gallimard, 1992) 3 vols.

Steven Vincent, K. & Klairmont-Lingo, A. (eds), *The Human Tradition in Modern France* (Wilmington, SR Books, 2000).

Stevens, A., *The Government and Politics of France* (Basingstoke, Macmillan, 1996 2nd ed).

Stoléru, L., *Les Français à deux vitesses* (Paris, Flammarion, 1982).

Stora, B., *La Gangène et l'oubli. La Mémoire de la guerre d'Algérie* (Paris, La Découverte,1992).

Stora, B., 'La Guerre d'Algérie quarante ans après. Connaissances et reconnaissance', *Modern and Contemporary France*, (2), 2, 1994, pp. 131–9.

Stovall, T., *France since the Second World War* (London, Longman, 2002).

Sur, S., *La Vie politique en France sous la Ve République* (Paris, Montchrestien, 1982).

Talbott, J. E., *The War Without a Name. France in Algeria, 1954–1962* (New York, Knopf, 1980).

Tarr, F de., *Henri Queuille en son temps, 1884–1970. Biographie* (Paris, La Table Ronde, 1995).

Teyssier, A., *La Ve République, 1958–1995. De de Gaulle à Chirac* (Paris, Pygmalion, 1995).

Thibaud, P., 'L'Homme au-dessus des lois', *Le Débat*, September–November, 1994.

Thody, P., *The Fifth French Republic. Presidents, Politics and Personalities* (London, Routledge, 1998).

Todd, O., *La Marelle de Giscard, 1924–74* (Paris, Robert Laffont, 1977).

Touchard, J., *Le gaullisme, 1940–1969* (Paris, Seuil, 1978).

Turner, R., 'The Presidency', in Perry, S. (ed.), *Aspects of Contemporary France* (London, Routledge, 1997).

Turner, R., 'Higher Education', in Perry, S. (ed.), *Aspects of Contemporary France* (London, Routledge, 1997).

Vaïsee, M., *La Grandeur. Politique étrangere du général de Gaulle* (Paris, Fayard, 1998).

Varouxakis, G., *Victorian Political Thought on France and the French* (Basingstoke, Palgrave, 2002).

Vershave, F.-X., *Noir silence. Qui arrêtera françafrique* (Paris, Lesarènes, 2000).

Viannson-Ponté, P., *Histoire de la république gaullienne* (Paris, Fayard, 1970) 2 vols.

Vinen, R., *Bourgeois Politics in France, 1945–51* (Cambridge, Cambridge University Press, 1995).

Vinen, R., *France 1934–1970* (Basingstoke, Macmillan, 1996).

Vinen, R., 'The parenthesis of the Fifth Republic', in McMillan, J. (ed.), *The Oxford History of Twentieth-Century France* (Oxford, Oxford University Press, 2003).

Virgili, F., *La France virile. Des Femmes tondues à la Libération* (Paris, Payot, 2000).

Wahl, N., 'De Gaulle and the Americans', in R. O. Paxton & N. Wahl (eds), *De Gaulle and the US. A Centennial Reappraisal* (Oxford, Berg, 1994).

Watson, J., 'The Internal Dynamics of Gaullism', unpublished University of Oxford D. Phil, 2001.

Weber, E., *The Hollow Years. France in the 1930s* (New York, Norton, 1994).

Weber, H., *Vingt ans après. Que reste-t-il de 68?* (Paris, Seuil, 1988).

Wharton, S., 'Progress. What Progress? The Gay and Lesbian Liberation Movement in the Fifth Republic', in Allison, M. & Heathcote, O. (eds), *Forty Years of the Fifth Republic* (Berg, Peter Lang, 2001), pp. 191–204.

Williams, P., *Crisis and Compromise. The Politics of the Fourth Republic* (London, Longman, 1964).

Williams, P., *Politics in De Gaulle's France* (London, Longman, 1971).

Winock, M., 'De Gaulle and the Algerian Crisis, 1958–1962', in Gough, H. & Horne, J. (eds), *De Gaulle and Twentieth-Century France* (London, Arnold, 1994).

Wright, V., *The Government and Politics of France* (London, Routledge, 1989 3rd ed).

Wolfreys, J., 'Neither Right nor Left? Towards an Integrated Analysis of the Front National', Atkin, N. & Tallett, F. (eds), *The Right in France from Revolution to Le Pen* (London, I B Tauris 2003 2nd ed).

Wolfreys, J., 'Shoes, Lies and Videotape. Corruption and the French State', *Modern and Contemporary France*, 2001, 9 (4).

Yacono, X., *Les Etapes de la décolonisation française* (Paris, Presses Universitaires de France, 1982 3rd ed).

Yonnet, P., Voyage au centré du malaise française (Paris, Gallimard, 1993).

Zeldin, T., *France 1848–1945* (Oxford, Clarendon Press, 1979–81) 2 vols.

Zeldin, T., *The French* (London, Collins, 1983).

Index